Micronesia
a travel survival kit

Glenda Bendure
Ned Friary

Micronesia - a travel survival kit
  1st edition

Published by
  Lonely Planet Publications
  Head Office: PO Box 88, South Yarra, Victoria, 3134, Australia
  Also: PO Box 2001A, Berkeley, California 94702, USA

Printed by
  Colorcraft, Hong Kong

Photographs
  Glenda Bendure
  Ned Friary

Published
  April 1988

Although the author and publisher have tried to make the information as accurate as possible, they accept no responsibility for any loss, injury or inconvenience sustained by any traveller using this book.

National Library of Australia
Cataloguing in Publication Data

Bendure, Glenda
  Micronesia, a travel survival kit.

  Includes index.
  ISBN 0 86442 019 6.

  1. Micronesia – Description and travel – Guide-books.
  I. Friary, Ned. II. Title.

919.6'504

Glenda Bendure grew up in California's Mojave Desert. Her first overseas travel was as a high school exchange student to India in 1969. A few years later a Trukese exchange student lived with her family, introducing her to Micronesia.

Ned Friary has travelled extensively throughout the US and Central America. He studied Social Thought and Political Economy at the University of Massachusetts in Amherst and upon graduating in 1976 headed west.

They met in Santa Cruz, California, where Glenda was attending university and Ned was working as a cook with the forestry. In 1978, with Lonely Planet's first book *Across Asia on the Cheap* in hand, they flew Freddie Laker to London and hit the overland trail across southern Europe, through Iran and Afghanistan, on to trains in India and treks in Nepal. The next six years were spent exploring Asia and the Pacific, with 3½ years of teaching English in Japan in between jaunts. They now live on Cape Cod in Massachusetts where Ned is the coordinator of a shelter for the homeless and Glenda writes a travel column for the *Cape Cod Times*.

Lonely Planet Credits

Editor	Lindy Cameron
Maps, design, cover design & illustrations	Valerie Tellini
Typesetting	Ann Jeffree

Thanks also to: Mark Balla and Katie Cody for proofreading and corrections; Debbie Lustig for index, contents, running heads & additional typesetting; Joanne Ryan for title page & additional illustrations; and Vicki Beale and Joanne Ryan for paste-up corrections.

Acknowledgements
Thanks to the people who gave assistance advice or tales of life on remote islands: Ray Aflague, Justus Alokoa, Elden Buck, Lee Boblitt, John Buchun, John Engbring, Margie Falunruw, Mike Flaherty, Kevin Foster, Francis Hezel SJ, Mark Howell, Dave Huskins, Teddy John, Julio Kazuo, Gerald Knight, Ray Kruger, Richard Macaranas, Samuel McPhetres, Marie Maddison, Madison Nena, Chutomu Nimwes, Jean Ogle, Ellen Opie, Lisa Parker, Ignacio Quichocho, Koichy Sana, William Stewart, Joe Suka, Elizabeth Udui, Dan Wales, Marie Wells, Emily Wen, Deo Wengu, Dave and Peggy . . .

and to all the others who helped us along the way.

Thanks also to tourist bureaus in the Marshalls, Kosrae, Pohnpei, Truk, Yap, Guam, Saipan and Palau; to the people in the Bureau of Land Management offices who stopped whatever they were doing to search out maps for us; to the many Peace Corps volunteers who shared their insights with us; and to those at the Alele Museum (Majuro), Micronesian Seminar (Truk), Micronesian Area Research Center (Guam), Belau National Museum (Koror) and the Micronesia Institute (Washington DC) who helped us with research.

A Warning & A Request

Despite clocks running on Micronesian time, not everything moves slowly in the islands. Small hotels and restaurants, even airlines, come and go with surprising frequency. Hotels turn into apartments, restaurants turn into video shops and so it goes. The best travel guides are kept up to date by travellers. If you find errors or omissions let us hear about them. If you visit an island we didn't cover let us know what it's like. As usual the best letters will be rewarded with a free copy of the next edition, or another Lonely Planet guide if you prefer.

Extracts from the best letters are also included in the *Lonely Planet Update*. The *Update* helps us make useful information available to you as soon as possible – it's like reading an up-to-date noticeboard or postcards from a friend. Each edition contains hundreds of useful tips, and advice from the best possible source of information – other travellers. The *Lonely Planet Update* is published quarterly in paperback and is available from bookshops and by subscription. Turn to the back pages of this book for more details.

Contents

MICRONESIA DEFINED

The boundaries of Micronesia are not cut and dried.

No one disputes the inclusion of the Mariana, Marshall and Caroline island chains. Those islands (with the exception of the US territory of Guam in the Marianas) have been known since WW II as the Trust Territory of the Pacific Islands, officially a United Nations territory but for all practical purposes an American colony.

The Gilbert Islands are often considered part of Micronesia, however the new nation of Kiribati includes not only the Gilberts but also the Phoenix and Line island chains which are part of Polynesia, so Kiribati is not included in this book.

The independent nation of Nauru, a small single island of phosphate which is being mined into oblivion to provide its inhabitants with one of the world's highest per capita incomes, is also often considered Micronesian. Nauru, just south of the equator and politically set apart from the other islands, doesn't encourage visitors and is not included here.

In this guidebook 'Micronesia' refers to Guam and to the islands of the dissolving UN Trust Territory which have emerged as the political units of: the Republic of the Marshall Islands; the Federated States of Micronesia – Yap, Truk, Pohnpei and Kosrae; the Commonwealth of the Northern Marianas; and the Republic of Palau.

Because these islands have in many ways been thought of as a single unit throughout four decades of US control, they have become for most purposes synonymous with the term Micronesia.

Introduction

Micronesia is entirely in the North Pacific, a term that doesn't exactly conjure up exotic images the way 'South Pacific' does. Yet all the idyllic island clichés fit perfectly: Micronesia has warm aqua waters lapping at pristine bleached sands, swaying coconut palms, lush tropical jungles, tumbling waterfalls and traditional thatched huts.

Micronesia's 2100 islands lie scattered between Hawaii and the Philippines. Though they cover an ocean expanse the size of the continental United States, their total land mass is less than Rhode Island, the smallest US state. Many world maps don't even bother dotting them in.

Four colonial powers have used these tiny specks of land as stepping stones between continents, first as provision ports on trade routes and later as military bastions. The island groups are now, however, emerging as 'island nations', each with some sort of political identity of its own, yet all still firmly locked into a future with the US.

Not only are they spread out over a great distance but each of the islands has its own culture and personality. The inhabited areas vary from idyllic villages with no cars or electricity to the high-rise resort developments of Guam and Saipan.

Steeped in a rich yet largely unknown history, the ruins of the great stone cities of Pohnpei's Nan Madol and Kosrae's Leluh are on an archaeological par with the stone statues of Easter Island and the Mayan ruins of Central America. You can still get a glimpse of these abandoned worlds by navigating the Venice-like canals of Nan Madol or walking Leluh's coral rock pathways.

Yap has giant stone money, grass skirts, men's houses and Micronesia's most traditional lifestyle. Visitors are rare, so with few hotel rooms and no developed tourist sights Yap offers the sort of unspoiled earthy attractions that independent travellers yearn for.

Now that jets fly into Kosrae, all the major district centres are linked by air.

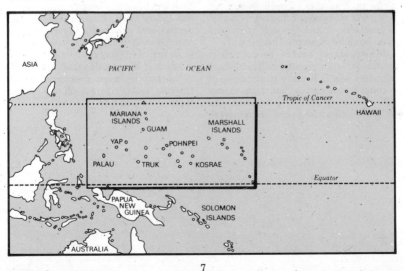

Kosrae itself is still a friendly backwater that until recently seldom saw more than a couple of visitors at any one time.

With more ocean than land, some of Micronesia's best sights are underwater. Around Palau, three ocean currents converge to bring in some of the most varied and dazzling marine life in the world – and it's all accessible from your own private beach on one of Palau's Rock Islands. Micronesia's clear 80°F (27°C) waters with coral gardens and zillions of tropical fish offer unsurpassed snorkelling and diving.

In Truk, the lagoon bed holds an entire Japanese fleet, frozen in time where it sank in February 1944. Complete with sake cups and skeletons, jeeps and tanks tied on board and fighter planes still waiting in the holds, the wrecks have been declared an underwater museum.

Some of the bloodiest battles of WW II were fought in Micronesia. On Peleliu, Saipan and Tinian, Japanese and Americans killed each other by the thousands. These days the battle scars and WW II ruins have been turned into sightseeing attractions and both US and Japanese war veterans and relatives of war dead make up a sizable (though dwindling) portion of Micronesia's visitors. Not a lot of people live on these islands, the saying goes, but a lot of people died here.

Micronesia is caught between past traditions and present realities. Many islanders who still make their homes of coconut fronds and sail outrigger canoes now also have electric generators and VCR's; visiting friends and neighbours to watch the latest video has become a popular pastime.

The Marshall Islands include more than a thousand flat coral islands with white sand beaches and turquoise lagoons. To some it's a tropical paradise but many Marshallese are struggling with the 20th century. Some have been victimised by nuclear testing while another 9000 live in a squalid ghetto on the doorstep of a US military base.

Throughout Micronesia young men, many with US college degrees and a craving for western lifestyles, are moving away from subsistence farming and fishing only to find high unemployment in the district centres. Alcoholism, discontent and high suicide rates are a real part of some islanders' lives.

Still, outside the larger towns, many of Micronesia's islands remain distant from the pollution and problems of the modern world.

Micronesia can be explored in depth or taken in small chunks; there is plenty of variety. You can take small prop planes or two-week ship journeys to some of the most remote and unspoiled islands on earth where you can stay in traditional huts and become a beachcomber; or you can island hop through the district centres, rent cars to drive around in and spend sunset hours on a beach lounge chair with a tropical drink in hand.

Much of Micronesia remains virtually untouched by mass tourism. For the traveller looking to get off the beaten track, it's a rare find.

Facts about the Region

GEOGRAPHY

It's no easy task counting the islands of Micronesia; there are more than 2100 of them. Some are just small flat specks that disappear and reappear with the tides; some are still growing, through coral build-up or volcanic flows; and most are uninhabited. With the vast majority of these islands covering less than one square mile each, they are aptly named Micronesia – 'small islands'.

Micronesia's islands are scattered over three million square miles of the western Pacific between Hawaii and the Philippines. They are divided geographically into three archipelagoes – the Marshalls, Carolines and Marianas.

All are in the tropics, except two of the Marianas which poke up just north of the Tropic of Cancer. The southernmost island is Kapingamarangi, one degree north of the equator.

Together the islands have a total land mass of 919 square miles (2352 square km). In comparison Hawaii totals 6450 square miles (16512 square km); Bali is 2147 (5496); and Tahiti is 402 (1029).

The islands of Micronesia are classified as 'high' or 'low'. The main islands in western Micronesia are high types and are actually the exposed peaks of a volcanic mountain ridge that runs from Japan through the Northern Marianas, Guam and Palau and on down to New Guinea. While basically of volcanic formation, some of the islands are partly or wholly capped with a layer of limestone. The Northern Marianas have some active volcanoes; Yap is a raised part of the Asian continental shelf; and Pohnpei, Kosrae and Truk, in the eastern Carolines, are also high volcanic islands.

High islands usually have good soil, abundant water and lush vegetation and make up the vast majority of Micronesia's land area. Guam is the largest island, followed by Babeldaob in the Republic of Palau.

The highest point in Micronesia is 3166 feet (950 metres) above sea level, on Agrihan Island in the Northern Marianas. A canyon, known as the Mariana Trench, runs for 1835 miles (2954 km) alongside the Mariana Islands and has the world's greatest known ocean depth. The canyon is more than seven miles (11 km) deep so, if measured from the ocean floor, the Mariana Islands would be the highest mountains in the world!

The Marshall Islands and the small islands of the central Carolines between Yap and Truk's high islands, as well as the small outer islands of Pohnpei and Palau, are low coral atolls.

Some are like the archetypal cartoon island – just a patch of white sand with a single coconut tree. Other islands group together to form the world's first, second and fourth largest atolls, namely Kwajalein in the Marshalls; Namonuito, part of Truk's Western Islands group in the Federated States of Micronesia; and Ulithi, which belongs to Yap, also in the FSM.

Low islands have practically no topsoil and the sand has a high salt content, so vegetation is limited. There are no springs or rivers so where rainfall is low, water is scarce.

Coral Atolls

Charles Darwin was the first to recognise that atolls are made from thousands of years of coral growth which has built up around the edges of a submerged volcanic mountain peak.

In a scenario played out over hundreds of thousands of years, coral first builds up around the shores of a high island producing a fringing reef. Then, when the island begins to slowly sink, the coral continues to grow upwards at about the same rate. This forms a barrier reef which

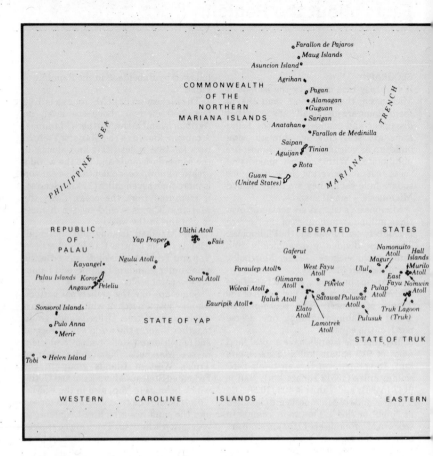

Farallon de Pajaros
Maug Islands
Asuncion Island
Agrihan
COMMONWEALTH
OF THE
NORTHERN
MARIANA ISLANDS
Pagan
Alamagan
Guguan
Sarigan
Anatahan
Farallon de Medinilla
Saipan
Aguijan Tinian
Rota
Guam
(United States)

PHILIPPINE   SEA

TRENCH

MARIANA

REPUBLIC
OF
PALAU
Kayangel
Palau Islands Koror
Angaur Peleliu
Sonsorol Islands
Pulo Anna
Merir
Tobi   Helen Island

Yap Proper
Ngulu Atoll

Ulithi Atoll
Fais

Sorol Atoll

FEDERATED   STATES

Gaferut
Faraulep Atoll
Woleai Atoll
Ifaluk Atoll
Eauripip Atoll

Olimarao
Atoll
West Fayu
Atoll
Pikelot
Satawal

Namonuito
Atoll   Hall
Magur   Islands
Ulul   East   Murilo
Fayu Atoll
Pulap Nomwin
Puluwat Atoll   Atoll
Atoll
Pulusuk   Truk Lagoon
(Truk)

Elato
Atoll
Lamotrek
Atoll

STATE OF YAP

STATE OF TRUK

WESTERN   CAROLINE   ISLANDS   EASTERN

is separated from the shore by a lagoon. By the time the island has completely submerged, the coral growth has become a base for an atoll, circling the place where the mountain top used to be.

The classic atoll shape is roughly oval, with islands of coral rubble and sand built up on higher points of the reef. There are usually breaks in the reef rim large enough for boats to enter the sheltered lagoon.

The coral is made up of millions of tiny rock-like limestone skeletons each one secreted by a separate coral polyp, to protect its soft body, using calcium deposits found in the water. Only the outer layer of coral is alive. As polyps reproduce and die, the new polyps attach themselves in successive layers to the empty skeletons already in place.

CLIMATE

Micronesia has some of the most uniform year-round temperatures in the world. Temperatures range between 70°F and 90°F (21°C to 32°C), with the average daily temperature for all of Micronesia about 81°F (27°C). Humidity percentages average in the high 70s.

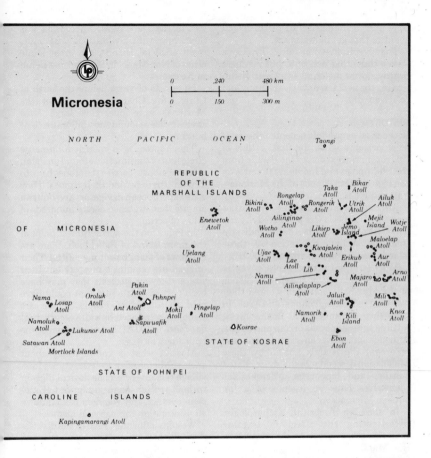

Micronesia

NORTH   PACIFIC   OCEAN

Taongi

REPUBLIC
OF THE
MARSHALL ISLANDS

OF   MICRONESIA

Bikar
Atoll

Taka
Atoll

Rongelap
Atoll   Rongerik
Atoll

Ailuk
Atoll

Bikini
Atoll

Utrik
Atoll

Enewetok
Atoll

Ailinginae

Mejit
Island   Wotje
Atoll

Wotho
Atoll   Likiep
Atoll   Jemo
Island

Maloelap
Atoll

Ujelang
Atoll

Kwajalein
Atoll   Erikub
Atoll   Aur
Atoll

Ujae
Atoll

Lae
Atoll   Lib   Namu
Atoll

Majuro   Arno
Atoll

Ailinglaplap
Atoll

Pakin
Atoll

Nama   Oroluk
Atoll   Losap
Atoll   Pohnpei

Jaluit
Atoll   Mili
Atoll

Namorik
Atoll   Kili
Island

Knox
Atoll

Ant Atoll   Mokil
Atoll   Pingelap
Atoll

Namoluk
Atoll   Sapwuafik
Atoll   Kosrae

Lukunor Atoll

Satawan Atoll

Mortlock Islands   STATE OF KOSRAE

Ebon
Atoll

STATE OF POHNPEI

CAROLINE   ISLANDS

Kapingamarangi Atoll

Generally the most comfortable months are January through March or, stretching the seasons, November through April. These months usually see a bit less rainfall, somewhat lower humidity and slightly cooler weather. Cool north-easterly tradewinds blow across much of Micronesia from December to March.

The average annual rainfall is about 85 to 150 inches (216 to 381 cm), but this varies from place to place. Some of the northern Marshalls get only 20 inches (51 cm) a year, while Pohnpei's rainforest interior gets over 400 inches (1016 cm) per year. Rainfall decreases in the Carolines from east to west.

A typhoon is a tropical storm in the western Pacific with winds over 75 miles (120 km) per hour. (The same storm, if found in the Atlantic or eastern Pacific, would be called a hurricane.)

Typhoons can occur in any month. Guam and the Northern Marianas are particularly susceptible, being directly in the storm track. For travellers staying in modern hotels it mostly means heavy winds and rains and the loss of a day outdoors. The real damage occurs with downed coconut trees and to thatched huts or tin-roofed shanties that get blown apart.

The silver lining comes after. Typhoons – even those that don't hit, but just pass nearby – draw moisture away with them, leaving the next few days clear, sunny and relatively dry.

HISTORY

In the most commonly accepted theory of Micronesian origins, the first settlers of this region canoed across the Pacific from the Philippines and Indonesia to settle on the high western islands of the Marianas, Yap and Palau.

Although some historians think that western Micronesia was populated as early as 2000 to 4000 BC, carbon dating indicates that the earliest habitation of those islands was on Saipan around 1500 BC.

Much later, so the theory goes, voyagers from Melanesia settled the eastern islands of the Marshalls and then worked their way west to Kosrae, Pohnpei and Truk. In time they continued still further west, settling the outer atolls of Yap and Palau. Although spread over an enormous expanse of ocean, the islands settled by these Melanesian descendants still share related cultures and languages. Micronesians themselves have no legends of a life outside Micronesia.

In 1986 an American archaeologist investigating the effect of ongoing radiation experiments on Bikini Atoll in the Marshall Islands discovered bone fragments and the remains of a village. These artifacts have been carbon dated to 1960 BC, making Bikini the site of the earliest human settlement yet discovered in all of Micronesia.

Pre-European Contact

Micronesia's inhabited island groups had thriving cultures and well-established societies long before the arrival of the Europeans.

As the islands had no metals, their most impressive archaeological remains are achievements in stone. While Europe was lost in the Dark Ages, Micronesia was flourishing with civilisations that built, upon artificial islands, the great stone cities of Nan Madol in Pohnpei and Leluh in Kosrae.

Hundreds of years before the birth of Christ, the Chamorros people of the Marianas were quarrying large *latte* stones to use as foundation pillars for their buildings.

The Yapese, who quarried immense circles out of the limestone found on Palau to use as money, carried the stones back to Yap on barges behind their canoes. They were superb ocean navigators and built an empire that stretched across hundreds of miles of ocean.

In Palau, on the northernmost point of the main island of Babeldaob, there are two rows of giant basalt monoliths. Their original use remains a mystery but their size and layout suggests they may have been part of a structure that could have held thousands of people. There are elaborately terraced hillsides nearby that date back to 100 AD but no one knows who built them or why.

Most of what is known today about ancient Micronesian societies comes from village remains or archaeological digs for without written languages, prior to European contact, the islanders passed down all information through oral histories.

Western influences, such as the diseases that killed off most of the population and the missionaries that converted the rest, shredded the traditional social fabric of the islands. The missionaries, by discouraging talk of the early religions and gods, contributed to the loss of oral traditions and in many places the old stories have been forgotten completely, resulting in a sort of cultural amnesia.

The First Europeans

In the late 1400s Portuguese explorers, in a quest for spices, established a trade route around Africa and across the Indian Ocean to the Spice Islands, or the Moluccas (Maluku), which are now part of present-day Indonesia. The Spanish, who were denied this Portuguese trade route by a decree from the pope, were forced to sail west to get to the east, so the search for an alternate route to the Spice Islands was on.

It led to a flurry of exploration beginning with Christopher Columbus who discovered parts of the Americas while floundering around the Atlantic looking for a route to the Pacific. The Americas were, however, just a pain in the arse for Columbus and the next few explorers because they became a massive obstacle in their search for the Spice Islands.

The first Europeans to actually set foot in Micronesia were with the Spanish expedition of Portuguese explorer Ferdinand Magellan in 1521. It had taken 30 years to successfully find a way around the Americas. Magellan became the first navigator to lead his ships around the tip of South America into the Pacific and the expedition was the first to circumnavigate the globe.

It was an indication of the vastness of the Pacific and the smallness of its islands that Magellan managed to sail across the entire ocean from South America's Cape Horn to the Mariana Islands, close to the Asian mainland, without encountering any of the scattering of islands along the way.

By the time they arrived in the Marianas, Magellan and his scurvy-ridden crew were eating rats and boiled leather to ward off complete starvation. Although the islanders provided the starving crew with food, drink and shelter, they also helped themselves to whatever they could carry off the ships. This led, of course, to retaliation by the Spanish.

Antonio Pigafette, one of Magellan's crew, wrote the following about the first encounter between Europeans and Micronesians.

' . . . the people of these islands boarded the ships and robbed us, in such a way that it was impossible to preserve oneself from them. Whilst we were lowering the sails to go ashore, they stole away with much address and

diligence the small boat called the skiff, which was made fast to the poop of the captain's ship, at which he was much irritated, and went on shore with forty armed men, burned forty or fifty houses, with several small boats, and killed seven men of the island; they recovered their skiff.'

This was just the first of many confrontations between explorers and Micronesians.

The Spanish Period

Numerous explorers soon followed in Magellan's path, beginning with the Spanish expedition under Juan Garcia Jofre de Loaysa in 1526. The tiny islands of Micronesia, devoid of cloves or gold, held little interest for the explorers other than as a quick stop-over to replenish water and food. Certainly no one ever set out to 'discover' Micronesia and it took more than 300 years for all the islands to be added to the charts.

In 1565 Spanish trade ships started making annual trips between Mexico and the Philippines. These 'Manila Galleons' picked up silk, spices and tea from Chinese traders in Manila and took them to Acapulco, where they loaded newly mined silver and carried it back to the Philippines.

The 'new' transpacific shipping corridors, established by the European traders to take advantage of favourable trade winds, actually followed routes the ocean-going Micronesians had been sailing for centuries. Because the ships attempted to stick to these precise routes very few Micronesian islands, outside these corridors, were discovered during the 16th and 17th centuries.

In one notable exception, after a mutiny in 1565, the Spanish ship San Lucas dropped a few degrees from the usual route to avoid other Spanish ships. In doing so it was the first European vessel to come upon a number of Marshallese atolls and Truk Lagoon.

Spain's interest in Micronesia at this time was centred almost entirely on the Marianas, where the galleons made regular stops to replenish supplies. Spanish missionaries arrived in the Marianas in 1668, accompanied by the military and government authorities sent to establish colonial rule. Spanish culture, language and Catholicism were forced upon the native Chamorros.

The Caroline Islands got their first Spanish missionaries in the early 1700s, but they had only a nominal presence. Outside the Marianas there were no significant European influences in Micronesia until the late 1700s when British, American and European traders began plying the waters for commercial purposes.

Whalers, Traders & Missionaries

Beginning in 1817 with Otto Kotzebue, French and Russian explorers began carefully exploring and mapping Micronesia's islands. They also wrote some colourful accounts of the island people and their lifestyles.

The first British whalers began to arrive in the early 1800s and American whaleships, out of New England, arrived a couple of decades later though in much greater numbers. During the whaling boom, in the 1840s, there were as many as 500 ships hunting whales in the Pacific.

Whaling was not a romantic business; it was back-breaking work. The whaleships were virtually factories which could stay at sea for years on end, boiling down blubber into oil and storing it in tanks on board. The islands were used to replenish food, water and wood. Desertion was common.

Traders were also infiltrating Micronesia at this time, setting up posts to deal in copra and beche-de-mer (sea cucumbers).

Whalers and traders were not usually the cream of civilised society. The sailors picked fights, taunted the natives and spurred massacres, although quite often it was the islanders who would do away with the crews. Kosrae had so much trouble with the 'degenerate whites' that jumped ship that the chief initiated a policy of putting deserters back out to sea on the next ship that pulled into port.

When the sailors came into port, usually after many months at sea, they were ready to party and they wanted women. In exchange they brought venereal and other contagious diseases to which the islanders, with no in-built immunities, were particularly susceptible.

Foreign diseases such as syphilis, smallpox, measles and influenza had devastating effects and caused a rapid depopulation of the islands. A single smallpox epidemic in 1854 killed approximately 50% of Pohnpei's population.

Prior to the arrival of the whaling ships, Kosrae's population was estimated to be about 6000. By the time the whalers had left the population had dropped to 300 and the Kosraeans were ripe for the prudish morality the Congregationalists were about to lay on them.

The American Board of Commissioners for Foreign Missions began sending missionaries to eastern Micronesia in 1870, after two decades of Protestant work had proven fairly successful in Hawaii.

The Protestant missionaries in the east, like the Catholic priests in the west, brought more than religion. They brought western clothing for the scantily clad islanders, as well as western laws and values. They were the first to put the native languages into a written form, primarily so the Bible could be translated, and they set up schools to teach the people to read and write.

The 1800s was a time of major change in Micronesia and the introduction of alcohol, firearms, new animals, new tools and new ideas all had a dramatic effect upon the islands.

The German Period

The start of the German period in Micronesia was more of a commercial venture than a fully fledged attempt to colonise. Disregarding Spanish claims in the region, the Germans arrived in Micronesia in the 19th century to develop the copra trade.

The first German company to set up

operations in Micronesia was Godeffroy & Sons. From their headquarters in New Guinea they opened an office in Yap in 1869.

Meanwhile 2200 miles to the east the Germans were negotiating a treaty with the numerous chiefs of Jaluit Atoll in the Marshall Islands. In 1878 Germany established a protectorate over the Marshalls.

Spain grumbled about German activity in the Carolines but did little else until 1885 when the dispute was taken to Pope Leo XIII for arbitration. The pope ruled that Spain owned the land and had administrative rights, but Germany had a right to establish plantations and commerce. For Spain, it was largely a face-saving decision as her days as a major colonial power were numbered.

In 1898 the United States, looking to get in on the action, abruptly declared war on a reluctant Spain. As an outcome of the Spanish-American War the US was ceded Spain's Pacific possessions of Guam, the Philippines and Wake Island (as well as Puerto Rico and Cuba). As part of the deal, the US paid US$20 million to Spain.

Not particularly keen on selling her remaining Micronesian possessions to gunboat diplomats, Spain went into secret negotiations with Germany for the sale of the Carolines and the remaining Marianas. In 1899 the Germans, now eager to become established as a colonial power, agreed on a purchase price of 25 million pesetas, or about US$4¼ million.

The period of German administration therefore began with a simple real estate transaction. It was to last a mere 15 years. Commercial development was mainly in terms of copra production, though there were also some phosphate mining operations. German interests were led by the Jaluit Company which controlled the copra trade in the Marshalls and eastern Carolines and governed the islands through local chiefs. In Yap and Palau the copra market was largely in the hands of Japanese traders.

The natives were encouraged to grow coconuts and were given seed, tools and long-term contracts. To increase manpower for German mines and plantations outer islanders were sometimes removed from their atolls. Communally held land, often seemingly idle, was redistributed to the new arrivals or leased by the government to private enterprise. Germany's main legacy in Micronesia rests in the social disruptions caused by forced relocations and altered land use policies.

Germany's presence, however, was limited to a small group of government officials, businessmen and missionaries. The total population of Germans in all Micronesia numbered well under 1000. Some of the businesses, such as the German South Seas Phosphate Company in Angaur and the Jaluit Company, made money but in the overall picture German government subsidies to faltering businesses usually outweighed the profits.

With the onset of WW I German forces fled Micronesia, allowing the Japanese fleet to sail in without resistance.

The Japanese Period

Japan had control of the whole of Micronesia, with the exception of Guam, between the two world wars; a period of about 30 years.

Throughout Germany's occupation, Japan had been tightening its economic ties with Micronesia and just prior to WW I maintained more than 80% of all trade with 'German Micronesia'. The Japanese imported turtle shell, mother of pearl, beche-de-mer and other products from the islands.

With the outbreak of hostilities in Europe, Japan made her move to bring Micronesia closer to home and in October 1914 the Japanese Navy seized possession of the German colonies under the pretext of alliance obligations with Britain. The Japanese then proceeded to occupy the islands, starting in the east with the Marshalls and moving westward, quickly developing the infrastructure and administration necessary for the complete annexation of Micronesia. Things were moving right along by the time the League of Nations formally mandated control of Micronesia to Japan in 1920.

By this time Saipan, the nearest island to Japan, was already home to a growing number of Japanese colonists and entrepreneurs who had sugar cane production underway. The South Seas Development Company bought them out in 1921 and rapidly became the dominant force in Micronesia's development and exploitation.

The Japanese left no doubt they were there to stay. Micronesia was an extension of the empire's boundaries, an expansion of its horizons. Their intent was to make Micronesia as Japanese as possible. They built Buddhist temples and Shinto shrines, geisha houses and public baths. Each administrative centre became a little Tokyo.

The building of roads, harbours, hospitals and water systems were followed by seaplane ramps, airfields and other fortifications; the latter in violation of the League of Nations mandate. The Japanese withdrew from the league in 1935 but remained firmly in control of Micronesia.

Administrative buildings were constructed of heavy concrete capable of withstanding not only typhoons but also direct aerial bombings. Many of these buildings, with their 20 inch (51 cm) thick walls and steel reinforcements, were to weather both.

Although the mandate called for the economic and social development of Micronesia, the Japanese geared this development not toward benefiting the local population but rather toward supporting and fortifying their own settlements. Expatriates came to outnumber the Micronesians. By 1940 the Japanese population in the Marianas, Carolines and Marshalls was more than 70,000, compared to about 50,000 Micronesians.

In the Marianas, railroads were built to carry the sugar from the plantations to the harbourside refineries and from there the sugar and alcohol was shipped to the Japanese homeland. Throughout Micronesia, fisheries projects, copra and tapioca production, phosphate and bauxite mining and trochus shell production were being developed and were thriving.

The Japanese, drawing from their own experiences of life on their resource-scarce home islands, created an astonishing level of agricultural activity in Micronesia. With exports greater than imports it was an economic viability that would never be remotely approached under the Americans. In terms of production it was Micronesia's heyday.

Not that all that necessarily made it the most pleasant of times for the Micronesians themselves, whose place in this profitable system was most definitely at the bottom. There was a two-tier system of education which saw Japanese children attending excellent schools while the three years of compulsory education for Micronesians was primarily geared to teaching them a servant's form of the Japanese language. This subordination prevailed in wage scales and social treatment as well.

Although it was an impressive economy, for the Micronesians it was a trickle-down economy and during wartime, when the trickle stopped, it was the native islanders who were the first to feel hard times and hunger.

The Japanese not only made the islands more productive than they had ever been before, they also set Micronesia on a shifting course from a traditional subsistence lifestyle to a moneyed economy with a penchant for imported goods.

In boom-towns like Garapan and Koror, the sudden development awed many locals and they developed a taste for the goods in the store windows. Many wanted a piece of the pie, or more precisely, they wanted the rice, canned food and sugar candies that only money could buy.

World War II

The war in the Pacific was launched with the Japanese air attacks on Honolulu's Pearl Harbor on 7 December 1941; and against the US territory of Guam on the same day, 8 December across the international date line.

Undefended, Guam surrendered two days later just hours after Japanese forces came ashore. With its capture, the Japanese possessed all of Micronesia and it was two years before any serious counteroffensive was launched by the US.

On 1 February 1944, US Admiral Chester Nimitz, Commander in Chief of the Pacific Fleet, started his drive across the Pacific with an attack on Kwajalein Atoll in the Marshall Islands, a major Japanese air and naval base.

By 4 February the US had captured Kwajalein and the undefended Majuro Atoll to the south and from these two outposts the Americans began air raids on Japanese bases in the western Carolines.

On 17 February the US made a surprise attack on a fleet of Japanese warships and commercial vessels harboured in Truk Lagoon. This supposedly impenetrable fortress was the Imperial Japanese Fleet's most important base in the central Pacific. The US hit more than 200 planes on the ground and sent nearly 60 ships to watery graves. The 200,000 tons of equipment sunk in the two days of fighting was to be a record for WW II. After the raid the few surviving Japanese ships evacuated Truk, leaving behind 30,000 Japanese troops who had little to do but wait out the war.

With the Truk base neutralised and no longer able to provide support to other Pacific bases, the US continued moving west, capturing Enewetok and other smaller atolls and islands in the Marshalls.

In June 1944, US forces moved west from the Marshalls with their Fifth Fleet, the largest armada ever assembled. Nearly 600 battleships, cruisers, destroyers and carriers carried a quarter of a million American troops across the Pacific.

The fight for the Marianas began with the US invasion of Saipan on 15 June. Tinian and Guam were invaded in July and all three islands were 'liberated' by the beginning of August. The battles there were some of the most brutal and costly but marked a major turning point in the war as the US finally had air bases within striking distance of Japan.

With the Marianas secured, only Palau was left, and in retrospect it would have been better off left alone. Though it was earlier feared that air raids from Palau would threaten a planned US invasion of the Philippines, Japanese air power in the western Pacific had nearly collapsed and the Palau bases had little significance in the declining days of the war.

Despite that however, the US attacked the Palauan island of Peleliu on 15 September. It was secured after a month of even bloodier battles than those witnessed in the Marianas.

With planes taking off from Micronesian airstrips, the air bombing of Japan began in force in November 1944. In August 1945 two planes, leaving from Tinian, dropped the first atomic bombs used in warfare on the industrial ports of Hiroshima and Nagasaki. The devastation of those cities and the awesome death toll was followed days later by the unconditional surrender of the Japanese.

The Micronesians had watched the impressive Japanese construction of fortified command posts, communications buildings, hospitals, airports and harbours. Caught in the crossfire, they watched as the US turned it all into crumbling rubble. Whole towns such as Koror, Garapan and Sapou were levelled, some of them never to be rebuilt. For Micronesia, the Rising Sun had also set.

In the months following the end of the war, thousands of Japanese were shipped home, most of them civilians or soldiers from uninvaded islands. The US took few military prisoners since most Japanese soldiers chose to fight to the death or commit suicide rather than surrender.

Many Japanese civilians killed themselves as well, rather than risk the torturing they had been told the Americans would inflict upon them.

Thousands of Americans and tens of thousands of Japanese died fighting in Micronesia. Thousands of Micronesians died too, though no one paid much attention to Micronesian body counts. In all the volumes written about WW II they are scarcely mentioned. Their islands were the stage but the islanders were not the players, merely the victims.

The Americans Move In

Even though Micronesians played no role in the Pacific conflict, the US government immediately began to treat Micronesia as their 'spoils of war'. The occupying forces were suddenly American instead of Japanese and when the war ended, the occupation continued.

The US Navy took command of the islands in 1945 and effectively sealed the area off to visitors. Some areas remained closed until 1962.

The isolation of the Micronesians and the fact that they were so few in numbers left them unseen, unheard and isolated to all beyond their shores. It was an isolation that the US military intended to maintain.

The Nuclear Age

Throughout Micronesia, islanders had been rocked by two military superpowers battling on their shores. Yet for the Marshallese, the destruction did not cease with the end of the Pacific conflict; for them the most fearsome display of firepower still lay ahead.

Soon after the end of the war, the US took over sections of the Marshalls to test nuclear weapons and the little-understood effects of radiation.

On 1 July 1946 the first nuclear device was exploded over Bikini Atoll. Experiments began at Enewetok Atoll in 1948. There would be 66 nuclear tests altogether that would leave some atolls uninhabitable and hundreds of islanders victims of radiation.

The most powerful bomb ever tested by the US was detonated over Bikini's lagoon in 'Operation Bravo' on 1 March 1954. The 15-megaton hydrogen bomb had a tonnage of TNT greater than the total tonnage of explosives used during the entire course of WW II. Operation Bravo's H-bomb was a thousand times more powerful than the bomb dropped on Hiroshima.

Pulverized coral from Bikini's reef was scattered, along with radioactive fallout, over an area of about 50,000 square miles. It filtered down upon the Marshallese on the islands of Rongelap and Utrik, upon US weather station personnel on Rongerik and upon the unlucky crew of the Japanese fishing vessel *Lucky Dragon*. More than 300 people and their offspring were affected. The US evacuated the islanders 48 hours later, but by that time many had already suffered severe radiation burns from 'Bikini snow'.

Nuclear experiments ended in 1958 with an international test-ban treaty. The US halted testing just prior to plans to blast nuclear warheads into space from Bikini Atoll; the warheads were instead launched from Johnson Island in 1961.

Trust Territory

In 1947 the United Nations established a trusteeship in Micronesia. Called the Trust Territory of the Pacific Islands, it had six districts: the Northern Marianas, Ponape (including Kosrae), Truk, Yap, the Marshalls and Palau. The United States was given exclusive rights for administering the islands.

The UN designated the area a 'strategic trust', allowing the US to establish and maintain military bases in Micronesia and prevent other nations from doing the same.

In 1951 the US Department of the Interior took over from the navy, moving the Trust Territory headquarters from Honolulu to Guam. The Northern Marianas were the only exception; they remained under military control until 1962.

Under UN guidelines, the US was obliged to foster the development of political and economic institutions with the goal of helping the Micronesians achieve self-government and self-sufficiency. Instead, 20 years of neglect were followed by 20 years of promoting welfare dependency.

Instead of developing an economic infrastructure and promoting industry, the US pumped in money for government-operated social services. Instead of encouraging farming and fishing, they passed out USDA food commodities. They built hospitals, schools, old age centres and other projects, creating an abundance of government jobs with no internal base capable of bankrolling it all. It was an economy reliant on imported greenbacks.

With anti-colonial sentiment high in the '60s, the US found itself, with its Micronesian possessions, to be one of the more blatant transgressors. To counter the mounting criticism, steps were taken for the islanders to assume a degree of self-government.

With this in mind, the Congress of Micronesia was established in 1965 to coordinate Trust Territory activities. It was a two-house legislature made up of elected representatives from all island groups. Executive authority in the Trust Territory, however, remained in the hands of the American High Commissioner and to make sure nothing got out of hand, the CIA kept tabs on island legislators by bugging the offices of the Congress of Micronesia.

Peace Corps

With the arrival of the Peace Corps in 1966 a new breed of Americans appeared on the scene. They were more concerned with the interests of the people of Micronesia than they were in the strategic interests of the United States. For the first time, Americans slept, ate and lived with the Micronesians; some even stayed on to marry into Micronesian life.

For awhile there was one volunteer for every 100 Micronesians and the US government no doubt saw the Peace Corps

as a way of spreading American influence. By putting a volunteer on every inhabited island, they brought English as a unifying language to the distant corners of Micronesia. What they hadn't calculated though, was the idealism and the critical outlook on American policies that the volunteers would also bring.

Volunteers worked in community development projects and as legal advisors. Peace Corps lawyers taught the Micronesians they had certain legal rights, including the right to challenge US government policies. The US Defense Department became particularly concerned with challenges to land policies. In response to the volunteers activities in Micronesia, the Nixon administration phased out the Peace Corps' legal services programme.

GOVERNMENT

When negotiations for self-government were first started, the US had initially expected that the six Trust Territory districts would join together as one Micronesian nation, but this was not to be.

In January 1978 the people of Northern Marianas opted to become American citizens with US Commonwealth status.

In July 1978 the remaining six districts (Kosrae had become a separate district in 1977) voted on a common constitution. It was not passed in the Marshalls or Palau.

The four central districts, Ponape (later renamed Pohnpei), Kosrae, Truk and Yap, who had voted in favour became the Federated States of Micronesia. Their constitution went into effect in May 1979.

The Marshallese drew up a constitution of their own, making the new Republic of the Marshall Islands a separate political entity. Their constitution also went into effect in May 1979.

Palauans, renaming their islands the Republic of Palau, voted for a constitution that went into effect in January 1981. It included a provision which totally banned the use, testing and storage of nuclear weapons and materials on its land and in its surrounding waters.

The internal governments of each of these new emerging nations are based on the US system of executive, legislative and judicial branches, with the exception of the Marshallese government which also incorporates elements of the British parliamentary system. Traditional village councils and high-ranking chiefs often retain some powers through advisory boards.

In 1982 all three new nations signed separate Compacts of Free Association with the US, all getting different economic deals. In theory the compacts allow the new nations to manage their internal affairs, although their relationships with other nations are subject to US restrictions. In return for millions of dollars to the islanders, the compacts allow the US to maintain sweeping military rights throughout Micronesia.

Before the Trust Territory could be dissolved, however, each compact had to be approved by four separate groups in turn: by the peoples of each new nation in a general election, by the legislatures of those nations, by the US Congress and by the UN Security Council.

The compacts of the FSM and the Marshalls were approved in plebiscites in 1983. The next step was ratification by the respective congresses. Finally the US Congress approved the two compacts, with the provisions going into effect in November 1986.

Unresolved issues in Palau, however, have stalled not only Palau's own political process, but the dissolution of the Trust Territory as well.

The compact between the US and Palau permits the US to transfer and store nuclear materials in the area, a clear violation of Palau's constitution. In vote after vote, Palauans have consistently approved the compact by the majority vote required, but with fewer than the 75%

required to overturn the anti-nuclear provision in the constitution. The compact and the constitution, both legally approved by Palauans, are in legal conflict with one another. In what many people see as a strongarm tactic, the US refuses to renegotiate the compact and remains steadfast on requiring nukes. The US Congress refuses to vote on Palau's compact until the issue is resolved by Palauan courts or voters.

The UN Security Council wants to make only one vote on dissolving the entire trusteeship, rather than disbanding it a portion at a time. That can happen only after all the islands have gone through the processes. This leaves the other nations waiting on Palau. In addition, there is the likelihood in the UN of a veto by at least the Soviet Union who's not keen on seeing the entire region stay in US hands and calls the compacts 'virtual slavery' for Micronesians.

After WW II the UN established 11 trusteeships of former colonial possessions. One by one they have attained self-governing status and with the independence of Papua New Guinea in 1975, Micronesia had the dubious distinction of being the only remaining Trust Territory. The US wants it to look as if these emerging Pacific nations are free to go their own way, but has done its best to make sure they can't go very far.

ECONOMY

The economy of Micronesia is heavily dependent on US appropriations, which makes it possible for island governments to employ roughly 60% of the total work force. Their payrolls form the backbone of the entire economy.

Hundreds of graduates are returning each year from overseas colleges to find the already bloated government departments unable to absorb them. The jobs just aren't there. Along with their degrees, many have acquired a taste for western lifestyles and are no longer satisfied with a subsistence life of farming and fishing.

They've become a new group of young, dislodged and disillusioned unemployed.

Actually, with the exception of those in the subsistence economy, Micronesians produce very little. Many of the private sector jobs that do exist deal largely in imported goods. Few, if any, of the products found in the department stores, markets, bars, office suppliers, petrol stations or Toyota dealers are locally produced. In a way the whole moneyed economy is an artificial one bankrolled by the US. It has no local base and no way of sustaining itself.

Exports are generally limited to copra, handicrafts, trochus shells and a few marine products. The total value of all exports doesn't generate enough income to even pay Micronesia's fuel bills.

As the trusteeship comes to an end, the US is finally completing a vast capital improvement plan in Micronesia, including new airfields, docks, water and sewerage systems, paved roads and hospitals. However, without training local labour in the maintenance of the sophisticated power, water and sewerage systems, the upkeep may well be beyond local capabilities, even if they could shoulder the estimated annual repair and operation costs of over $35 million for these new projects.

Although they have created a fair amount of hustle and bustle, most often the projects are contracted out to foreign firms, providing minimal benefits to the local economy. Recently for example, the Chinese under a Japanese contractor built a new multi-million dollar hospital in Saipan and the tab was picked up by the US.

The nature of US expenditures in Micronesia has created a dependency, rather than fostered self-sufficiency. Micronesians have little to barter except their water and their land, the latter for US military bases, the former to tuna fleets who want fishing rights within their 200-mile (322 km) economic zones.

PEOPLE & CULTURE

Micronesia's population is about 270,000, with 110,000 of those living on Guam. Micronesian societies can be divided into two groups: those on the high islands and those on the low islands.

On the high islands, people developed a land-based subsistence lifestyle, tending to be homebodies. Food sources were reliable and it was an easier lifestyle that supported larger populations. The high islanders developed stable and elaborate societies, some highly stratified with caste hierarchies, chiefs, royalty, commoners and the like.

Low atoll islanders also share a similar lifestyle, eking their living out of the sea rather than the land. They have traditionally been expert navigators, sailors and fishers. They travelled great distances and though their next door neighbours were sometimes hundreds of miles away, visits were not infrequent.

Canoe journeys between islands brought trade, warfare and new ideas. Islanders near each other share things in common and can often understand each other's languages, whereas islanders at opposite ends of Micronesia are quite different and their languages mutually unintelligible. It is among the low islanders that the commonalities of culture and language are spread over the greatest distances.

Micronesian societies are made up of clan groupings descended matrilineally (except Yap, which is patrilineal) from a common ancestor. The head clan on each island can trace its lineage back to the original settlers of the island and members of that clan usually retain certain privileges.

Extended families are the norm and it's not uncommon for grandparents, cousins, children and an adopted clan member to live under the same roof. If one family member gets a good job other relatives may well move in and live off the income. In general, people visiting other islands simply look up a member of their clan to stay with.

Canoes & Navigation

Some of the greatest navigators in the Pacific came from the resource-scarce low islands of Micronesia. With their sandy soil offering limited food supplies they took to the oceans. In general, the smaller the islands, the more ocean-going the islanders.

Without compasses or maps, Micronesians used a combination of natural aids to direct themselves around the Pacific.

The long Marshallese atolls, fairly close together in north-south lines, interrupt the large swells that move across the Pacific from east to west. Marshallese navigation depended largely on learning to feel and interpret the patterns of the currents and waves that were deflected around the islands.

The Carolinians' main focus was on the sky. Because most travel was in an east-west line, they could keep on course by watching the sun and by identifying individual stars that would rise or set over particular islands. They sang ancient chants which contained information on star patterns and other directions on how to navigate.

The Micronesians also used a variety of patterns and clues that together with swell interpretations and celestial compasses formed highly refined methods of navigation.

For instance, to see if land was near, they would watch for birds returning home to their island nests in the evening. A single stationary cloud off in the distance was often moist ocean air hovering over a high island; and although coral atolls are too flat to be seen from far away, their shallow aqua-coloured lagoons reflect a pale green light onto the undersides of clouds.

Micronesian canoes have a single outrigger. In protected areas islanders used simple dugout canoes, made from a single tree trunk. On the open ocean they used huge canoes, up to 100 feet (30 metres) long, constructed of planks tied together with cord made from coconut husk fibres. These ocean-going vessels were often larger and faster than the ships of the early European explorers and could hold 100 passengers or more.

LANGUAGE

Micronesian languages are in the Austronesian language group. The major native languages are: Marshallese; Palauan; Chamorro, in Guam and the Northern Marianas; Yapese, Ulithian and Woleaian in Yap; Pohnpeian and Kapingamarangi-Nukuoro in Pohnpei; Trukese and Mortlockese in Truk; and Kosraean. There are several more dialects spoken on the outer islands.

English is widely spoken throughout Micronesia and elderly people often speak Japanese.

RELIGION

Micronesia has been almost completely Christianised. Spanish Catholics got to the Marianas and the western islands first and New England Protestants converted the Marshalls and the eastern islands. They met somewhere in the middle, with Truk and Pohnpei turning out about half Catholic and half Protestant.

HOLIDAYS

Most of Micronesia takes advantage of US public holidays and then throws in a few of its own. The additional holidays vary from island to island but the usual standards are:

January
    New Year's Day
    Martin Luther King's Birthday (3rd Monday)
February
    President's Day (3rd Monday)
April
    Good Friday
May
    Memorial Day (last Monday)
July
    US Independence Day (4th)
September
    Labor Day (1st Monday)

October
   Columbus Day (2nd Monday)
   United Nations Day (24th)
November
   Veteran's Day (11th)
   Thanksgiving (4th Thursday)
December
   Christmas Day (25th)

Holidays and special events specific to island groups are listed in those sections.

FAUNA & FLORA

The closer an island group is to the Asian land masses, the more numerous its birds and animals. High islands have a greater variety and support larger populations than coral atolls. The Marshalls therefore have few creatures other than seabirds and shorebirds while Palau, predictably, has the greatest variety.

The only land mammals native to Micronesia are bats. Fruit bats, with wingspans of up to three feet (one metre), are found on all island groups except the Marshalls. They are common at dusk in Palau's Rock Islands and on Truk, Pohnpei and Yap. Due to a Chamorro penchant for eating the furry flying beasts, they are now on the endangered list in Guam and rare in Saipan and Tinian. Imported fruit bats sell for $14 per frozen pound in Guam.

Animals that have been introduced into the islands include dogs, cats, mice, rats, pigs, cattle, horses and goats. Angaur in Palau has monkeys; and sambar deer are found on Pohnpei, Rota, Guam and Saipan, though they are seldom seen.

Guam has *carabao* (water buffalo), which were probably brought in by Jesuit missionaries in the 1600s. Carabao are most often seen in the southern part of Guam where they are used on small farms as beasts of burden. They are large clumsy animals and not always good-tempered with strangers.

Palau has estuarine crocodiles (and a few New Guinea crocodiles) that frequent both saltwater and freshwater areas, favouring muddy mangrove swamps. They are primarily nocturnal, but may bask in the sun during the day. Adult crocodiles average 12 feet (3.6 metres) in length and can be dangerous. After a spearfisherman, hunting fish not crocs, was eaten in the late 1960s, Australian hunters were bought in to pick off the larger reptiles. The crocodile that actually killed the fisherman was captured and part of the man's arm and flashlight were found in its stomach. Palauans occasionally hunt crocodiles with guns or spears, eating the meat and selling the skins, though technically they are now endangered and protected.

You might come across monitors (sometimes incorrectly called iguana) sunning themselves on the roads or hanging out in caves or muddy swamps. These predatory lizards can reach up to six feet (1.8 metres) in length but are more commonly half that size.

Genus Tibia

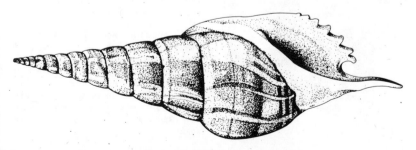

Turtles, including hawksbills, green turtles and leatherbacks, lay eggs on uninhabited sandy beaches and have been an important food source in Micronesia for centuries.

Micronesia has a variety of crabs, including coconut crabs and mangrove crabs which both make good eating. Coconut crabs are sometimes caught by islanders and kept in cages while they grow to a meatier size. They are strong enough to tear open a metal rubbish bin and pry apart the bars of a steel barbecue grill. And yes, they can also rip through coconut husks and shells!

Other than venomous but non-aggressive sea snakes and worm-sized blind snakes, Micronesia's only legless reptiles are on Guam and Palau. Palau has the Pacific Island boa in its forests; the Palau tree snake in its small trees and shrubs; and the dog-faced water snake in its mangrove swamps. None pose a threat to people.

The brown tree snake, accidentally introduced to Guam in the late 1940s, has wiped out virtually all of Guam's forest birds. In the 1960s it was noted that the number of birds was declining and by the

Red-mouth Frog Shell (Bursa B...)

Laciniate Conch (Strombus sinuatus)

late 1970s many species survived only in a small forested area in the north. While pesticides and avian disease were suspected, it wasn't until the 1980s that the snake was identified as the primary culprit. For most birds it was too late. The Guam flycatcher, bridled white-eye, rufous-fronted fantail and nearly all Guam's native forest birds are now considered extinct.

Meanwhile there are now believed to be a million brown tree snakes living without predators on Guam, roaming the forest trees at night and polishing off birds and eggs, or at least what's left of them. With so few birds left to eat, the snakes are resorting to chicken eggs, rodents and lizards.

Micronesia has a number of native skinks including a green variety, which can grow to one foot long; and others with iridescent blue tails. The endearing gecko, a small common house lizard that scampers along walls and ceilings by means of suction-cup-like feet, has a loud call. It prefers to live indoors with people, paying its way by eating mosquitoes and other pesky insects.

Ramose Murex (Chicoreus ramosus)

Giant Frog Shell (Bursa bufos)

Orange Spider Conch (Lambis ?scuta.)

Micronesia has about 7000 varieties of insects. Mosquitoes, beach gnats and cockroaches are the most common annoyances. Large numbers of butterflies are particularly noticeable on Guam, perhaps because the geckos and skinks that once preyed on the caterpillars are now prey themselves for the brown tree snake.

Birds

The cardinal honeyeater, a small bright red and black bird, is endangered in Guam but easily seen elsewhere. It's found in gardens and forests, poking its curved bill into the centres of hibiscus and other flowers. The Northern Marianas have a golden honeyeater.

White-tailed tropicbirds, distinguishable by two long white tail feathers, are often seen riding the air currents around the cliffs where they build their nests.

The white or grey Pacific reef heron is common on reefs and in shallow water where it uses its long beak to hunt for fish and small crabs. Cattle egrets are sometimes seen in open grassy areas.

Kingfishers in Micronesia seldom fish. These pretty, blue and white birds, with cinnamon-coloured touches, are found on Pohnpei, Palau and in the Marianas and their diet consists mainly of insects and lizards.

Micronesian starlings are common and widespread. Starlings like to eat papayas and some islanders like to eat starlings.

The best place to see the endangered Micronesian megapode is in Palau's Rock Islands, where some of these ground-living birds have built their nests on the picnic beaches. The megapode does not incubate its eggs, but lays them in the ground, warming them with dirt and decaying matter. Endemic to Micronesia, this species is now extinct on Guam and Rota. There is a small group near Saipan's Suicide Cliff in the Northern Marianas.

The koko, a type of rail or wading marsh bird, is a flightless bird indigenous to Guam that now survives only in zoos. Palau has a banded rail.

Some of the more commonly seen shorebirds, especially during spring and autumn migrations, include: the lesser golden-plover, wandering tattler, grey-tailed tattler, whimbrel and ruddy turnstone. Common seabirds include the brown noddy, black noddy and white tern.

More than 200 species of birds have been recorded in Micronesia and about 85 species breed in the area. Serious birdwatchers should get hold of a 12-page listing titled *Checklist of the Birds of Micronesia*, by Peter Pyle and John Engbring. It's available for $2 from the Hawaii Audubon Society, Box 22832, Honolulu, Hawaii 96822.

A Field Guide to the Birds of Hawaii & the Tropical Pacific by H D Pratt, P L Bruner and D G Berrett (Princeton University Press, New Jersey, 1987), is probably the best general bird guide to the area.

Flora

The coconut palm tree is Micronesia's most important plant. Copra, the dried meat of the nut from which coconut oil is made, is its most important export. The nut also provides food, drinking liquid and sap for making palm wine. Rope is made from the green coconut husks and fuel and charcoal are made from mature husks. The wood is used for lumber and carving, the fronds for thatch, baskets and grass skirts.

Breadfruit trees provide timber (lumber) and their large green globular fruits are a major food source. Timber also comes from mahogany and other trees including the betel nut tree (Areca palm), although the latter is more treasured for its nuts. Pandanus is eaten and the leaves are used for making mats, baskets and fans.

Other traditional food plants include taro, yams, tapioca and bananas. The lush heart-shaped leaves of the taro plant, which is cultivated in mud flats, are big enough to use as umbrellas. Tapioca looks a bit like tall marijuana plants.

Mangrove swamps are common along the shores of many of the high islands. The most unique thing about mangroves are their looping prop roots that arch above the water before reaching down into the mud. Mangroves help to extend the shoreline as their roots extend away from shore and sediments collect around them.

Colourful tropical plants and flowers are abundant in Micronesia, especially on the high islands. Common varieties include hibiscus, bougainvillea, purple-flowered beach morning glories, plumeria, lilies, lantana, crotons and others. The Marianas are especially noted for their flame trees (royal poinciana) which have scarlet blossoms.

Plants such as coleus, caladium and philodendron, which in colder climates are painstakingly nurtured indoors in pots, grow in wild abandon in Micronesia, reaching gigantic proportions. Look at ground level for the insectivorous pitcher plant or for the 'sensitive plant', a small green ground cover with thin compound leaves that close up when touched.

Facts for the Visitor

PASSPORTS & VISAS

US citizens don't need a passport to visit Micronesia, though it makes things simpler to carry one. Without a passport, some other proof of US citizenship, such as a birth certificate, is required.

All other nationalities must carry a valid passport.

Visas are not required to visit the Northern Marianas, Marshalls, FSM or Palau for stays of up to 30 days in each. Each FSM state has its own immigration procedure so you automatically get a new entry permit, usually good for 30 days, each time you land in a new district centre.

We were always given the full visa automatically, except in Yap. If they actually ask how long you want to stay, go for the maximum, even if you're not planning on hanging around for a whole month. That way you won't have to bother about getting an extension if you do decide to stay on a bit longer.

For stays of more than 30 days in any one FSM state, entry permits are supposed to be obtained in advance from the Chief of Immigration, Department of Resources and Development, FSM National Government, Pohnpei, FSM 96941.

The Marshalls, Palau and the FSM require all visitors to have a return or onward ticket. The Northern Marianas requires the same only of non-US citizens. On our last trip, they checked for onward tickets in Yap, they asked and took our word in Palau, and in the Marshalls, Pohnpei and Truk they didn't bother at all. In Kosrae, the immigration didn't even make it to the flight.

All non-US citizens, except Canadians, need an American visa to visit Guam and immigration procedures are the same as for entering other US ports.

Guam has applied for a visa waiver programme which would make it possible for people to enter Guam for 15 days for business or pleasure without having to get a US visa. The waiver would be valid for one entry only and would apply to citizens of Australia, New Zealand, Japan, the UK, Nauru, Papua New Guinea, Western Samoa, the Solomon Islands, Vanuatu, Indonesia, Malaysia, Singapore, Hong Kong, Burma and Brunei. The waiver is expected to go through sooner or later, though no one knows when. If it affects you, check it out with the Guam tourist office or a US embassy or consulate.

CUSTOMS, ENTRY & EXIT

Sometimes customs officers carry out baggage checks, but they're usually brief and cursory. As everywhere, Micronesian nations prohibit the entry of drugs, weapons and large quantities of alcohol. But mostly they're worried about visitors bringing in fruit, plants or animals that might contain insects or diseases harmful to crops.

The Marshalls have a $5 departure tax; Palau charges $3.

MONEY

American dollars are the only accepted currency in Micronesia. Except in the outer islands, US dollar travellers' cheques are accepted everywhere and you'll rarely have to wait in a bank queue to change them as most hotels, restaurants and larger stores will accept them as cash.

There are commercial banks on Majuro, Kosrae, Pohnpei, Moen (Truk), Yap, Koror (Palau), Saipan, Rota, Tinian and Guam. On the outer islands you should always bring enough cash with you to get you through your stay.

Plastic addicts will be pleased to know that major credit cards (Master Card, Visa, American Express) are accepted all over Guam; at most hotels and car rentals on Saipan; at the two resort hotels on Rota; at Palau Pacific Resort, D W Hotel and major car rental agencies on Palau; at Palm Terrace, the Village and Cliff Rainbow hotels on Pohnpei; and by Air Micronesia everywhere. The Truk Continental Hotel, South Pacific Island Airways and some of the commuter airlines in the Marianas, accept only American Express.

No credit cards are currently accepted in Yap, Kosrae or the Marshalls, except by Air Micronesia agents or offices. If you do try to buy an airline ticket in a place like Yap, they have to radio the card in for approval and it takes a day. That's presuming they get all the numbers right; if they don't it takes another day for them to try it again.

Personal cheques, from US dollar accounts, are accepted at a few places, including Pacific Missionary Aviation.

INFORMATION

All the island groups have packets of brochures, maps or other standard tourist information. You can pick them up once you're there or, if you write in advance, they will mail the info to you.

Micronesian Tourist Offices

Marshalls
Tourist Office, Ministry of Resources & Development, Majuro, Republic of the Marshall Islands 96960
Kosrae
Division of Tourism, Department of Conservation and Development, Kosrae, FSM 96944
Pohnpei
Tourist Commission, Box 66, Kolonia, Pohnpei, FSM 96941
Truk
Tourist Commission, Box 280, Moen, Truk, FSM 96942
Yap
Division of Tourism and Industries, Box 36, Colonia, Yap, FSM 96943
Palau
Palau Tourist Commission, Box 256, Koror, Republic of Palau 96940
Northern Marianas
Marianas Visitors Bureau, Box 861, Saipan, CNMI 96950

Guam
Guam Visitors Bureau, Box 3520, Agana, Guam 96910

Overseas Offices

Japan
Guam Visitors Bureau (tel 02-212-3630), Kokusai Building, 3-1-1 Marunouchi, Chiyoda-ku, Tokyo 100
Taiwan
Guam Visitors Bureau, 68 Chung Shan Nt Rd, Sec 2, Taipei
Europe
Guam Visitors Bureau, Korneliusmarkt 10, D-5100 Aachen-Kornelimunster, West Germany

Micronesia Institute

The Micronesia Institute (tel 202-387-7525), 2152 Wyoming Avenue NW, Washington DC 20008, was founded a few years ago by people concerned with the failures of the US government in Micronesia.

Their main focus is to serve as a resource unit to support Micronesian self-help and development. They're getting involved in public health programmes, small business seminars and historical preservation work. They produce a newsletter for Micronesians, called *Resources*, which concentrates on small business and the building up of local island economies. Their Micronesia headquarters are in Pohnpei.

GENERAL INFORMATION
Post

All of Micronesia is under the umbrella of the US Postal Service, which handles Micronesia's international mail. Micronesia has US zip codes and US domestic postage rates apply to all mail between America and the islands. Service is quite efficient between major islands and the outside world, although mail delivery to and from the outer islands depends on the frequency of field trip ships and/or flights.

Guam has more than a dozen zip codes and post offices; the Marshalls have two;

and Palau, each FSM state and the three main islands in the Northern Marianas have only one post office and one zip code each.

All mail is picked up from the post office and businesses usually have private post office boxes. Outside Guam, even if you don't have someone's box number, the islands are small enough that if you were to just send a letter with the name, the post office and zip, whoever you're writing to would probably get it anyway.

If you're writing to someone on an outer island, you need to include their island's name, in addition to the district centre's address and zip code.

In the information given on the individual islands later in the book, most addresses (except for those in Guam) just have the box number in parentheses after the hotel or business. In all cases that means the PO box number and in all cases there is only one possible zip code.

The following, are the zip codes for the 10 postal areas in Micronesia, excluding Guam.

Koror
    Republic of Palau 96940
Pohnpei
    Federated States of Micronesia 96941
Truk
    Federated States of Micronesia 96942
Yap
    Federated States of Micronesia 96943
Kosrae
    Federated States of Micronesia 96944
Saipan
    Commonwealth of the Northern Marianas 96950
Rota
    Commonwealth of the Northern Marianas 96951
Tinian
    Commonwealth of the Northern Marianas 96952
Majuro
    Republic of the Marshall Islands 96960
Ebeye
    Republic of the Marshall Islands 96970

You can have mail sent to you c/o General

Delivery at any of these post offices. For Guam, use: General Delivery, Agana, Guam 96910. Use the Majuro zip code for all mail to the Marshalls outside Ebeye.

Guam and the Northern Marianas use US stamps, but the Marshalls, FSM and Palau print their own stamps which can only be used from those particular island groups.

Stamp collectors can order Palauan commemorative stamps and first day covers from the Palau Philatelic Bureau, Box 59628, Washington DC 20012.

Telephone

Long-distance telephone services are available in the major district centres, usually via COMSAT satellite stations. Rates average about $3 to $4 per minute to almost anywhere outside Micronesia. There is usually a three-minute minimum. Calls within the FSM cost $3 for every three minutes. From Guam and the Northern Marianas, calls are a bit cheaper on Sundays.

Local phone services are of variable quality and outside Guam and the Northern Marianas the telephone system is not very extensive. Outer islands can be reached by radio, which are sometimes solar-powered.

Electricity

Electricity is 110/120 volts, 60 cycles; the same as in the US.

Time

Going from the US to Micronesia you cross the International Date Line and lose a day. On the return you gain a day.

Micronesia has four time zones. Guam is 10 hours ahead of Greenwich Mean Time.

So, when it's 12 noon in Guam, the Northern Marianas, Yap and Truk it is: 1 pm in Pohnpei and Kosrae; 2 pm in Majuro; and 11 am in Palau. It is also 12 noon in Port Moresby, Sydney and Melbourne; 11 am in Tokyo; 10 am in Manila and Hong Kong; 2 am in London; and 4 pm the day before in Honolulu.

Business Hours

Business hours vary throughout the islands, but 8 am to 4.30 pm is fairly common. Banking hours also vary, though 10 am to 3 pm Monday to Thursday and 10 am to 5 or 6 pm on Fridays is usual.

The last weeks of the year are very difficult for doing business. Not only do Christmas and New Year holidays and parties interfere, but for many government employees leftover annual leave must be taken by the end of the year or lost, so lots of people scoot off for a quick vacation.

Weights & Measures

Micronesia, like the US, uses the imperial system of measurement. Distances are in inches, feet, yards and miles; weights in ounces, pounds and tons. For those accustomed to the metric system of measurement, there is a conversion table at the back of this book.

MEDIA
Newspapers

Micronesia's only daily newspaper is Guam's *Pacific Daily News*, which is flown to capital towns all around Micronesia.

In addition, Guam has a bi-weekly newspaper, the *Guam Tribune*; the Marshalls have a weekly newspaper, the *Marshall Islands Journal*; the Northern Marianas have the weekly *Marianas Review* and the *Marianas Variety News*; and the FSM has two official government newsletters, *Pohnpei Reports* and the *FSM National Union*. There are also a couple of college publications. Other than that, local papers seem to have a hard time getting off the ground, though now and again someone gives it a try.

Magazines

Guam & Micronesia Glimpses (Box 8066, Tamuning, Guam 96911), is a full colour bi-monthly magazine with quality features and photographs. The emphasis is on local destinations, historical events, community projects, the arts, education and personalities.

Air Micronesia's inflight magazine, titled *Islands*, is published quarterly and is glossy and slick. It usually has a couple of good feature articles in English, but these days most of the magazine is in Japanese.

Pacific Magazine (Box 25488, Honolulu, Hawaii 96825), and the *Pacific Islands Monthly* (GPO Box 3408, Sydney, NSW, 2001, Australia), cover the entire Pacific region with an emphasis on politics, business and development. Of the two, *Pacific Magazine* has the most coverage of Micronesia.

Radio & Television

Guam has five radio stations, three local TV stations and the standard US cable connections including HBO, live news from the US mainland and the Disney and Playboy stations.

All the main district centres have active radio stations, usually with both local and American music.

Outside Guam, TV stations are more temperamental. Sometimes they're on, sometimes they're off, sometimes they're just down for long periods of time. When they're running they usually show video-taped US programmes that are several days or weeks old, complete with commercials from Honolulu or Los Angeles.

HEALTH

In general, Micronesia is a healthy place to visit. Still, infections, sunburn, diarrhoea and intestinal parasites all warrant precautions.

If you're new to the heat and humidity you may find yourself easily fatigued and more susceptible to minor ailments. Acclimatise yourself by slowing down your pace. The climate is one of the reasons Micronesia is so laid-back, so learn to go with the flow.

Immunisations

The only immunisations required in

Micronesia are for cholera and yellow fever, but that's only if you're coming from an infected area. Although not required, tetanus shots are recommended and, if you're going to the Marshalls, typhoid and paratyphoid shots are also a good idea.

Water

Tap water is not always safe to drink. There are a lot of parasites in Micronesia, including giardia and amoeba, and unclean water is a great way to discover them.

Often the problem derives not so much from impure water as from poor water distribution. Sometimes sewer and water pipes are laid alongside each other and when the water is turned off, sometimes for several hours for rationing purposes, cross-seepage often occurs.

When in doubt stick with readily available hot drinks, canned beverages or bottled water.

To avoid dehydration, you should make a conscious effort to drink an ample supply of liquids to replace the body fluids you quickly lose in the heat and humidity of the day. Drinking coconuts are not only a good source of uncontaminated water, but they're also an excellent rehydration drink, full of vitamins and minerals.

Health Precautions

Malaria The good news is that Micronesia has absolutely no malaria. On rare occasions mosquitoes transmit dengue fever, but it's not usually severe.

Gastrointestinal Problems If you have an attack of diarrhoea, the most important thing to do is replenish you bodily fluids to avoid dehydration. A diet of bland foods such as rice, bread and weak tea is a good treatment.

If you also have a fever, then your ailment may be something more serious, such as amoebic dysentery, which is common in Micronesia. Have it checked out as soon as possible because medication is essential. Treatment usually consists of a

week's prescription of *Flagyl*, with a dosage of six tablets per day. *Flagyl* is both an antibiotic and an anti-parasitic drug and the symptoms usually clear up in a few days. Be aware that alcohol mixed with *Flagyl* could be deadly and that this drug should not be taken by pregnant women.

Colds You may be surprised to discover that the common cold is alive and well in tropical Micronesia, and a large number of travellers seem to get persistent coughs. Probably the most effective way to avoid susceptibility is to be in prime condition before you travel.

Over-zealous air-conditioning can be a particular problem. In a restaurant you may have to position yourself in a corner away from the blast; and at night you should adjust the air-con vent so it's not aimed directly at your bed and keep a blanket within reach.

Fungi & Infections The same climate that produces lush tropical forests also promotes a prolific growth of skin fungi and bacteria.

Keeping your skin cool and allowing air to circulate is essential. Choose cotton clothing rather than synthetics and sandals over shoes. If you're susceptible to fungus, athlete's foot or skin rashes, bring medicated powder.

Cuts are more easily infected in hot and humid climates and those infections can be persistent. Keep open wounds clean and protected.

Cholera Cholera is spread through poor sanitation conditions. The minimum precautions where cholera is suspected include drinking bottled liquids and not eating raw fish. Also avoid swimming in polluted lagoons, especially near populated areas.

Truk has had sporadic outbreaks of cholera in the past. In the last epidemic, in 1982 to '83, there were 2254 reported cases and 17 deaths. After years of neglecting the region's public utilities this last epidemic, and the resulting negative publicity, finally spurred the US to install extensive public water and sanitation systems on Truk's main islands of Moen and Dublon.

During the 1983 epidemic, all passengers flying from Truk to any other FSM state needed proof they had been treated in Truk with tetracycline for three days prior to departure.

In February 1984 the last two cases of cholera in Truk were diagnosed and the World Health Organization has since declared Truk cholera free.

Taking the Heat

Sunburn is a definite possibility in this region because the islands are so close to the equator, where fewer of the sun's rays are blocked by the atmosphere. Don't be fooled by what appears to be a hazy overcast day and dress sensibly. Sunscreen is recommended if you're not already tanned and a hat is a good idea at all times. If you're snorkelling, you should wear a T-shirt if you plan to be out in the water for a long time.

Medical Care

Each main population centre has a hospital, clinic or dispensary and treatment is usually at nominal rates.

Many remote outer islands have no health services available so if you're going to head out, it's a good idea to take along a first aid kit with some of the more common medical supplies.

FILM & PHOTOGRAPHY

The high temperatures in the tropics, coupled with high humidity, greatly accelerate the deterioration of film. The sooner you have exposed film developed, the better the results. Sending off your film in pre-paid mailers is a good way to avoid carting it around.

Don't leave your camera in direct sunshine any longer than necessary. A locked car can heat up like an oven in just a few minutes.

Another problem that often arises is moisture condensing on film and lenses that have been taken from air-conditioned rooms into the warm, moist outside air. One way to avoid this is to keep your camera in an area of the room less affected by the air-con, such as a closet or the bathroom. Or try keeping it wrapped inside a camera case or carry-bag for an hour or so after leaving a place with air-con.

Sand and water are intense reflectors and in bright light they'll often leave foreground subjects shadowy. You can try compensating by adjusting your f-stop or attaching a polarising filter, or both, but the most effective technique is to take photos in the gentler light of early morning and late afternoon.

Print film is available on the main islands. Slide film isn't as readily available but can be purchased at the duty-free shops in Saipan and Palau, at Robert Reimers' store in Majuro and camera shops in Guam. Film is fairly expensive in Micronesia and you have to be careful about how it has been stored. Check the expiry dates.

BOOKS & BOOKSHOPS

The only real bookshops in Micronesia are in Guam, and even those are limited in their selection of books about the area. Try the Faith Book Store in the Agana Shopping Center near the Sizzler Steak House.

A small but select collection of books about Micronesia is available from the Alele Museum (Box 629, Majuro, Marshall Islands 96960). You can either get them while you're in Majuro or write for a book list and order by mail.

On Pohnpei, Gene Ashby's books and *Birds of Micronesia* by Harvey Gordon Segal are available at Palm Terrace Hotel and Joy Restaurant. The museum in Palau also has a small book section.

Theses, short papers and reprinted articles on current issues are available from the Micronesian Seminar (Box 250, Truk, FSM 96942) for a 10 cent per-page photocopying fee. Selections include such

Top Left: Pandanus – Majuro
Top Right: Orchid
Bottom Left: Bougainvillea
Bottom Right: Carnivorous Pitcher Plant – Yap

Top: Boy on outrigger canoe, Mangrove Coast
Left: Eten Island from Mesa Wharf – Fefan Island
Right: Stone pathway, Leluh Ruins – Kosrae

titles as *The Role of the Beachcombers in the Caroline Islands, Education For What?* and *Suicide Epidemic Among Micronesian Youth.*

The Micronesian Area Research Center (MARC, University of Guam, Mangilao, Guam 96913) also has theses and short papers available for a minimal photocopying fee. Both places will send a list of available publications upon request.

Hawaii's East-West Center publishes, or has access to, a lot of obscure titles like *Pohnpei: Household Income, Expenditure, & the Role of Electricity* and *Nuclear Activities & the Pacific Islanders.* Their selection ranges from free, reprinted articles to expensive books. You can get a listing from the Distribution Office, East-West Center, 1777 East-West Rd, Honolulu, Hawaii 96848.

The Bishop Museum (Box 19000-A, Honolulu, Hawaii 96817) also has its own catalogue of Pacific-related books and articles.

History

The First Taint of Civilization, by Francis X Hezel SJ (University of Hawaii Press, Honolulu, 1983), is an excellent anecdotal history of the Caroline and Marshall Islands during the the pre-colonial era from 1521 to 1885. Hezel, a long-time resident in Micronesia and head of the Micronesian Seminar, presents some poignant insights into the culture of the islands.

Micronesia: Winds of Change, edited by Francis X Hezel SJ and M L Berg (Government of the Trust Territory of the Pacific Islands, 1980), is a colourful history taken from the accounts of early explorers, missionaries and others involved in Micronesia between 1521 to 1951. It features terrific old etchings and photos.

Politics

There are a number of books assessing US involvement in Micronesia.

Micronesia: A Trust Betrayed, by Donald McHenry (Carnegie Endowment for International Peace, New York, 1975), is an insightful history of the Trust Territory and the events leading up to the Compacts of Free Association.

Micronesia at the Crossroads, by Carl Heine (University of Hawaii Press, Honolulu, 1974), is an appraisal of Micronesia's political dilemma in its relationship with the US government. This is one of the few books on the situation from the viewpoint of a Micronesian.

The American Touch in Micronesia, by David Nevin (W W Norton & Co, New York, 1977), looks at fumbling American colonialism and the effects of power, money and corruption in Micronesia.

Culture

There are a good number of scholarly anthropological works about Micronesia, many written by individuals who have lived on remote islands and studied a single group of people in depth. The following books are the ones geared more to the general reader.

An Introduction to the Peoples & Cultures of Micronesia, by William H Alkire (Addison-Wesley Publishing Co, Redding, Massachusetts, 1972), is a comprehensive study resulting from Alkire's 3½ years of field work in the islands. Alkire is an authority on Micronesian societies and this book is a sort of bible of Micronesian cultural anthropology.

Man This Reef, by Gerald Knight (Micronitor News & Printing Co, Majuro, 1983), is a translated collection of tales and legends as told by an elderly Marshallese storyteller. Knight is curator of the Alele Museum in Majuro.

Book of Luelen, (University of Hawaii Press, Honolulu, 1977), is a record of Pohnpei's history and traditions. It was given by an elderly Pohnpeian man who wanted Pohnpei's stories to remain alive and was translated and edited by John L Fischer, Saul H Riesenberg and Marjorie G Whiting.

Diving

The *Diver's Guide to Guam & Micronesia*, by Guam journalist Tim Rock (Guam Publications, 1986), describes in detail 35 dives in Guam; 12 dives each in Truk and Palau; and a handful of dives in Yap, Saipan and Rota. He even throws in information on diving in Bali.

Ghost Fleet of the Truk Lagoon, by William H Stewart (Pictorial Histories Publishing Co, Missoula, Montana), is an account of the American attack on the Japanese naval base in Truk Lagoon during WW II. Stewart includes maps and photographs showing how and where the more than 60 ships were sunk.

General

A Reporter in Micronesia, by E J Kahn (W W Norton & Co, New York, 1966), is a very readable log of Kahn's travels around the islands. His journeys were mostly by field ship, as Micronesia then had no jet traffic, no tourist hotels and very few visitors.

Micronesia: The Breadfruit Revolution, by Byron Baker (East-West Center Press, Honolulu, 1971), features black-and-white photographs by Robert Wenkam offering glimpses of Micronesian life. It's a hardcover coffee-table book giving an excellent overview of the islands.

Micronesia: Island Wilderness, by Kenneth Brower, also features photography by Robert Wenkam. This is also a handsome coffee-table book, this time with some stunning colour plates.

Micronesia: The Land, the People & the Sea, by Kenneth Brower (Mobil Oil Micronesia, 1981), covers the relationship between the Micronesians and the sea. There are good sections on navigation, canoes and ruins.

Pohnpei – An Island Argosy, by Gene Ashby (Rainy Day Press, Box 574, Pohnpei 96941), is an in-depth study of Pohnpei's history, government, culture, flora, fauna and island sights.

Micronesian Customs and Beliefs, also compiled by Gene Ashby (Rainy Day Press), is a collection of legends and stories by the students at the Community College of Micronesia.

This Living Reef, by environmentalist Douglas Faulkner (Quadrangle/The New York Times Co, New York, 1974), is a beautiful book, heavy on colour photographs of coral, fish and underwater life.

ACCOMMODATION

Hotels

There are hotels in all the major island centres in Micronesia, with accommodation varying quite a bit from island to island.

A few of the major islands, such as Majuro, Pohnpei and Guam, have some very basic accommodation, in the $6 to $18 range, but they're rock bottom and not particularly clean or enticing. These sort of places include dormitories for single men, love hotels and the sort of local place where the manager's extended family sleeps in the lobby and head-lice picking is a common sight.

Once you get out of the district centres however, there are a few delightful surprises. The rustic thatched huts on Pohnpei's Joy Island cost only $5 a night and you get a white sand island practically to yourself. You can enjoy Micronesian hospitality at pleasant guest houses in a few scattered places, including on Peleliu and Angaur, for $10 to $15.

Although Micronesia doesn't have a lot of real cheapies, there are many rooms which cost from $20 to $35. In this price range you can choose between western-style hotels, found in all the district centres, or get a taste of island flavour at a handful of small family-run places. For the most part, rooms are comfortable and have private bathrooms and either air-con or fans.

One of the region's most pleasant and most Micronesian-style hotels is the *Hotel Pohnpei*, which has thatched hillside cottages for $20 a night. Similar cottages on the beach on Kosrae cost $25.

Some islands have fine upscale hotels for about $35 to $50. The handful of places that fall into this category are locally owned and their overall atmosphere is usually much more congenial than the neighbouring resort hotels.

Guam, Saipan, Palau and Truk have more luxurious resort-style hotels, ranging from about $60 a night to well over $100. They have all the modern amenities you'd expect resort hotels to have and are usually right on the beach. A couple of them are beautifully situated and tastefully laid out while others resemble bustling inner-city highrises that process package tourists in one end and out the other.

Some hotels offer discounts to government employees, Peace Corps volunteers, the military and businesspeople. It never hurts to ask if a hotel (or car rental agency for that matter) has business or 'corporate' rates. You can call yourself a travelling salesperson, researcher, or whatever you fancy yourself to be. Few people ask for proof although a dozen personalised business cards can quickly pay for themselves.

Outer Islands

Few of the outer islands have hotels or guest houses for accommodating foreigners. It's generally best to make some sort of arrangement in advance, through the island's mayor or chief magistrate. Although you could try doing it by mail before you go, remembering that mail service to the outer islands can take a long time, it's often less confusing to just radio ahead through the governor's office or tourist office in the district centre. A few outer islands, particularly in Yap and Truk, simply don't want visitors.

If you do just fly out to one of the islands or get off a boat somewhere, you'll probably be able to get help from the local school principal who may allow you to stay in the schoolhouse, especially if school's not in session. You can also approach the local mayor or chief or perhaps a Peace Corps volunteer.

Usually people are warm and friendly and will help you out. However, because islanders feel obligated to provide for

visitors, foreigners can sometimes impose without realising it. Be careful not to take advantage of Micronesian hospitality. While islanders readily welcome each other into their homes, it's a long-established system founded on reciprocity and kinship obligations and the casual visitor should not expect the same rights.

If you stay with a family you should offer them something, but unless money is requested, giving coffee, rice or other gifts is probably a more appropriate way to pay for your stay.

Camping

Throughout Micronesia most of the land, including the beaches, is privately owned and uninvited campers are about as welcome as they would be if they walked into your backyard at home and started pitching a tent. So if you want to camp, get permission from the landowners first.

In any case, camping is very uncommon in most places, especially throughout the FSM, and you're likely to collect a crowd of curious onlookers.

Some of the best, and locally accepted, camping in Micronesia is on the Rock Islands, Angaur and Peleliu in Palau; and on Tinian and Rota in the Northern Marianas. For more details refer to those sections.

If you decide it's worth your while to carry camping gear, you won't need a sleeping bag but you'll sleep more comfortably with some sort of covering that is gnat and mosquito-proof.

FOOD

Considering the geographic spread, it is surprising how similar the food is throughout Micronesia.

Fish is plentiful, fresh and delicious. Grilled tuna is often one of the best and cheapest meals available, while another good choice is reef fish, especially in the Marshalls and Truk where it is grilled and served whole.

Western foods like hamburgers, sandwiches, fried chicken and steak are found on most menus. Almost equally as common is Japanese food, such as sashimi, teriyaki and ramen. Breakfasts are typically western style, with toast and coffee, eggs and bacon (or Spam!) or french toast.

Fish, shellfish, coconuts, pandanus, breadfruit, taro, tapioca and bananas are Micronesian staples. Traditional local dishes are not often served in restaurants, although mangrove crab and fried breadfruit find their way onto a few menus.

Breadfruit is prepared much like potatoes – either boiled, fried, mashed, roasted or baked. Preserved (fermented) breadfruit, which was traditionally a provision food for long canoe journeys, is definitely an acquired taste. Taro root is baked or boiled, rather than smashed up into a Hawaiian-style poi.

Turkey tails are a really hot item, particularly in Truk and the Marshalls. You'll often see them amidst the hot dogs and reef fish on picnic barbecue grills.

Rice, canned fish and high-salt, high-fat canned meats are popular imported foods, as are chocolate chip cookies, donuts and candy bars. In grocery stores, banana cake mix may be easier to find than bananas. If you're buying provisions watch out for wormy food and check the expiry dates.

If you've imagined a wild abundance of exotic tropical fruits, you'll probably be disappointed. You can buy bananas, papayas and coconuts in local markets and on a lucky day you might find citrus, passion fruit, soursop or mangoes. But despite year-round sun, many fruits in Micronesia are seasonal and unfortunately, fresh fruit is rarely served in restaurants. Families often grow just enough for their own use and use the surplus to feed the pigs, so those sweet papayas you were hoping to see on the breakfast menu might well be going to the family porker instead.

Fresh vegetables, especially crisp salad types, are also scarce. Many have to be imported so the more remote the island,

the scarcer they are. What you do find often looks ready for composting.

In Micronesia 'green salad' usually refers to a small clump of shredded cabbage and occasionally some cucumber slices, with a dribble of Thousand Island salad dressing.

Dog is a popular food in Pohnpei, but you don't have to worry much about having it thrust upon you by surprise. It's mainly regarded as a specialty food, served primarily at occasions such as funeral feasts.

Some of Micronesia's more exotic dishes include crocodile (Palau), fruit bat (Guam and the Marianas), mangrove crab, coconut crab and sea turtle.

Having a meal in Guam is quite a different experience to eating in the rest of Micronesia. There's a great deal of variety, including spicy Chamorro food, good salad bars, Mexican food and Korean, Chinese and other Asian cuisines.

Tipping is expected on Guam, and is usually 10% to 15%. It's beginning to catch on in some places in Saipan and Palau but is generally not the custom elsewhere in Micronesia.

DRINKS

Water is probably safe in most district centres but it's still a good idea to boil it when you're unsure, or avoid it altogether. Tap water is safe in Guam and bottled water is sometimes available in grocery stores throughout the islands.

Soft drinks, coffee and tea are easy to get everywhere.

Although coconuts are plentiful, unless it's your habit to carry a machete everywhere you go so you can whack one open at any time, you're restricted to buying them from stalls, markets or shops. If you've got a coconut that's already husked, look for the three dots that resemble a face with two eyes and a mouth. It's easy to poke a hole through the 'mouth' with a pointed object to get to the juice inside.

Alcohol

Alcohol is available almost everywhere in Micronesia, the major exception being a few dry islands in Truk and the Marshalls. Budweiser is truly the king of beers in Micronesia, so whoever has the Bud concession must be making a killing!

For island drinks, *tuba*, which is labouriously made from coconut sap, is the most common.

Then there's *yeast*, which is coconut water or USDA fruit juice, mixed with sugar and bakers yeast. It's consumed straight away and the fermenting takes place in the stomach. The high continues until the fermenting stops – up to 24 hours later. It's a cheap way to get drunk, though apparently not always a pleasant one.

Other Highs

Sakau, extracted from the roots of a pepper plant, is a mild narcotic that can give the drinker a pretty good buzz. For the most part the mind stays clear and the body numbs up. These days in Micronesia, it's only available in Pohnpei where there are a number of *sakau* bars.

There's still debate as to whether Peace Corps volunteers introduced marijuana to Micronesia or whether Micronesian students returning home from school in the States brought the first seeds. One way or the other its cultivation is widespread in the islands. Attitudes and procurement procedures vary from place to place and for the most part people are pretty tolerant, although in Guam things can get a little more heavy-handed. In a place like Pohnpei older kids will sometimes approach you, while in Palau it's sold under the counter in a select group of small shops. The price is usually about $1 for a pre-rolled joint.

Betel nut is readily available in Yap and Palau and anywhere else there are Yapese and Palauans. Unlike places in Asia where it's chewed dry and brown, Micronesians like it green, mixed with a little lime and wrapped in a pepper leaf. It produces a very mild short-lived buzz.

THINGS TO BUY

Micronesia has less of a variety of handicrafts than you'd probably expect, although there's some really fine basketwork and weaving to be found throughout the islands, and some wood carving is quite good.

Yap has the most interesting traditional crafts, including hibiscus fibre skirts and other functional items that the Yapese people still use. The Marshalls have stick charts and baskets; Palau has carved storyboards; and Truk has carved love sticks and masks. The Northern Marianas and Guam are devoid of any real native handicrafts.

Pohnpei's specialties are gourmet pepper and island-made coconut soaps and oils, usually packed in gift baskets of woven coconut fronds. Truk and Yap also make coconut soap; while the Marshalls, FSM and Palau sell their own postage stamps on first day covers.

Sea turtle shells make beautiful jewellery – too beautiful, in fact, for the welfare of the turtles. Although the islanders have taken turtles for subsistence purposes for centuries, a worldwide demand for the shells has thrown sea turtles onto the endangered species list. Tortoise shell jewellery, as well as the whole shells, are prohibited entry into the US and many other countries.

The purchase of coral, which is often dynamited from its fragile reef ecosystem and sold in chunks or made into jewellery, should also give pause to the environmentally conscious.

WHAT TO BRING

Travelling light, a good policy anywhere, is easier in the tropics as sleeping bags, heavy jackets and bulky clothing are totally unnecessary.

At most, one long-sleeved shirt, lightweight cotton jacket or windbreaker might be useful against indoor air-con and outside insects. Speaking of bugs, there are mosquitoes in Micronesia so if you use insect repellent, bring some.

Dress is definitely casual. For men, dressing up means wearing a Hawaiian-print shirt; and for women, a cotton dress is as formal as it gets. Lightweight cotton clothing breathes best in hot humid weather.

Most islanders walk in the warm rain unprotected, but if that bothers you bring an umbrella or rain jacket.

Footwear in Micronesia is predominately rubber *zories* (thongs) which are sold everywhere, or other casual sandals. Sand shoes can be useful for hiking off the beaten path and are advisable for walking along rough coral reefs.

A flashlight is good to have on hand for the occasional power blackouts and is essential if you want to fully explore caves. A Swiss Army knife, as every traveller knows, is worth its weight in gold. If you plan to do a lot of snorkelling, it's a good idea to bring your own gear.

You should consider a passport pouch or money belt, to wear around your neck or waist, to ensure your passport and money are always safely close at hand.

Zip-lock plastic sandwich bags in a couple of sizes are indispensable for keeping things dry. You can use them for your film and camera equipment and to seal airline tickets and your passport.

A one-cup immersion heater, usually available for a few dollars from hardware or department stores, and a durable lightweight cup can come in very handy. Not only can you sterilise your own water and make coffee and tea in your room but you can use it make up a quick meal if you carry a few packets of instant oatmeal, ramen, soup or the like.

Medical supplies and toiletries are available in most places, but outside Guam and Saipan the selection may be limited. Although you'll find it in Guam, contact lens cleaning solutions and supplies may be unavailable everywhere else. Bring sunscreen.

Air Mike planes are specially designed to carry more cargo than most planes. Because of this there are no overhead compartments and all hand luggage has to fit under the seat in front of you.

DIVING & SNORKELLING

What Micronesia lacks in land, it makes up for in water. Some of the region's most spectacular scenery is underwater and the traveller who never looks below the surface is missing out on some incredible sights.

Micronesia's water temperature is about 80°F (27°C), which is much warmer than Hawaii's. Wet suits are not required for warmth, although some divers wear them as protection against coral cuts.

Divers the world over know about Truk's underwater museum and Palau's great drop-offs. These are, without doubt, the finest diving spots in Micronesia and among the very best locales in the world.

There are many other superb, though less famous diving opportunities in Micronesia, including unspoiled reefs, forests of towering sea fans, coral gardens, underwater caves and the scattered wrecks of whaleboats and WW II ships and planes.

Dive shops in Guam, Saipan, Truk, Palau, Pohnpei and Majuro are able to rent gear to divers who show up with nothing more than their diving certificate and a swimsuit. Experienced divers who know the islands, however, recommended that you bring your own buoyancy compensator and other personalised equipment with you.

Some places, like Yap and Kosrae, can provide filled tanks but divers have to bring everything else, including weight belts. Details on diving facilities are given in each island section.

If you've never been scuba diving before, here's your chance to learn. Some dive shops offer non-divers a one-day introductory dive, with full scuba gear down to about 30 feet, which costs from $60 to $70. You can become fully certified in several places in Micronesia for as low as $150 for the full course.

On the other hand you can just pack a mask and snorkel and enjoy it all for free.

It's nice to have your own fins too, though they are a bit heavier to carry around. If you really want to travel light, snorkelling gear can be rented from many places for $5 a day or less.

For information on diving holiday packages to various parts of Micronesia, refer to the Tours section in the Getting There chapter.

MARINE LIFE
Micronesia has an incredible abundance and variety of fish in every imaginable, and some quite unimaginable, colour and shape. There are hundreds of types of hard and soft coral, anemones, colourful sponges and many varieties of shellfish, including giant tridacna clams.

Sea cucumbers, particularly common in the Marianas, dot the bottom of shallow waters near shore. Their entrails squish underfoot if you happen to step on one, but they're harmless. These creatures are the *beche-de-mer* that traders were after in the 1800s. When boiled, dried and smoked they are considered delicacies and aphrodisiacs in China and South-East Asia.

Micronesia has hawksbill and other sea turtles, sperm whales, beaked whales and porpoises. Palau has the rare dugong, or sea cow, which is a whale-like sirenian (aquatic and herbivorous) mammal.

Nautilus Pompilius

MARINE DANGERS
Most underwater experiences in Micronesia are safe and while you shouldn't miss out for fear of monsters lurking in the depths, it is important to be aware of the potential dangers.

Sharks
The probability of shark attacks on humans has been greatly exaggerated. Still, they *are* out there in the deeper waters and it doesn't hurt to have a healthy respect for them.

The few attacks that do occur in Micronesia are usually during spearfishing. When the shark tries to chomp down on a bloody, just-speared fish, the spearer sometimes gets in the way. Still, even these incidents are rare. If you need more reassurance though, according to the Yap Institute of Natural Science, people eat sharks 600,000 times more often than sharks eat people!

Sharks are attracted by shiny things and by anything bright red or yellow, which might influence your choice of swimsuit colour. Those popular day-glo orange life jackets are said to be known as 'yummy orange' in shark circles.

Poisonous Fish
More than 300 species of fish are poisonous to eat. Sometimes the same species can be safe in some areas and poisonous in others, so get local advice before eating your catch.

The symptoms, if you do eat the wrong fish, can include nausea, stomach cramps, diarrhoea, paralysis, and tingling and numbness of the face, fingers and toes. Vomit until your stomach is empty and get immediate medical help.

Coral Cuts
All cuts are more apt to become infected in the tropics than they are anywhere else. Coral cuts are even more susceptible because tiny pieces of coral can get imbedded in the skin. Most coral cuts occur when swimmers are pushed onto the coral

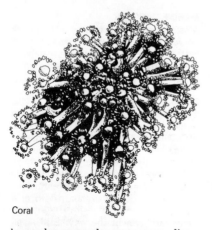

Coral

by rough waves and surges so many divers wear wetsuits to protect themselves. At the very least, wearing flippers and/or sand-shoes and diving gloves is a good idea.

Jellyfish

Take a peek into the water before you plunge in, to make sure it's not jellyfish territory. These gelatinous creatures are fairly common around Guam, where even the dangerous Portuguese man-o-war and sea wasps have occasionally been sighted.

The sting of a jellyfish varies from mild to severe, depending on the variety. You can at least partly neutralise the venom of a sting by washing the skin with ammonia or urine, then rinsing with soap and water. For serious stings, which are usually followed by swelling, bleeding, stomach spasms, difficulty in breathing, chest pains or the like, seek immediate medical attention.

Stings & Punctures

Incidents with venomous sea creatures are pretty rare. You should, however, learn to recognise such venomous varieties as the turkey fish, lionfish, scorpion fish and stonefish. The latter two are sometimes seen in quite shallow water and all can inject venom through their dorsal spines.

The sting causes a sharp burning pain, followed by numbness around the area, nausea and headaches. Immediately stick the affected area in water as hot as bearable (be sure not to unintentionally scald the area due to numbness) and go for medical treatment.

There is no safe way of picking up a live cone shell, as the animal inside has a long stinging tail that can dart out and reach anyplace on its shell to deliver a sometimes-fatal puncture wound. Immediate medical attention is essential.

Sea urchins and crown of thorns starfish have long spines that can puncture the skin and break off, causing burning and possible numbness. Try to remove the spines with tweezers or by soaking the area in warm water and epsom salts.

Strong Currents & Rip-Tides

Be careful of water funnelling off the reefs into the channels when the tide's going out as it can have a very strong pull.

You can quickly use up all your energy and lose ground if you try to fight a strong current. It's easier to swim across a current than against it. If you do find yourself being carried out through a reef passage, once outside the reef you should be able to move down along the reef and cross back over it to a calmer area.

CONDUCT & SAFETY
Dress

Outside Guam or the beaches of resort hotels, skimpy swimsuits are apt to get you more attention than you'll want.

In some areas, particularly Yap and Kosrae, it's considered offensive for women to expose their upper thighs. Although it's OK to wear a swimsuit in the water, women are expected to put on a skirt when they get out. Off the beach in many places, bathing suits, short skirts and even shorts are deemed inappropriate for women. Follow local custom.

For the most part it's acceptable for men to wear shorts throughout Micronesia, even on islands like Pohnpei and Moen where just about all the local men seem to be sweating it out in long pants.

Property

In Micronesia, most things are shared and individual property in the western sense is a rather foreign concept. If you don't want visitors, particularly when you're out, be careful to leave your doors locked. The more remote the place you're staying, the more likely you'll have the village kids just walking in.

Don't tempt anyone. If you have anything that looks appealing, lock it up in your bags. The old adage 'out of sight, out of mind' holds true in Micronesia.

The simplest way to feel at ease is not to bring anything which you mind parting with. Keep your passport and air tickets on you, and if you have a camera, you should bring a day pack to carry it in.

Privacy

The concept of privacy is also a different affair in Micronesia compared to most western societies. You can often tell which house in a village has a VCR by the crowds standing outside looking in the windows; it's an acceptable way to watch a movie.

If you stay with a local family and are given your own room it won't be uncommon for groups of the extended family to come by and join you for impromptu visits. You should see this, not as an intrusion, but as an indication that you're being honoured and accepted as part of the family.

Hassles

Although most places shouldn't be a hassle, women travelling alone may occasionally get some unwanted attention.

Duly earned or not, Truk seems to have the worst reputation. Although it's largely their demeanor, some young Trukese males may seem to have surly macho stares. Women travelling alone are particularly likely to hear a few come-ons and under-the-breath innuendos. Foreign women aren't exactly singled out but neither are they left out. Trukese women have their own defense, which largely consists of maintaining an aloofness and pretending they don't hear. Although it doesn't make a very favourable impression, it's all part of their game and women are not necessarily any more likely to be in physical danger here than elsewhere.

Payday Weekends

Throughout most of Micronesia every other Friday is payday. From payday until Sunday a number of Micronesian males go on a drinking binge and, for the most part, they don't make happy-go-lucky drunks. Alcohol is not part of their culture and often acts as a key that unleashes many suppressed feelings. Domestic violence, suicide and the desire to settle pent-up accounts all tend to come to a head on this weekend. A few places like Moen have responded by enacting prohibition. The rest of Micronesia just sits it all out. The problem tends to be worse in district centres.

Getting There

AIR

Gateways to Micronesia include Honolulu, Guam, Japan, Manila, Hong Kong, Bali, Nauru, Fiji and Kiribati. Travellers coming from elsewhere need to first find their way to one of these connections.

FROM THE US

Continental Air Micronesia (known throughout the islands as Air Mike) is the only airline that island hops between Honolulu and Guam. The route is: Honolulu, (Johnston), Majuro, (Kwajalein), Kosrae, Pohnpei, Truk, Guam.

Flights leave Honolulu four mornings a week, crossing the international date line before arriving at Majuro, the first destination where civilians can disembark. You lose a day, arriving one day later than you leave.

The plane refuels on Johnston but no stopovers are permitted on this small, flat coral island which is shaped like an aircraft carrier. Nuclear testing was carried out there after WW II and it now serves as a storage site for chemical munitions and remains a field command of the US nuclear defense agency.

Kwajalein is another military base and home to the airfield you use if you're going to Ebeye Island. If you want to visit Ebeye you need to get military clearance from Majuro first.

The one-way 'island hopper' fare allowing all stopovers between Honolulu and Guam costs $450. Air Mike's family plan allows an accompanying spouse to pay half the regular fare, only $225, and is the main discount on this route.

The same ticket between Los Angeles or San Francisco and Guam costs $635 ($318 for spouse). Stopovers are allowed in Honolulu and it's a one-year open ticket.

If you're going the full distance you'll definitely save money by buying the island hopper as opposed to point-to-point tickets. For example, Honolulu to Majuro one way costs $447, just $3 less than the whole island hopper route to Guam. Majuro to Kosrae flights cost $212; and Kosrae to Pohnpei is $107.

The island hopper service connects with Kosrae only once weekly, stopping on Fridays going west from Honolulu and Mondays going east from Guam.

On Sunday evenings there's a special flight from Guam to Truk to Pohnpei, and vice versa, with a 50% discount on fares. On this flight one-way fares are $75 between Pohnpei and Truk, $150 between Pohnpei and Guam and $100 between Truk and Guam. Air Mike doesn't really promote this flight outside the islands, but it's been going on for years.

If you're booking in the US you can use Continental's toll-free international number: tel 800 231 0856. They generally try to rush you into booking and don't always volunteer information on the cheapest fares so you may need to be persistent. If you don't like the answers they give you, call back and get another agent.

As schedules go, Air Mike's island hopper really hasn't changed much over the years, yet for some reason Continental agents in the US swear that printed timetables do not exist. They do of course, but you'll probably have to wait to get to Micronesia to get your hands on a copy.

Relations between Continental and Air Mike have been stormy in the past. Continental is but one of Air Mike's shareholders and has had long-standing disputes with its partners. Continental feels it took the lion's share of losses in establishing a Micronesian air service in the 1960s. Now with Air Mike's numerous new flights doing fully-booked package tour jaunts from Japan, Continental wants a larger share of the profits.

Air Mike is the islands' carrier and once you're finally flying with them you'll find a certain down-home quality quite in touch with Micronesian flavour. If you island hop, you'll see the same faces over and over and half the people on the flights always seem to know each other.

To Guam via Majuro South Pacific Island Airlines (SPIA) flies from Honolulu to Majuro to Guam. The Honolulu to Majuro or the Majuro to Guam connection costs $196. From Honolulu to Guam it costs $299. On SPIA's family plan, the accompanying spouse flies for $196; and there's also a $249 student ticket.

When things get slow SPIA sometimes attempts to fill up the planes by offering cheap Honolulu-Guam tickets. Last time we were there they cost $199 between Thanksgiving and Christmas. Check with SPIA for their current fares.

SPIA also connects Honolulu with Papeete, Apia, Pago Pago and Rarotonga.

Direct to Guam Continental charges $325 one way for direct flights from Honolulu to Guam ($217 spouse); and $495 one way from Los Angeles to Guam ($330 spouse). A return ticket costs double.

The regular fare from Honolulu to Guam, on Northwest Orient, is $435 one way. With seven days advance purchase it's $650 for the return trip. From Los Angeles, it costs $930 return or $630 one way.

If you're considering a round-the-world ticket, Guam can be added on to some of them.

FROM GUAM TO YAP & PALAU
You can continue from Guam to Yap and Palau (Koror) via Air Mike. The full fare from Guam to Palau, with a stopover in Yap, is $251 ($188 spouse).

Direct flights between Guam and Palau cost $125 on Sunday, Monday and Friday evenings. Other direct Guam-Palau flights cost $150.

The full fare between Guam and Yap is $173, except on Thursdays when it costs $100.

The Thursday flight from Yap to Palau

(in that direction only) costs only $50. Other days it's $103 either direction.

So, $275 is the cheapest side trip to both Yap and Palau from Guam, leaving on Thursday for Yap, flying on to Palau the following Thursday and eventually returning from Palau on one of the evening flights to Guam.

If you want to do this, you'll have to purchase at least your first two tickets in Guam, to be able to show Yap customs an onward ticket. Apparently there's no problem later applying these tickets to a more expensive flight or getting them refunded.

SPIA has an on-again, off-again flight between Guam and Palau. The last time it was flying it cost $99 one way. On this route they've been notorious for cancelling flights when there aren't enough passengers. If you're in Koror you're probably better off buying your ticket at the airport counter after you've seen the plane come in.

FROM GUAM TO SAIPAN
Continental Air Mike and JAL fly between Guam and Saipan, in the Northern Marianas. Maui Airlines and SPIA also have numerous daily commuter flights between these two cities, some of which stopover on Rota. For more details on the local air service connections refer to the Getting Around chapter or the relevant island section later in the book.

FROM PAPUA NEW GUINEA
Continental Airlines have started a new service between Micronesia and Papua New Guinea. The cost of a one-way economy fare between Guam and Port Moresby is $360.

FROM INDONESIA & HONG KONG
Garuda has a flight between Bali and Guam for $180 one way. Air Nauru flies weekly from Hong Kong (via Manila) to Guam for $299 one way.

FROM THE PHILIPPINES

Continental Air Mike flies between Manila and Palau. The one-way flight costs $125, the return trip is $250.

Continental also flies from Manila to Guam. The one-way fare is $345. An excursion ticket, valid for seven to 45 days, costs $508 and allows a stopover in Palau.

Air Nauru flies from Koror to Manila for $124 and from Guam to Manila for $191.

FROM JAPAN

There are multiple daily flights from Japan to Saipan and Guam. Many flights stop in Saipan en route to Guam.

Air Mike and Northwest Orient fly non-stop between Tokyo and Guam; and Japan Air Lines (JAL) and Air Mike have Tokyo, Saipan, Guam flights.

JAL does an Osaka to Saipan to Guam route; and Air Mike has daily flights between Nagoya and Saipan and Guam.

The fare between Guam and Japan is $210 one way; $341 for a three-week excursion ticket; and $420 for a full-fare, one-year return ticket – but that's if you buy the tickets in Saipan or Guam.

Coming from Japan, it's an incredible government-sanctioned ripoff. They will take the $210 full-fare one-way ticket, multiply that by an 'airline-industry dollar exchange rate' of Y296 and then charge you Y62,160 for a one-way ticket to Guam.

You have to buy the ticket in yen and, with the real exchange rate currently under Y145 to one US dollar, the ticket will cost you about US$430. This is the law and all international airline tickets sold in Japan are calculated this way. The government-owned national carrier (JAL) benefits most, but none of the other carriers cleaning up in the Japanese market are complaining!

Travellers flying from Europe to Japan can add Guam on to some tickets for as little as $20. At any rate, even if you have to pay full fare you'll be better off getting your Japan-Guam ticket before arriving in Japan.

Reservations are almost impossible to make around Japan's New Year's vacation (24 December to 6 January), the Golden Week period (the last week of April and the first week of May) and during Obon (mid-August), as the Japanese have holidays and almost all the seats are pre-booked for package tours.

If you're heading back to the States from Japan, or vice versa, island hopping through Micronesia is a great alternative to a non-stop transpacific flight!

FROM THE SOUTH PACIFIC

The Airline of the Marshall Islands (AMI) connects Majuro with Nandi in Fiji, via Tarawa in Kiribati, once a week. The one-way fare between Majuro and Tarawa costs $150, and between Majuro and Nandi costs $450. There's also a $625 return excursion fare between Nandi and Majuro. AMI will send you a current flight schedule upon request.

Air Nauru connects Majuro, Guam and Koror with various places in the South Pacific via Nauru. From Nauru one-way tickets cost $80 to Majuro, $190 to Guam, $274 to Koror.

From Nauru it costs about $197 to Noumea, $179 to Nandi, $198 to Apia, $384 to Sydney and $475 to Auckland. As Nauru uses Australian dollars the fares given here, in US dollars, are not exact.

FROM AUSTRALIA & NEW ZEALAND

There are no direct flights from Australia or New Zealand to Micronesia but there are various routes you can take to get to Guam or Majuro.

Air Nauru flies from Melbourne or Sydney to Nauru for A$360. You can then fly on to Majuro, in the Marshall Islands, for an additional A$98 or to Guam for an extra A$190. Return fares are double. Air Nauru also flies from Auckland to Nauru.

Another alternative is to go via Denpasar, in Bali, or Jakarta from where it costs $180 one way to Guam. From Melbourne or Sydney to Bali it costs A$380 one way (low season) or A$590 return. To Jakarta it costs A$425 one way

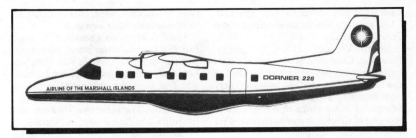

or A$67 return. All these flights into and out of Indonesia are with Garuda.

INTERNATIONAL AIRLINES
The addresses, in the US and around the Pacific, for the airlines which operate in and out of Micronesia's main island centres are:

Continental Air Micronesia (Air Mike)
Japan – Suite 242, Kokusai Building, 3-1-1 Marunouchi, Chiyoda-ku, Tokyo, (tel 03-592-1631; Nagoya, tel 052-962-1563)
Micronesia – Box 8778, Tamuning, Guam 96911 (tel 646-0220/1/2/3)
  Kolonia, Pohnpei, FSM 96941 (tel 424)
  Moen, Truk, FSM 96942 (tel 424)
  Kolonia, Yap, FSM 96943 (tel 2127)
  Box 138, Saipan, Mariana Islands 96950 (tel 234-6491)
  Majuro, Marshall Islands 96960 (tel 3209)
  Koror, Palau 96940 (tel 448)
Philippines – Philbanking Building, Ayala Avenue Cor Herrera St Makati, Metro Manila, (tel 818-8701)
USA – 1600 Kapiolani Boulevard, Suite 1215, Honolulu, Hawaii 96814
  Air Mike's toll free number within the US (mainland), Hawaii and Canada is tel 800-231-0856
Airline of the Marshall Islands (AMI)
Micronesia – Box 959, Majuro, Marshall Islands 96960 (tel 3373, 3216)
Air Nauru (Nauru Air & Shipping Agency)
Australia – Nauru House, 80 Collins St, Melbourne, 3000 (tel 653-5709)
Hong Kong – Kai Tak, Commercial Building, 317 Des Voeux Rd (tel 3-722-1036)
Micronesia – Ada Building, Ground Floor, Agana, Guam 96910 (tel 477-7106/7)
  Koror, Palau 96940 (tel 837)
Nauru – Republic of Nauru, Central Pacific (tel 3418)

Philippines – Legaspi Tower Building 300, Ground Floor, Roxas Boulevarde Cnr of Vito Cruz St, Pasay City, Metro Manila, 3194 (tel 574-011-34, ext 215)
USA – Davies Pacific Center, 841 Bishop St, Suite 506, Honolulu, Hawaii (tel 808-531-9766)
South Pacific Island Airways (SPIA)
Micronesia – Guam (tel 646-0381)
  Majuro (tel 3287)
USA – 733 Bishop St, Honolulu, Hawaii 96813 (tel 808-526-0844)

BOAT The Nauru Pacific Line provides passenger service from Melbourne to Nauru and the boat fare is not that much more than the airfare. Apparently the boat sometimes goes on to Majuro and Tarawa (Kiribati), but it is not clear whether passengers are allowed to continue on past Nauru. For information, contact Nauru House, 80 Collins St, Melbourne, Australia 3000 (tel 03 653-5709).

Nauru Pacific Line used to have a passenger service between Honolulu and Micronesia, but no longer.

TOURS
Conventional package tours by either air or cruise ship are rare in Micronesia. There are however, a number of diving plans or 'adventure' tours available, though most are expensive.

Poseidon Ventures, (505 N Belt, Suite 675, Houston, Texas 77060), offers dive tours to Truk, Palau and Pohnpei.

Ed-U-Dive, (Box 724, Libby, Montana 59923-9990), offers dive/study tours to Palau and Truk, sometimes in conjunction with museum or aquarium research. Their package has optional extensions to Pohnpei and Yap.

Ocean Voyages, (1709 Bridgeway, Sausalito, California 94965), has a 36-foot cutter called *Snowdrop* which is based in the Marshall Islands. The boat can carry up to four people and generally cruises the Marshalls' outer atolls of Wotje, Likiep, Aur and Maloelap. It can be chartered for longer trips to Pohnpei or Truk.

Society Expeditions, (723 Broadway East, Seattle, Washington 98102), offers 'adventure cruises' to the Carolines,

usually Yap and Palau, that continue on to Borneo and other locales.

The *S S Thorfinn*, (Seaward Holdings Ltd, 2314 Commissioner Street, Vancouver, British Columbia, Canada VSL 1A4), is a luxury ship that cruises between Pohnpei and Truk from November to May. Diving possibilities are emphasised.

See & Sea Travel Service, (50 Francisco St, Suite 205, San Francisco, California 94133), organises diving vacations to Truk and Palau. In Palau they have 10-day cruises aboard the *Sun Tamarin*, a live-aboard dive boat.

Getting Around

AIR

Air Mike links Micronesia's eight major district centres of Majuro, Kosrae, Pohnpei, Truk, Guam, Saipan, Yap and Palau.

Some island groupings also have domestic airlines connecting the district centre to some of the outer islands. The government-supported Airline of the Marshall Islands (AMI) is by far the most extensive, linking every inhabited Marshallese atoll.

On Pohnpei, Pacific Missionary Aviation (PMA) links Pohnpei with Pingelap and Kosrae, and also flies between Yap and Ulithi. Although their flights aren't particularly cheap, they do some impressive rescue and medical evacuations on the outer islands. If you fly with them, you help to subsidise it all.

On Palau, competition between several domestic airlines has left Palau Paradise Air the winner. They fly six and eight-seater planes from Koror to the outer islands of Peleliu and Angaur. There are usually two return flights per day, in the early morning and the late afternoon, which allows for day trips between these islands. Sometimes extra flights are added if there's a demand and Wednesdays are usually reserved for charter flights. The fares are very reasonable and the trip takes you over the Rock Islands on the way.

In the Marianas, a handful of commuter airlines fly daily between Guam, Saipan, Rota and Tinian. One-plane airlines pop up with regular frequency, tending to keep the market hot and the fares low. You should be able to get to all these islands from Guam for under $100 return. There are also lots of deals including off-peak, round-trip and stopover packages.

On Maui Airlines, for example, the full-fare from Guam to Rota and then Rota to Saipan totals $100. But if you take their midday 'Paseo Barato' flight, you'd pay only $54 by taking a $39 Guam-Saipan flight, with a stopover on Rota for an extra $15.

ISLAND AIRLINES

Airline of the Marshall Islands (AMI)
    Box 959, Majuro, Marshall Islands 96960 (tel 3373, 3216)
Maui Airlines
    Guam – Box 23367 GMF, Guam 96921 (tel 646-0231)
    Rota – tel 532-3427
    Saipan – tel 234-8321
Pacific Missionary Aviation (PMA)
    Guam – Box 3209, Agana, Guam 96910
    Pohnpei – Box 517, Pohnpei, FSM 96941 (tel 796)
    Yap – Box 460, Yap, FSM 96943
Palau Paradise Air
    Box 488, Koror, Palau 96940 (tel 348)

Addresses and telephone numbers for Air Mike, Air Nauru and SPIA are given in the Getting There chapter.

BOAT

Field Trip Ships

Field trip ships link the district centres with their outer islands, carrying both supplies and passengers and loading copra for the return journeys. Some of the routes have the ships out for weeks, and they're often behind schedule, while the shorter routes, such as Pohnpei to Pingelap, take only a few days.

Don't expect much in the way of comfort – these are definitely not cruise ships, though all vessels have both deck and cabin class. Deck is cheaper, but the cabins aren't terribly expensive. Check to see if you have to be on a meal plan if you go cabin class.

The meals usually consist of monotonous dishes of rice, canned fish and canned meat so you'll probably want to bring at least some of your own food.

Commuter Boats

There's an extensive weekday system of commuter boats linking Moen with the other islands in Truk Lagoon. Palau also has public boat services that take

47

passengers from Koror to Peleliu, Melekeok and Kayangel, among others.

Fishing Boats
Fishing boats often double as passenger carriers, especially in Palau and Truk. As often as not the large ones are expensive new boats that are government-owned and contracted out to the individual islands to promote fishing co-ops. There are, therefore, fairly regular services between, say, Moen and the Mortlocks, as the fishermen run their boats back and forth.

The fares are quite reasonable (usually just a few dollars) but, on the private boats particularly, they are sometimes set at whim. Women often get a better deal than men.

You can catch these boats when they're in port, but they don't really run on any schedule. There are also a few small cargo boats which take passengers, including vessels which ply a regular route between Saipan and Tinian. Just go down to the docks and ask around.

Speedboats
There are lots of private speedboats, particularly commuting back and forth between islands within the same lagoon. Depending on how rough the seas are, traffic sometimes crosses open ocean to neighbouring islands as well.

Hitching a ride on one of these boats is not all that difficult if you're friendly and offer a few dollars to help pay for the petrol.

LOCAL TRANSPORT
Most of the major islands have extensive road systems. Usually the main drag around town and the road out to the airport are paved but beyond that it varies, and unpaved roads are more common than not.

In some places you can just cruise along, while other roads are little more than pitted washed-out obstacle courses, challenging you to get through without bottoming out. To challenge you even further, the car agencies often rent low-riding small cars. The truly amazing thing is you don't find a lot of cars stuck in mud holes on the side of the road.

On some of these dirt roads you'll pass heavy machinery running up and down smoothing over the ruts. They keep particularly busy between the washouts caused by heavy rain storms.

Car Rental
Rental cars are available on the major islands, though their actual availability is sometimes limited. Because most cars are rented on a 24-hour basis, you can get two day's usage by renting at midday and driving around all afternoon, then heading out in a different direction the next morning before the car is due back.

There's usually no mileage charge and the minimum rate averages between $25 and $30 per day. The cars are seldom more than three years old but then again, between the salt air and the roads, that's about their average life expectancy.

With the major rental companies in Guam and Saipan, it's a good idea to reserve a vehicle in advance, or you may find the cheaper cars already rented out. They'll hold your reservation and there are no cancellation penalties.

Officially you need a US or international driver's license to drive.

In many places it's hard to find cars with insurance. It's a mixed bag – you save a few bucks, but as someone at the rental booth said: 'you hit it, you buy it'.

Taxi
Majuro gets the prize for its inexpensive system of shared taxis that cruise constantly up and down the main road, making it one of the easiest places to visit without having to rent a car. As long as the taxi is not full, it can be waved down and another passenger taken on. Rates are charged for each person according to their own destination.

Pohnpei and Truk (Moen) also have shared taxis, which are usually the back of pick-up trucks, and the prices are cheap.

In Palau (Kolonia area), Saipan and Guam, taxis are private and rates are comparable to western fares.

Hitching

The usual hitchhiking precautions apply, especially for women, but with the exception of Guam, getting lifts in Micronesia should not be too difficult.

Kosrae, for example, has no taxis but drivers nearly always offer rides to people walking along the road; a courtesy which is pretty common throughout the region.

Be careful, however, of getting dropped off in remote locations that see little traffic, unless you're prepared to walk back.

In backwaters like Rota and Kosrae, passengers arriving at the airport commonly ask around for someone going into town to catch a ride with.

Bus

Public bus transportation is available only to a *very* limited extent on Majuro, Saipan and Yap.

Republic of the Marshall Islands

The Marshalls consist of more than a thousand small coral islands. They are particularly narrow and they are all, without exception, flat. Most can be walked across in a couple of minutes.

The Marshall Islands have little fertile topsoil and are devoid of rivers and underground water supplies. Aside from coconuts, pandanus and breadfruit, few crops grow in the salty sand of most atolls so the Marshallese long ago turned to the sea for their resources. They became, by absolute necessity, expert fishers and navigators.

The Marshalls had little to tempt conquerors or settlers and because they hadn't much food, water or wood to offer, even whalers and explorers seldom stayed long.

However, as a gentle people in an isolated part of the Pacific, the Marshallese and their islands were easy prey as nuclear testing subjects after WW II. The bomb tests have stopped, but today the Marshallese are still grappling with the lingering effects of radiation as well as ongoing US missile tests and appalling health conditions. No other Micronesians have suffered under US colonialism to the extent that the Marshallese have.

Although the capital Majuro is not a resort area it has some nice sandy beaches though unfortunately, particularly around the population centre of D-U-D, the shoreline is strewn with trash. Most of the outer islands however still retain the more pristine nature you'd expect to find in the tropical Pacific.

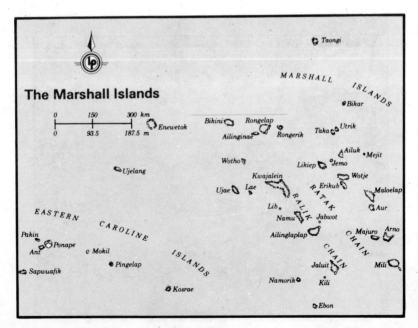

Geography

There are 1152 islands and islets in the Marshalls. Only five are single islands. The rest are grouped into 29 coral atolls.

The atolls run roughly north-south in two nearly parallel chains about 150 miles (241.5 km) apart and 800 miles (1288 km) long. The eastern chain is called *Ratak* which means 'toward dawn' and the western chain is *Ralik*, 'toward sunset'.

The total land area is 70 square miles (179 square km), stretching over more than 500,000 square miles, or 1280,000 square km, of ocean. True to classic atoll form the islands are narrow and low and encircle central lagoons. The widest island, Wotje, is less than a mile across and the highest elevation, of just 34 feet (10 metres), is on Likiep.

The southern islands have more vegetation than those in the north and virtually all of them have gorgeous white sand beaches.

Climate

In Majuro, the average daily temperature is 81°F (27°C). It's usually a few degrees warmer at night than it is during the day because most heavy rains fall during the daytime.

The northern Marshalls are quite dry, averaging just 20 inches (50.8 cm) of rain each year. Rainfall increases as you head south, with some islands getting up to 160 inches (406 cm) a year.

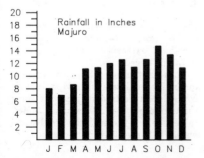

20
18   Rainfall in Inches
16   Majuro
14
12
10
8
6
4
2

J F M A M J J A S O N D

On Majuro, the wettest months are September through November (about 14 inches monthly) and the driest period is January through March (with about eight inches a month).

Full-blown tropical storms or typhoons are rare, but can be devastating when they whip across the low unprotected islands. Smaller storms however, are common in March, April, October and November.

History

The Marshalls were never unified under a single leader, though one chief often controlled several atolls and at times the entire Ralik chain was under a single chief. Chiefs had absolute authority though their wealth and power depended upon the loyalty and tribute payments made by the commoners.

Living on such narrow stretches of sand, land control was always, and still is, an extremely important issue for the Marshallese. Islanders married for land, went to war for land and when all else failed, they employed magic to get land.

Pandanus was an important food in the northern islands, breadfruit equally so in the south, while coconut production and fishing were important everywhere.

The Marshallese developed some of the best canoe-building and navigational skills in the Pacific.

Stick Charts The low elevation of the Marshalls and the distances between the atolls make them particularly difficult to sight from sea. In travels between islands, early inhabitants learned to read the patterns of the waves by watching for swells which would show that land was ahead.

Stick charts were used to teach the secrets of navigation. They were made by tying flat strips of wood together in designs which imitated the wave patterns. Shells were then attached to these sticks to represent the islands.

Three different kinds of charts were used. The *mattang* showed wave patterns around a single island or atoll and was used first to teach the basic techniques. The *medo* showed patterns around a small group of atolls and the *rebillit* mapped an entire chain, showing the relationships between the islands and the major ocean swells.

Stick charts were not actually taken on journeys. All the information they contained was memorised. Few people understand them today though due to their popularity as souvenirs many islanders can still make them.

European Contact Because the Marshalls were off the main trade routes they received few visits from early European explorers.

In 1525 a Spaniard named Alonso de Salazar became the first European to sight a Marshallese island. Although other Spanish expeditions landed in the Marshalls during the 1500s Spain did nothing to colonise the area.

The islands were named after the English sea captain John Marshall who in 1788 sighted Arno, Majuro, Aur, Maloelap, Wotje and Ailuk and docked at Mili. His visit was probably the first made by Europeans in the Marshalls in 200 years and the exchange between the English and the 'Marshallese' was friendly.

Otto von Kotzebue and other Russian explorers made the first good maps of the islands in the early 1800s.

Whalers, Traders & Missionaries Traders and whalers first showed up in the region in the early 1800s but they avoided the Marshalls once the islanders' reputation for violence spread. A 30-year period from the mid-1820s was a time of especially brutal attacks on European and American traders. The kind-hearted Marshallese had suddenly become, for westerners, the most feared people in Micronesia.

In case after case the captain, or surviving officers, of vessels putting into port at various atolls in the Marshalls had to record the death of a captain or crew members in the ship's log. Sometimes the scouting parties that went ashore just completely disappeared and in the early 1850s the entire crews of three trading ships were massacred at Namorik, Ebon and Jaluit.

Some of the fighting was prompted by the stealing of island women. The high chief of the southern Ralik chain was partly responsible for attacks in his area in revenge for the death of his brother during an earlier encounter.

Violence was on the decline when the first Protestant missionaries arrived on Ebon in 1857. The missionaries were at first welcomed, or at least tolerated, by the chiefs. Schools and churches were opened side by side and conversions came quickly. By the time the chiefs realised their traditional authority was being usurped by western values and the Christian god, it was too late. Getting rid of the missionaries would not solve the problem. By 1872 Marshallese graduates of their own mission schools were running most of the churches themselves.

The German Period Germany annexed the Marshalls in 1885, but didn't move government officials in until 1906. Instead, island affairs were left to the Jaluit Gesellschaft, a group of powerful German trading companies.

Coconut plantations and copra facilities had been set up as far back as the 1860s, including a coconut oil factory on Ebon in 1861 and trading stations on Mili, Ebon, Jaluit, Namorik, Majuro and Aur atolls.

The Japanese Period The Japanese took control from 1914 and colonised the Marshalls extensively, developing and fortifying large bases.

They also took over the copra business, but unlike the Germans the Japanese sold copra directly to traders instead of going through local chiefs. This policy undermined, even further, the traditional authority of the chiefs in the islands.

World War II The first Micronesian islands captured by the Americans in WW II were at Kwajalein Atoll in February 1944. Roi-Namur, the main Japanese air base in the Marshalls, fell first followed by Kwajalein Island with its almost completed airstrip.

Majuro Atoll, left undefended, was taken next. From the air base at Kwajalein and using Majuro as a base for fast carriers, the US then staged attacks on the Carolines.

The US bypassed four atolls still in Japanese hands, but within weeks had captured Enewetok Atoll and about 30 more Marshallese islands before heading west.

Americans & Atomic Bombs

After the war, the Americans immediately moved in and started atomic bomb experiments on Bikini and Enewetok atolls. Kwajalein Atoll was later established as a missile testing site.

Some of the islanders who breathed radioactive air or lived on contaminated land have died from radiation-related ailments while others have lingering health problems. Many wonder if they were deliberately used as test subjects for monitoring radiation's long-term effects on humans.

Bikini Atoll Bikini, site of the earliest known habitation in Micronesia, was the first atoll to be nuked back to the Stone Age.

According to legend, Bikini was the favourite island of Loa, creator of the Marshalls. Loa used the words *iia kwe!*, 'you are a rainbow', to describe Bikini. Eventually the term grew to describe anything lovely and is said to be the source of the current greeting *yokwe*.

Early in 1946 a US Navy spokesman met with the religiously fervent Bikini islanders, following church services, to inform them that their islands were needed for 'a greater good'. After deliberations, their chief, Juda, responded that if the US wanted to use Bikini for the 'benefit of all mankind' his people would go elsewhere. Still awed by the American firepower which had recently defeated the Japanese Imperial Navy, the Bikinians may not have felt in a position to balk. Undoubtedly the Americans also knew that protesting is not a Marshallese custom.

The 161 Bikinians were relocated on the assurance they could move back once the tests were over. A few months later a nuclear device was exploded 500 feet over Bikini's lagoon, the first of 23 nuclear tests that would leave the islands uninhabitable, the Bikinians displaced and their society disrupted.

The Bikinians were first moved to Rongerik Atoll, a place of bad reputation in Marshallese legend. They got sick from eating poisonous fish in the lagoon and nearly starved from inadequate food supplies. Two years later they were moved to Kwajalein Atoll and then later to Kili Island.

In the 1970s the Bikinians were told it was safe to move back home and a resettlement programme began. The Bikinians, who had been dreaming of the day they could return, were shocked to find two entire islands blown away and most of the others treeless, blasted apart and covered with wreckage and debris.

In 1978 US tests showed that by eating food grown in the caesium-contaminated soil the Bikinians had collected high levels of radioactivity in their bodies, so they were moved off again.

Scientists from the Lawrence Livermore Lab in California are currently using Bikini to study ways to clean up radiation, including tests to see which plants soak up the most caesium. By their estimates Bikini's 24 islands could be made habitable in four years at a cost of about $100 million.

In case you're wondering, the bikini swimsuit was first named *atome* by its French designer, a year after the first atomic bomb tests at Bikini.

Enewetok Atoll Enewetok islanders were evacuated to Ujelang Atoll before atomic bomb tests began in 1948. Over a 10-year period 43 atomic bombs were detonated from Enewetok.

In 1980, after a $120 million clean-up programme, the islanders were allowed to return to Enewetok Island, in the southern part of the atoll.

The more highly contaminated island of Engebi in the northern part of the atoll has a ban on visits of longer than a couple of hours duration.

Between the two is Runit Island, where contaminated items from the atoll were stashed under a huge 18-inch-thick concrete dome nicknamed Cactus Crater. The radiated debris and soil is supposed to be safe in 50,000 years. The concrete may last 300!

A 9.8-megaton hydrogen bomb which exploded in 1958 on Enewetok was the focus of a recent multi-million dollar geological study which showed the bomb had blasted a mile-wide, 200-foot-deep (60 metre) crater in the lagoon and fractured the rock to a depth of 1400 feet (420 metres) beneath the crater's surface. The geological impact of such massive bending and breaking of the earth's bed remains unknown.

Rongelap Atoll The immensely powerful hydrogen bomb 'Bravo' that exploded on Bikini in March 1954 sent clouds of deadly radioactivity toward inhabited Rongelap Atoll, 100 miles to the east. The fallout came down as powdered ash six hours after the blast.

Immediate signs of radiation sickness included nausea, hair loss and severe radiation burns. Three days after the blast the US military evacuated the Rongelapese to Kwajalein for decontamination, returning them to their atoll in 1957.

The Rongelapese have health problems that include high rates of mental retardation, leukemia, stillbirths and miscarriages. Almost 75% of the children who were under the age of 10 on the day of the blast have had surgery for thyroid tumors.

Despite an aerial survey showing that some of the islands of Rongelap were as 'hot' as islands in Bikini, and a ban on eating shellfish because of accumulated radiation, the US continued to insist that Rongelap was safe and refused to help resettle the approximately 350 islanders.

In 1985 the Greenpeace ship *Rainbow Warrior* moved the Rongelapese to a new home on Mejato Island in Kwajalein Atoll, 110 miles to the south. The boat was later sunk in New Zealand by French agents who hoped to stop *Rainbow Warrior's* activities aimed at ending nuclear testing in the South Pacific.

Half Life, a film by Australian director Dennis O'Rourke, tells the plight of the islanders and convincingly presents a picture of the Rongelapese being used as nuclear guinea pigs.

Utrik Atoll Though their plight is not as well known, the islanders of Utrik Atoll also received fallout from the Bravo test and have been developing radiation-related medical problems.

Government

The Marshallese began pulling out of the Congress of Micronesia as early as 1973, intent on going their own way – though not too far. As with the other Trust Territory districts they were to sign a Compact of Free Association with the United States. Their constitution became effective on 1 May 1979 and they are now known as the Republic of the Marshall Islands.

The Marshallese government is modelled after a combination of both the British and US systems. It has a unicameral 33-member parliament called Nitijela, a Council of Iroij (chiefs) which is basically an advisory board, and a cabinet headed by a president. Each inhabited atoll has a local council.

The compact with the US was not overwhelmingly popular. The Bikinians were afraid that the conditions of the compact meant the US would deny further responsibility for cleaning up Bikini, minimising compensation. Although 89% of Bikinians voted against it, the compact was passed in September 1983 with 58% approval. It went into effect in 1986.

Economy

In addition to compact monies, the US has to pay $170 million rent for Kwajalein bases and $80 million for development projects on Kwajalein Atoll over 30 years.

Some local income comes from copra production, tourism and handicrafts. Cultivation of giant clams obtained from Palau has begun on a commercial scale.

A Danish-built milk processing plant, owned by the Marshallese government, uses imported powdered milk and butterfat combined with Majuro water to make plain and chocolate milk and four flavours of ice cream. It's sold in local stores under the Pacific Maid label.

A Japanese company in Majuro produces *katsuobushi*, made by a process of boiling and smoking skipjack tuna.

People

The population in the Marshalls has more than doubled over the past 20 years and population growth is a major problem. The estimated 1986 population was 37,000, with most people living on Majuro and Kwajalein atolls.

The Marshallese are a soft-spoken, good-natured people with musical talents. Most women wear bright, floral print *muu-muu* dresses.

The Protestant 'Boston Mission' that started converting the Marshallese in the mid-1800s effectively wiped out the ancient religion of the islanders. About 80% now belong to the Christian Church of the Marshall Islands, an independent Protestant denomination.

Language

Marshallese is the official language, but English is taught in schools and is widely understood. The islanders' gentleness is reflected in their traditional greeting *yokwe yuk*, which means 'love to you'. 'Thank you' is *kommol tata*.

Holidays

Majuro celebrates the usual US holidays as well as Constitution Day on 1 May.

Health Problems

Much of Micronesian society has been traumatised by its inability to rapidly absorb massive doses of westernisation. Dietary health problems in the Marshalls are one of the most blatant examples.

Although the Marshallese eagerly took to a new diet heavy in processed sugars, genetically they have been unable to assimilate it. The sugar-laced cereals, soft drinks, and the extensive variety of packaged junk food that crams supermarket shelves have left 30% of the population potentially diabetic. At Majuro's new hospital, 75% of inpatients are diabetic.

Malnutrition is also severe. There have been cases of blindness from vitamin A deficiency, even though vitamin-A-rich pandanus, papaya and pumpkins are locally grown. Suprisingly, a high percentage of deaths related to malnutrition are amongst the people of agriculturally productive Laura Village on Majuro. Rather than eating the produce, some families take it to the market to sell to get money to buy more tantalising junk food.

Majuro

Most travellers to the Marshalls only get to Majuro Atoll, the political and economic centre.

The atoll has 57 small islets curving 63 miles (101 km) in an elongated oval shape. The larger islets have been connected by a single 35-mile (56 km) stretch of paved road, making it appear that most of Majuro is one long narrow island. The highest point is 20 feet (six metres).

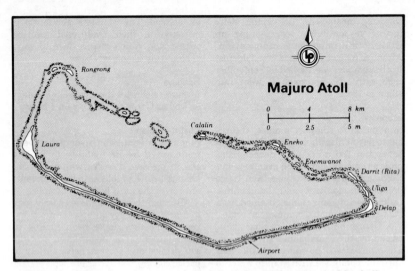

These narrow sandbars have no way of coping with the packaging of western culture. Tin cans, junked cars and disposable nappies (diapers) are piled by the roadside and spill into the lagoon.

Although Majuro is more westernised than other islands in the Marshalls, there's a lot you can learn about life in this region just from this one atoll.

You can grasp what it's like to live on a ribbon of land so thin that as often as not you can see the ocean on both sides, and by visiting Laura Village in the north you can see rural life somewhat similar to the outer islands.

The name Majuro means 'many eyes' and it has always been one of the more populated Marshallese atolls.

Information

The tourist office (tel 3206), is in with the Ministry of Resources and Development in the green buildings next to the RRE Hotel parking lot in Uliga. They have free postcards, maps and information sheets.

Majuro's only post office is next door to Robert Reimers Enterprises. It's open from 8 am to noon and 1 to 4 pm on weekdays and from 9 to 11 am on Saturdays. All mail to the Marshalls goes through Majuro and uses the zip code 96960, except for mail to Ebeye which uses 96970.

The Bank of Guam is on the first floor of the RRE Hotel and the Bank of the Marshall Islands is next to the post office. Banking hours are 10 am to 3 pm Monday through Thursday and 10 am to 5 pm on Fridays.

Long distance calls can be made from the office near the COMSAT station in Delap. The RRE Hotel switchboard will place calls for non-guests but charges everyone $1 for the service. There's no service charge for calls from the Marshall Sun Hotel.

There are several laundromats around town, the nicest is in Rita.

The library next door to the museum has a Pacific room with a surprisingly comprehensive selection of books, magazines and journals on Micronesia. It's open from 10 am to noon and 1 to 5 pm Monday to Friday.

The *Marshall Islands Journal* is published on Fridays, costs 40 cents and is easy to find in stores around town. Guam's *Pacific Daily News* is available at the RRE Hotel and at larger stores.

Majuro has three radio stations and a TV station.

D-U-D Municipality

Three of Majuro's islands – Delap, Uliga and Darrit – are joined into one municipality with the unappealing moniker 'D-U-D'. (Pronounce each letter separately, rather than spitting out the single syllable 'dud'.)

D-U-D is the nation's capital and most of Majuro's 12,000 residents are concentrated there. The lagoon around D-U-D is polluted and not good for swimming. The poor sanitation conditions are compounded by causeways and bridges that close up the lagoon and contribute to poor water circulation.

Delap The main government buildings are in Delap as is President Amata Kabua's house, which is the pink building with the spiffy tennis courts to the right just before the bridge leaving D-U-D going towards Laura.

Next to the new dock where the field trip ship pulls in, is a copra processing plant. The people there will gladly talk about the plant and someone will probably offer to give you a little tour. Get them to show you the warehouse where the copra is piled. Believe it or not, all that gritty brown coconut meat will be transformed into pure transparent oil!

Uliga The Alele Museum and the public library share a modern building next to the courthouse.

The museum is small but has quality exhibits of early Marshallese culture. One highlight is a collection of photographs of the Marshalls taken at the turn of the century by the son of a Portuguese whaler who lived on Likiep Atoll.

The museum is open from 10 am to noon and 3 to 5 pm Monday to Friday. There's no entrance fee.

Rita US forces stationed on Majuro during WW II gave the island of Darrit the nickname 'Rita', after one of their favourite pin-up girls Rita Hayworth, and the name has stuck. They also named Laura.

Die-hard sightseers may want to seek out the Japanese bunker, which is Majuro's only remaining WW II fortification, or the overgrown Action Wave Memorial raised after a tidal wave destroyed the area in November 1979. Neither is particularly interesting nor easy to find. The bunker is beyond the high school and is reached by tramping through people's yards.

At low tide people commonly wade over the reef to and from the islands north of Rita. If you catch the lowest tide, the water is less than a foot deep. Remember to start before low tide if you want to come back the same way. The inside page of the local newspaper has a tide chart.

Laura

Laura, 30 miles away, is a quiet green refuge from the bustle of D-U-D. It's the atoll's agricultural centre and has a pretty white sand beach at its tip.

The road to Laura passes the airport, the runway of which is sloped to allow it to serve as Majuro's main water catchment source. A dirt path to the left, immediately past the runway, goes straight out to the beach where there's a shipwreck on the shore.

Further up the road on the right is Peace Park Majuro built by the Japanese. Its amphitheatre, cement monument and flagpole all look rather lonely and out of place on the beach but there are shady spots for picnicking.

The Taiwanese have an experimental agricultural station where corn, cabbage, soybeans, cucumbers, papaya and other crops are grown, and pigs and chickens are raised. It's on the left just as you enter Laura and you're welcome to take a look around.

The Japanese have raised a stone memorial marker for a major typhoon that hit Laura in 1918. To find it, drive to

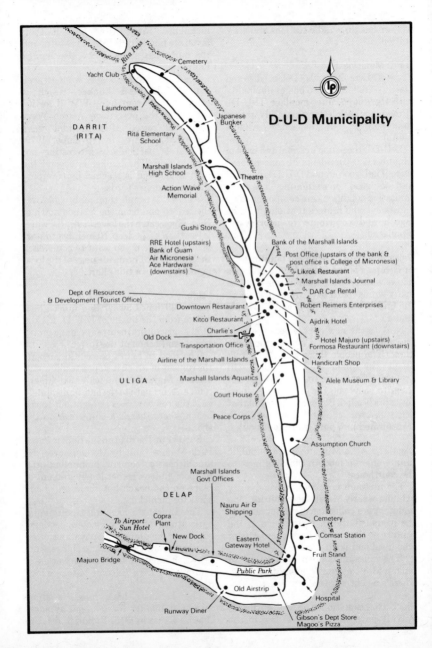

D-U-D Municipality

Rita Pass

Cemetery

Yacht Club

Laundromat

Japanese Bunker

DARRIT (RITA)

Rita Elementary School

Marshall Islands High School

Theatre

Action Wave Memorial

Gushi Store

RRE Hotel (upstairs)
Bank of Guam
Air Micronesia
Ace Hardware (downstairs)

Bank of the Marshall Islands

Post Office (upstairs of the bank & post office is College of Micronesia)

Likrok Restaurant

Marshall Islands Journal

DAR Car Rental

Dept of Resources & Development (Tourist Office)

Downtown Restaurant

Robert Reimers Enterprises

Kitco Restaurant

Ajidrik Hotel

Charlie's

Old Dock

Transportation Office

Hotel Majuro (upstairs)
Formosa Restaurant (downstairs)

Airline of the Marshall Islands

Handicraft Shop

ULIGA

Marshall Islands Aquatics

Alele Museum & Library

Court House

Peace Corps

Assumption Church

DELAP

Marshall Islands Govt Offices

To Airport
Sun Hotel

Copra Plant

Nauru Air & Shipping

New Dock

Cemetery

Comsat Station

Eastern Gateway Hotel

Majuro Bridge

Fruit Stand

Public Park

Old Airstrip

Hospital

Runway Diner

Gibson's Dept Store
Magoo's Pizza

the end of the paved road, continue about 400 yards on a dirt road and turn left.

Diving & Snorkelling

Majuro is a good place to find rare varieties of tropical fish. If you're looking for sharks you can find them too.

Diving is possible year-round, though the best months are May to October when the water is calmest. There's good diving in the channels around Majuro and good diving and snorkelling off the islands between Rita and Calalin on the lagoon side. Snorkellers can also try Laura Village and in front of the Sun Hotel.

Matthew Holly (tel 3669; Box 319) of *Marshall Islands Aquatics* offers Majuro's only dive services. He charges $25 to $30 per person, per dive; $200 per day for six people with two dives each; or you can negotiate something in between. Snorkellers pay $20 per day.

Matt does underwater photography, charters for diving at other atolls (Mili, Maloelap and Arno are popular) and boat tours. He rents filled tanks for $5 each, a full set of diving gear including tank for $15 per day and snorkelling gear for $5 per day. Matt can certify NAUI in seven dives for $150 and says the Marshalls is an easy place to learn to dive.

You can buy snorkelling gear at Gibson's or Ace Hardware.

Places to Stay – bottom end

The cheapest places are locally owned, right in the centre of town and rather dingy. Don't expect much for your money.

The *Majuro Hotel* (tel 3324; Box 185), above the Formosa Restaurant, has 11 rooms. It costs $18 a single for a room with fan and shared bath, $21 with private bath, $25 with air-con. It's $5 more for a second person.

The *Ajidrik Hotel* (tel 3171; Box E) has 15 air-con rooms with mini-refrigerator and private bath for $25 a single or $28 a double. When not filled with long-term renters, the Ajidrik's older rooms cost $22

single or $26 double. The hotel is tucked behind the Downtown Restaurant. They can provide airport transfers.

Places to Stay – middle

If you want to be right on the beach stay at the Japanese-run *Marshall Sun Hotel* (tel 3118; Box 1215), halfway between the airport and D-U-D and less than a 10-minute ride each way. With its 35 air-con rooms with private baths, it is quiet, relaxing and friendly, but don't be misled by their brochure. The beach bar and restaurant are both good places to meet other travellers and resident foreigners. Rooms cost $33 a single and $44 a double. Sun Hotel has unlimited free laundry service and they'll let you use their snorkelling gear. Repeat customers get a 10% discount and the hotel has a free shuttle bus which meets Air Mike flights.

Places to Stay – top end

The *RRE Hotel (Hotel Robert Reimers)* (tel 3250; Box 1) is a comfortable modern 18-room hotel above the Bank of Guam. Rooms have stocked mini-refrigerators, telephones and rattan furnishings. It's the only hotel in Majuro with baths and TVs. Rooms on the inside corridor (no windows) cost $40 a single or $45 a double. The smaller rooms with lanais and lagoon view cost $50 a single and $55 double. Airport transportation is free.

The multi-story *Eastern Gateway Hotel*, a project financed by the Republic of Nauru, has been under construction for years. When it's finally done it will be Majuro's first luxury resort hotel. Plans call for 56 rooms, tennis courts and a top floor restaurant. In the meantime there are older bungalows on the ocean side that get cool breezes and construction noise. Rates there are $42 a single and $47 a double, or they may be negotiable. You get the feeling that hotel guests are rather in the way. There's a small restaurant patronised by the construction crew.

All hotels add a tax of 3% plus $2 per room per night.

Places to Eat
Food in Majuro is cheap, fresh fish is found in most restaurants and you might even see *won*, or turtle steak, chalked up as a dinner special.

The *Kitco Restaurant*, in the middle of town, is cheap. You can get curry chicken for $2, ham and eggs with pancake for $1.50 and a full chalkboard of other dishes in the $1 to $3 range.

If you like big breakfasts between 6 and 7 am, *Downtown Restaurant* has an early bird special of two eggs, bacon and toast or pancake for $1. Their tuna steak (or reef fish) plate costs $3 and is good and *ni*, or coconut juice, costs 40 cents.

The *Litrok Restaurant*, behind the post office, has very good food in the same price range as the cheap restaurants on the main street and it's light, airy and has an ocean view to boot! Try reef fish for $2.50 or the salad bar with fruit for $1.50. You can have a good hearty breakfast with coffee for under $2.

The *Yacht Club* in Rita has outdoor tables on a grassy area next to the lagoon, but no yachts. The pool tables and bar make it a popular hang-out and meals start from around $3. The tiny cheese pizza is disappointing for $5. Check the calculation on the bill.

The *Formosa Restaurant* is a typical Chinese restaurant where you can get chicken chow mein with rice and soup for $2.95 and other standard Chinese dishes in the $3 to $6 range.

The *Sun Hotel Restaurant* is the place where folks go when they want a special treat. It has authentic Japanese food, such as tempura with miso soup and rice for $5.50 and sashimi for $3.50, and western dishes.

The *Runway Diner* out on the old airport runway, not far from Gibson's department store, has Marshallese food.

You can buy fruit from the red stand with the large fish sign near the COMSAT station. Coconuts are 35 cents.

Majuro has some typhoid problems so drinking water should be boiled first.

Entertainment
Charlie's, next door to Kitco Restaurant (no sign), is the most popular place to knock back a few beers in the evening.

Uncle Sam's, The Pub and the *Lanai Club* all have discos and sometimes live bands for a $2.50 cover charge. Uncle Sam's is a popular spot with young working women. The women ask the guys to dance and it's rude to refuse. Thursday nights are 'ladies' nights' and there are always more women than men so the guys end up dancing all night long. Nothing gets going until around 11 pm but the bars close at 2 am.

A small movie theatre in Rita shows popular Hollywood movies.

Another option is to go along with the novel suggestion in the official tourist brochure:

'Sometimes it would be very wonderful to purchase a case of beer and go to a beech, sit, watch and enjoy the moon comes over the ocean while consuming the beer.'

Special Events
The Marshall Island's Fishing Tournament is held over the 4th of July weekend and there's an annual billfish tournament in mid June.

The Alele Museum sponsors a Folk Art Festival with traditional crafts, song and dance during the last week of August.

On Christmas Day people gather at the churches for singing, dancing and skits that last all day long.

Things To Buy
The best-known Marshallese handicrafts are stick charts, carved models of outrigger canoes and intricately woven items such as baskets, wall hangings and purses made from pandanus leaves, coconut fronds and cowrie shells. Marshallese handicrafts are among the best in Micronesia both in quality and price.

The handicraft cooperative behind the museum is open from Monday to Friday and there's another shop down by the

Catholic church. You can often catch women working on handicrafts at either place. They also open two handicraft booths at the airport during flight times.

You can get colourful commemorative postage stamps and first day covers at either the post office or the museum. The cover and stamp of the Baker Day Atomic Bomb Test makes a provocative souvenir for $1.

The Alele Museum sells books on Micronesia, audio tapes of Marshallese chants and stories for $5.50, video tapes of the same for $30 and T-shirts.

Majuro is *the* place to buy 'Nuclear Free Pacific' or 'Bikini – Paradise Lost' T-shirts, as well as more standard designs. Men's Hawaiian-style shirts are about the same price here as in Hawaii.

Majuro stores are more modern than those in the FSM, so if you're continuing on in that direction buy anything you might need before you leave. If you should run out of film, this is one of the better places in Micronesia to buy it.

The locally produced *Marshalls Island Guidebook* is $4.50 at Gibson's department store. It's got colourful information about the Marshalls and a long list of Marshallese vocabulary.

Getting There
South Pacific Island Airlines (SPIA) flies both Honolulu-Majuro and Guam-Majuro. The one-way fare for either flight is $196.

If you're flying Air Mike from Honolulu to Majuro you might as well buy a ticket all the way on to Guam, as the complete island hopper at $450 is only $3 more than the Honolulu-Majuro ticket.

Airline of the Marshall Islands (AMI) flies from Nandi, in Fiji, to Majuro for $450. They also have an excursion ticket for $625. Going to Majuro, passengers must layover one night in Tarawa. A Tarawa-Majuro ticket costs $150.

Air Nauru has flights between Nauru and Majuro for $80.

Majuro has a $5 departure tax.

Getting Around
An excellent paved road runs from Rita to Laura.

Airport Transfer Most hotels provide a free minibus service to and from the airport. Taxis cost $2 from the airport to D-U-D or $1 to the Sun Hotel.

Taxi Majuro has a fine, inexpensive shared

First Day Cover – Marshall Islands

taxi system. You stand at the side of the road and wave at the taxis and if they're not full they stop.

The taxis are sedans, clearly marked with taxi signs. They don't have meters but it costs just 30 cents to go anywhere within D-U-D and from 50 cents to $1 between D-U-D and Sun Hotel.

Bus Minibuses run between D-U-D (from the RRE Hotel parking lot) and Laura. The one-way fare is $1.

Car Rentals Domnick Auto Rental, or DAR (tel 3680), charges $25 per day for a standard sedan with no air-con or $27 with air-con. Short-term rentals are $5 per hour and insurance is $3 per day extra. They operate from inside a video shop near the Litrok Restaurant.

Hotels can also arrange rentals. The Sun Hotel gets cars for $28 and the RRE Hotel charges the same as DAR but their insurance is $5. There's a rental booth at the airport too but they don't always have cars available.

Mopeds You can rent mopeds from the Jemenei store in Uliga for $10 for 24 hours.

Boats The larger hotels can arrange boat rentals or you can try to save money by cutting out the middleman and making arrangements yourself with someone who has a speedboat. Bargain the price. Marshallese are generally very fair and won't cheat you but if you throw money around they'll take it.

Kwajalein Atoll

Nowhere in Micronesia is the US military presence so ominous as on Kwajalein Atoll, a missile testing range operated by the US Department of Defense.

Kwajalein is the world's largest coral atoll. Its 97 islands have a total land mass of just 6½ square miles (16.5 square km), but they surround a 900-square-mile (2304 square km) lagoon.

The lagoon, sometimes called 'the world's largest catcher's mitt', is the target and splash-down point for intercontinental ballistic missiles (ICBMs) fired from Vandenberg Air Force Base in California, 4500 miles (7245 km) away.

The missile tests, which are generally announced a few days beforehand, occur at night and often light up the sky with a brilliant display of explosions, burning debris and sonic booms.

Recently Kwajalein has also been used as a test range for anti-ballistic missiles and strategic defense systems, on the cutting edge of the 'Star Wars' programme. In 1984 a missile shot from Kwajalein Atoll intercepted and exploded another missile shot from California, the first successful interception of an ICBM in space.

The Kwajalein Missile Range includes Kwajalein Island in the southern part of the atoll, Roi-Namur Island in the north and some smaller islands between the two. It's a world of radiation shields, radar systems, microwave dishes and sophisticated computers and tracking equipment.

Although Kwajalein is on the same side of the International Date Line as the rest of Micronesia, it uses the same date as the USA to avoid potential goof-ups between missile launchers in California and missile retrievers in Kwajalein. When it's noon Sunday in Majuro, it's noon Saturday in Kwajalein.

The Americans stationed on Kwajalein Island include an active group of divers who probably know quite a bit about the more than 30 Japanese ships at the bottom of the lagoon, but their main function is diving for missile pieces after a splashdown.

Getting permission from local landowners to visit the smaller islands in the area is more difficult in Kwajalein Atoll than elsewhere in Micronesia. Apart from the islands under direct US military control there are others in the north and south that have been taken over as tracking stations. The US pays rent to the Marshallese government for the use of the tracking station land. Most of the rent money goes to the Kwajalein Atoll Development Authority (KADA), a group comprised of the landowners who own the islands being used by the US.

So, despite the US presence, here as elsewhere in Micronesia there are different landowners for different islands, so you should always ask permission to visit another island – even for a picnic on the beach. The locals will be able to tell you who owns what.

The islands closest to Ebeye are day trip distance. As far as we know none of them have any established places for staying overnight.

KWAJALEIN ISLAND

About 3000 American civilian contract workers and their families live on Kwajalein Island.

Recreational facilities include two swimming pools, three baseball diamonds, tennis courts, movie theatres, handball and basketball courts, a bowling alley and a dart league. Everything is free to residents, including taxi vans to get around.

There's also a dinner club, restaurants and snack bars, a chapel, schools from kindergarten through high school, a supermarket and a modern department store. As much as possible, it is American suburbia transplanted.

EBEYE ISLAND

About 600 Marshallese labourers work on Kwajalein Island and live on the 78-acre (31-hectare) Ebeye Island, three miles (4.8 km) to the north. They support an additional 9000 relatives and friends in squalid, overcrowded conditions.

The contrasts between the two islands are startling. Workers are shuttled by boat between their ghetto homes and their affluent work sites. Marshallese are not allowed to shop at Kwajalein's fancy subsidised stores, make use of its modern 25-bed hospital or swim in its 'public' pools. They can look at the good life but they can't touch.

In 1935 Ebeye had 13 people in three households. With the development of the Kwajalein Missile Range in the early 1960s, Kwajalein Island residents were evacuated to Ebeye. Other Kwajalein Atoll islanders joined them as the 'mid- corridor' islands were also evacuated to free up most of the lagoon to catch missiles.

The US Army constructed apartment units, a saltwater sewerage system, a power plant and a freshwater system on Ebeye – but allotted no money for maintenance. The systems soon fell into disrepair.

As if concentrating all the atoll's people on tiny Ebeye wasn't problem enough, the menial jobs that opened up on the base tended to attract Marshallese from other atolls, particularly those who had relatives on Ebeye. Traditional Marshallese custom dictates that members of each extended family take in relatives in need. The neat little apartments built by the military were on their way to becoming Micronesia's most overcrowded ghetto.

In 1968 Marshallese workers began receiving US minimum wages. By 1970 Ebeye had 4000 people and by 1978 the population had swelled to 8000. The island came to be known as the 'Slum of the Pacific'.

Because of the inadequate catchment facilities on Ebeye, water had to be sent over by barge from Kwajalein Island. A new sewerage system built in 1979 broke down soon after its completion. Residents became accustomed to frequent power shortages and water restrictions. The supply of water was sometimes limited to only 15 minutes a day.

By 1984 there were 630 dwellings for 8500 people, on an island just one mile long and less than 200 yards wide (1.6 km by 182 metres).

One-room shacks and lean-tos of plywood, tin, cinder block and plastic sheeting are jammed side by side. Stores sell few fresh fruits or vegetables and are stocked instead with expensive packaged junk foods. Alcoholism is rampant and beer cans litter the roads. There are no trees – there simply isn't room.

Needless to say Ebeye is strewn with trash and sanitation is poor. Dirty nappies float in a lagoon too polluted for swimming, yet those same waters are the children's only playground. Dysentery, typhoid, diabetes and malnutrition are all in epidemic proportions. Infant mortality and suicide rates are high.

There's talk of building a causeway that will stretch six miles northward from Ebeye and join six other islands, using them as a spillover for Ebeye's population.

Under provisions of a lease agreement granting the US continued use of Kwajalein Atoll, the US is providing a new power plant and an Israeli-designed water desalination plant that may produce as many as 300,000 gallons of freshwater daily, innovatively using waste heat from the power plant.

Obviously Ebeye is not a big tourist spot, but it is a real eye-opener. The people are generally very friendly, especially the children.

ROI-NAMUR & SANDO ISLANDS

Fifty miles north of Ebeye, Roi-Namur houses radar and other tracking equipment. Like Kwajalein, it's a restricted military facility and another 'little America' with modern amenities once again available to Americans only.

Sando is the home of Marshallese workers commuting to Roi-Namur, much like Ebeye is to Kwajalein. The Japanese had communications facilities on Sando and large bomb shelters still stand, though they were damaged by heavy bombing during WW II. Live shells are still occasionally found on Roi-Namur and Sando.

The US built a modern bomb shelter for the 400 people of Sando for use during missile tests. Though the islanders once dutifully practiced drills, they no longer bother to go to the shelter during the tests.

MEJATO ISLAND

Mejato, in the north-west part of the atoll is now home to the Rongelapese, many of whom were irradiated in US nuclear testing.

The problems of the Rongelapese have been compounded by food shortages, a lack of sanitary facilities and problems in bringing in enough supplies from Ebeye, 70 miles (112 km) to the south.

Places to Stay

The *KADA Hotel* (tel 3100) on Ebeye is, at the moment, Kwajalein Atoll's only hotel and it gives priority to government guests and businesspeople. There are just two rooms, both dormitory style, one with three beds, the other with five. Each has air-con, a bathroom with hot water and a shower and, amazingly, water 24 hours a day. Beds cost $15 and can be reserved in advance by phone or by mail through KADA, Box 5958, Ebeye, Marshall Islands 96970. The secretary, Ernestine, is very helpful.

Two other small hotels are now under construction. Because of the extreme overcrowding, families on Ebeye have no room to spare for visitors.

If you have permission from the military commander to stay on Kwajalein Island there are dormitory rooms with two to three beds, hot water and bath for about $11. You may need a sponsor on the base to use these facilities however.

Places to Eat

On Ebeye there are many small restaurants but the best is the *Ebeye Restaurant* right by the dock. It has good clean food at a good price. The *Formosa Restaurant* is also a good choice, serving Chinese food at moderate prices.

Entertainment

Nightlife is limited on Ebeye but there are three dancing spots on Thursday, Friday and Saturday nights.

The Islander is the hottest night spot, with a $2 cover charge and beers for $1.75.

Top: Coconut Seller – Moen
Left: Storyboard maker – Palau
Right: Making a thatched floor – Kosrae

Top: Reef Island – Truk Lagoon
Bottom: Pingelap Atoll – Pohnpei

RYCA's, where the beer costs $1.50, is the wee-hours spot though it's small and has no air-con. The *MonKubok* is a quieter place frequented by an older crowd. Avoid the small bars and always avoid drunks – they can be dangerous. If possible, hang out with a friend at night.

Getting There

Although Kwajalein Island is a closed military base, it is the transit point if you're entering Ebeye by air.

If you want to visit Ebeye you have to apply for a permit at the Marshall Islands government complex in Delap (Majuro). It shouldn't be difficult to get. A fellow traveller on a writing assignment for Greenpeace was granted a permit without any hassle.

Air Mike stops on Kwajalein Island as part of the island-hopper flight.

Airline of the Marshall Islands flies to Kwajalein daily, except Tuesdays and Sundays, for $90 one way.

To get to Ebeye, once you're on Kwajalein, go to Dock Security Checkpoint and wait for a boat. There you will be asked again to show your permit to enter Ebeye. The ferries to Ebeye, which are refitted WW II landing crafts, are free and leave Kwajalein at 12.45, 5 and 7.30 am and 2.30, 4.45 and 7.30 pm.

Field trip ships stop at Ebeye. The one-way deck fare is $14.10.

Getting Around

Taxi From Ebeye's dock you can get a taxi to anywhere on the island for 25 cents. Most taxis are extended-cab pick-up trucks and you ride in the cab or hop in the back, wherever there's room.

Boat Large boats, that can carry 30 people, rent for about $650 for the round trip from Ebeye to Mejato or Sando. You can also rent smaller boats, but you'll have to bargain for the price. Ask around and be sure to talk directly to the boat owner. Radio ahead for permission before visiting either island.

Trips to closer islands are cheap. You should get permission from the landowner on Ebeye first, but it isn't hard to do. Avoid military installations around the lagoon as you'll be arrested for trespassing.

Outer Islands

Something of Marshallese traditional island life still remains in the quiet village communities away from Majuro and Kwajalein. The pace on the outer islands is relaxed and s-l-o-w.

Usually a few people on each island speak English and nearly everyone is friendly. Because of the language barrier some people may appear shy while others will strike up a conversation just to practice their English.

If you're visiting somebody special you might even rate a real Marshallese welcome. On these occasions a group of women singing in harmony and bearing baskets piled with food will surround the visitors. The women give the guests flower headbands and leis and then everybody stands around exchanging compliments.

One Peace Corps volunteer, describing a visit by her brother, told how some of the older village women welcomed him by rubbing baked breadfruit on his stomach and chanting about how good-looking he was. For better or worse, this isn't something the average traveller will encounter!

Although some outer islanders still use the *korkor*, a dug-out fishing canoe made from a breadfruit log, 'boom-booms', or motorboats, are steadily gaining in popularity. Both kinds of boats are used for frequent *jambos*, trips or picnics, to uninhabited atoll islands.

MILI ATOLL

Mili is a good choice for travellers who want to see more than just Majuro. It's a friendly atoll with good beaches and it's close to Majuro and cheap to get to. Even better, there's a place to stay.

After Kwajalein, Mili has the most land area of the Marshallese atolls – just over six square miles (16 square km). The population is about 800.

Mili played a part in one of the bloodier and most famous mutinies of the whaling years. In 1824 the captain and officers of the Nantucket whaleship *Globe* were murdered and the mutineers, led by Samuel Comstock, chose Mili as their hideout. Other crewmen, however, stole the ship and abandoned the mutineers on the island. A US naval ship that came ashore two years later learned that Comstock and all but two of his crew had been killed by the islanders, apparently in retaliation for their cruelty.

The mysterious circumstances surrounding the disappearance of famed US aviator Amelia Earhart in this part of the Pacific in 1937 has led to lots of speculation. She was reportedly seen in Mili long after her disappearance.

Mili was also a Japanese base and there are many abandoned weapons and bombed-out structures still scattered around. Where the plane lands, you'll see an old rusted WW II gun adorned with lush green vines. Local kids are quite curious to see who's arrived on the 'balloon', as they call the plane.

Unless you happen to run into the one pick-up truck on the island, it's a pleasant ¼-mile walk to the hotel. Along the way you'll see large bomb craters now covered with vines and coconut trees. Mili has a serious mosquito problem as these bomb craters make perfect spawning grounds. Bring mosquito repellent or coils or both with you. (Mosquito coils and coffee also make nice gifts for people on Mili.)

There's a good beach across the road from the hotel and the little shacks behind are used to make copra. The whole lagoon side of the island is trimmed with sandy white beaches, while shell collecting is good on the ocean side. At low tide you can easily walk along the reef to the neighbouring islands, some of which have only a single house upon them.

Places to Stay & Eat

The *Mili Hotel* has four little thatched houses nestled back from the lagoon amid a cluster of coconut trees. Each has one big room with a bed and a tiny bathroom with plumbing, although there's no hot water. Make your reservations while you're still on Majuro through Beverly and Gushi Chutaro, the owners of Gushi store in Rita. The rates for the Mili Hotel are $15 per night plus $1 for breakfast, $2.75 for lunch and $3 for dinner. Although the meal prices are relatively cheap, you might get stuck eating a lot of canned corned beef and rice.

Unfortunately there are almost no vegetables on the island, and people on Mili don't fish much. You can make special arrangements with Beverly and Gushi for a more balanced diet or bring food with you.

The hotel has a VCR run by generator in a large main building where people also eat. Movies are usually action-packed karate and monster flicks.

Getting There

AMI makes the 20-minute flight from Majuro on Wednesdays for $40 one way.

It costs about $3 to go from Majuro to Mili in a small boat called the *Lee Milok* which is owned by Gushi Brothers (ask at the Gushi store in Rita). The story going round is that it takes half a day and a few trips to the edge of the boat before getting to Mili. It's only for the intrepid traveller, by the sound of it.

MALOELAP ATOLL

Taroa (Tarawa) Island, in Maloelap Atoll, was the main Japanese airbase in the eastern Marshalls during WW II and most visitors these days come to see war relics. There are numerous twisted wreckages of Zeros and Betty bombers, pillboxes, guns and the remains of an airfield, narrow-gauge railroad and a radio station. The southern tip of the island has coastal defense guns, including a 127 mm anti-aircraft gun and a Howitzer on wheels.

You can stumble across some of it on your own, but a lot of the stuff is hidden under thick jungle foliage and is difficult to find. A few islanders are willing to trek with visitors and show them the sites, so if you're interested just ask around.

Off Taroa's lagoon beach the Japanese freighter *Toroshima Maru* lies half submerged where it was sunk by B52s. Periscopes and the mast can still be seen, but it's pretty well stripped, except for seven live depth charges. If you swim out around it, watch for the grouper (a type of perch) that is said to be as large as a human. The lagoon also has its share of sharks, so watch out for them too.

After the war ended, Taroa was not settled again by Marshallese until the 1970s. Now it's the centre of atoll activity because of its airport, stores and copra cooperative. Maloelap has about 700 people.

Legend has it that Taroa used to be in the centre of the lagoon in a spot where it was easy for all canoes to sail to. But the legendary figure *L'etao*, who demanded food from each of the atoll islands, got upset with the unsatisfactory service given by the Taroa islanders. To demonstrate his extreme displeasure he kicked Taroa to where it is now.

Taro used to be widely grown on Taroa until the crops were destroyed by an aggressive breed of imported New Zealand pigs which also, apparently, had a notorious reputation for chasing women and children up coconut trees. Fear not though, it seems successive generations have mellowed out!

The atoll has four other inhabited islands. Airok is 16 miles south of Taroa; and Ollet, Jang and Kaben are respectively six, 18 and 32 miles to the north-west. Not many Japanese were stationed on the other islands so they don't have the same amount of war junk as Taroa.

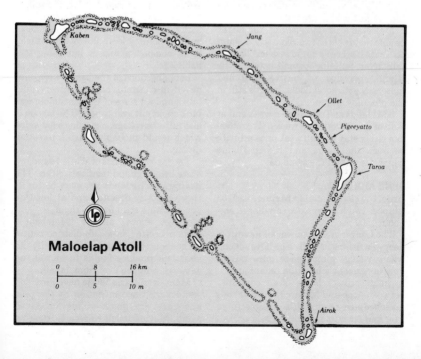

Maloelap Atoll

Maloelap has two chiefs. One is head of Taroa, Ollet, Jang and Kaben, as well as the northern atolls of Wotje, Utrik and Ailuk; and the other presides over Maloelap's Airok Island and parts of Aur Atoll.

Private speedboats and inboard motorboats owned by individual islands are used for inter-island commuting. A diesel inboard boat ride to Kaben from Taroa costs about $15 to $20 and takes around 4½ hours, depending on the roughness of the water in the lagoon. Ask for Jibo Erra on Taroa if you want to charter a speedboat.

To Airok it takes about one hour by speedboat or just over two hours by diesel inboard. The cost is $10 to $15 one way.

Just a few miles from both Taroa and Ollet is uninhabited Pigeeyatto, which is sometimes called 'Papaya Island' because of its fresh fruit. It has ruins of a wartime radio transmitter station where cables ran to Taroa's radio receiving station. You need to ask the owner, Minor, for permission to visit. Minor lives on Taroa and you can find him by just asking around.

Maloelap is used to visitors. You might be able to stay at the two-room schoolhouse on Taroa if school's not in session. There's talk about building a small hotel on the island, perhaps of native thatched materials with coral floors, but it's still in the planning stages.

AMI lands at Taroa once a week and at Kaben once every two weeks. Travellers can either stay the full week or coordinate between the Taroa and Kaben flights which are not on the same day.

ARNO ATOLL

Arno, the closest atoll to Majuro, has 133 islands, two airstrips, three villages and about 1500 people.

The Longar area is known for its superb deep-sea fishing as well as its 'love school' where young women were once taught how to perfect their sexual techniques.

Small private boats often commute between Arno and Majuro though there's no scheduled service. It's possible to go over and back in a day.

LIKIEP ATOLL

Likiep, made up of about 60 islands around a shallow lagoon, has a population of about 500.

During the German era two Europeans, Jose deBrum and Adolph Capelle, bought the atoll from the high chief who owned it. They planted coconuts and fruit trees and started profitable copra and ship-building companies. Copra production remains important on Likiep.

Jose's son Joachim designed ships and homes, and the mansion he built for his family still stands. He was also a photographer with a keen historian's perspective. More than 2300 glass plate negatives, taken between 1885 and 1930, and hundreds of documents and diaries have been recovered from the mansion and are being catalogued and reprinted for display in Majuro's Alele Museum.

WOTJE ATOLL

Wotje, the main island in Wotje Atoll, is literally covered from one end to the other with remnants of WW II. Huge Japanese-built structures loom out of the jungle, some bombed to pieces but some still habitable.

Large portions of the island were once paved in concrete, and machinery, fuel tanks and all sorts of unidentifiable war junk sticks out everywhere. The lagoon is also full of wreckage, including a few ships which would probably make interesting diving.

The lagoon beaches of Wotje Island are quite beautiful and relatively clean. The nearby small islands are even better as they're mostly deserted and at low tide you can walk right over to them.

Wotje, known as the 'Marshallese garden centre', is a sub-district centre with about 550 people. Supposedly its abundant produce is due to topsoil the Japanese shipped over from Japan.

Many families on Wotje have provided visitors with accomodation in the past and they are quite willing to do so again. Mayor Hellen Kobaia is friendly, speaks fluent English and can help you find a place to stay.

MEJIT ISLAND

Mejit is a single coral island with about 350 people. Fishing and the unloading of field trip ships around Mejit can be quite perilous as the island does not have a protective lagoon. This is especially true in November and December, months which also have pleasantly cooling winds. From May through July it's very humid and the mosquitoes are out in full force.

Mejit has a small freshwater lake that the locals, for some unknown reason, call 'the river'. It's safe to swim in and has no fish. The best beach for swimming is California Beach on the north-east corner, next to which is a good place to snorkel.

Mejit has lots of tuna (in season), as well as lobster and octopus and, unlike other islands, no poisonous fish. The Mejit men go out fishing in their canoes on Saturdays. They are hesitant to take foreigners out fishing and consider it plain bad luck to have a woman on board.

The island is known for its beautiful quality mats which the women weave from pandanus leaves.

Mejit has one of the best outer island schools and quite a few people speak fluent English. There's a government council house where you might be able to stay, but you should offer to pay something to the council for the privilege.

JALUIT ATOLL

Traditionally Jaluit was the home of the high chief of the southern Ralik islands. Today it's a sub-district centre with a population of about 1500 people and a large high school for islanders of this and nearby atolls.

Jaluit, and especially its main island of Jabwor, was the area headquarters of the German copra traders. It later became the German capital and Marshallese from other islands moved in, attracted by the schools, churches and higher standard of living.

When the Japanese took over they

fortified the islands and started a fishing industry. The US captured the atoll during WW II but then mostly ignored it, so the ruins of Japanese buildings and bunkers still remain. In the 1950s Catholic and Protestant missions were set up and Jabwor began to prosper again.

In 1958 Typhoon Ophelia swept waves and wind over Jaluit, flooding the islands with water several feet deep, washing away most of the homes and coconut trees and killing 16 people. Jaluit is not a good place to be during typhoons; one in 1904 swept away at least 60 people.

You can see the wreck of the ship *Alfred* still on the reef at Jabwor Pass where it sank in 1899.

KILI ISLAND

The single island of Kili is now home to about 500 Bikinians, most of whom have lived there since 1948. They consider Kili a place of exile.

The Bikinians soon learned that the canoes they had brought with them to Kili were useless as the island has no access to the sea; there is no lagoon, no port - not even a nice beach. Once a society of famed navigators, their seafaring skills are dying with the older Bikinian men.

The Micronesian Institute in Washington DC is coordinating efforts to set up a Bikini music library. Anyone who wants to help can send new or used cassette tapes of any kind of music to the Mayor, Kili Island, Marshall Islands 96960.

OTHER ATOLLS

Many Marshallese claim that **Wotho**, with a population 85, is the most beautiful atoll in the world. It's where Amata Kabua, the president of the Marshalls, has said he intends to retire.

Although flying fish are caught throughout the Marshalls, they are especially associated with **Ailuk Atoll**, figuring in Ailuk's music, dance and legends. The fish are caught at night using lights and scoop nets and Ailuk is known for its delicious flying fish cuisine.

Ailinglaplap Atoll, the Marshall's biggest copra producer, may soon be mined for its high-grade phosphate deposits. It's the Marshall's third largest atoll measuring, in land area, 5½ square miles (14.5 square km). It is home to about 1500 people.

Bikar, Taka and **Bokaak** atolls and **Jemo Island** are uninhabited by people, but are home to birds, coconut crabs and turtles.

Places To Stay

The Marshallese in the islands and atolls away from Majuro and Kwajalein are used to weekly flights dropping off the occasional person now and again. Although most atolls do not have arrangements for visitors, the Marshallese are warm, hospitable people and you should be able to find a family to stay with or at least a place to camp. You need to get permission before setting up a tent though, as all land belongs to someone.

You could write to the mayor of the atoll you wish to stay on before you arrive in Micronesia. Just direct it to, for example: Mayor of Maloelap, Maloelap Atoll, Marshall Islands 96960.

If you're already in Majuro, the best thing to do is to radio ahead. It's not an absolute necessity but it's common courtesy to let them know you're coming.

If there's a Peace Corps volunteer on the island (you can find out from their Majuro office), they might welcome the company or at least be able to help you find a place to stay.

Sugar, coffee, cigarettes and candy (no health problems here!) are gifts that will win you friends and encourage someone to let you stay on their property or in their home. Don't expect this to be a freebie. Many islanders are quite fond of money and you should be prepared to pay.

Trade items can often be more useful than cash though, especially if they are things not readily available from the field trip ships. Printed T-shirts, jeans, baseball caps, lighters, flashlights, pocket knives and cassette tapes of western music are popular items.

Most outer islands do not have electricity, running water or flush toilets. Some houses are of concrete and others are made of thatch with coral rock floors. Instead of beds, pandanus mats are piled on the floor.

The Marshallese take excellent care of guests and will share what they have.

Eating & Drinking

Restaurants don't exist outside the major atolls. You can make do with local store provisions, eat with the family you stay with or bring food with you from Majuro which you can then either eat or trade for local fresh foods.

Usually there are a couple of small stores with a very limited inventory of staples, such as rice, flour, tea and canned meats. Island meals usually consist of a combination of those items and local foods like breadfruit, pandanus, pumpkin, taro and fish.

Most of the outer islands are dry, though alcohol is illegally made and consumed. Visitors who drink are not usually appreciated.

To be safe, all water should be boiled even if it's from catchments and without fail if it's not.

Getting There

Air The government-owned Airline of the Marshall Islands operates services to about two dozen islands, touching down at every inhabited atoll. You can write ahead for a schedule or pick one up at the Majuro office. AMI has two planes, a 48-passenger HS748 and a 20-passenger Dornier 228.

From Majuro flights go five times a week to Kwajalein and once a week or every two weeks to other atolls.

One-way fares from Majuro are $20 to Ine and $24 to Tinak (both on Arno Atoll), $50 to Maloelap, $60 to Jaluit, $70 to Wotje or Kili, $88 to Mejit and $90 to Likiep.

Flights hop across islands a couple at a time making it possible to visit different islands without returning to Majuro each time. For example, you could fly from Majuro to Wotje one Tuesday, pick up the Wotje to Maloelap flight the next Tuesday and return to Majuro the Tuesday after. AMI or smaller private planes can be chartered, but the cost is high.

Boat The field trip ship *Micro Pilot* has an irregular schedule which aims for nine runs a year to the outer islands, though once every two months is probably closer to the truth. Typically two or three days is spent at each stop.

There are six different routes. The longest run is the western field trip which goes to Kwajalein, Lae, Ujae, Wotho, Enewetak and Ujelang, a round trip distance of about 1510 miles (2431 km). The southern route takes two weeks, covering four atolls and 680 miles (1094 km). The eastern route is 175 miles (281 km).

The fare is six cents per mile on deck. Cabins cost 10 cents per mile and have two beds, toilet and shower but no air-con. Meals are about $10 per day. Scheduling information is available from the Transportation Department (tel 3037), at Majuro's old dock opposite the museum.

Boats leave from the new dock near the copra processing plant.

Getting Around

Outer islands usually have at least one motorboat and trips to other islands in the atoll can usually be arranged if visitors are willing to pay for petrol and maybe a little extra. Each situation is different, but the price for locals to an island one hour away by motorboat might be about $20 round trip, regardless of the number of people.

Sometimes the uninhabited atoll islands are used for copra production or to raise livestock. The more remote islands often have the best beaches and sometimes thatched shelters to sleep in. It's cleaner swimming away from the village centres.

For a price, it should be fairly easy to get someone to take you fishing, lobstering, coconut-crab hunting and the like. Check with the mayor to see if there is a local fishing ordinance and fee. There often is, though it's not usually much and you may only need council approval. Mostly it's a courtesy that will make you friends.

Some islands have vehicles, but most of the time people just walk.

Federated States of Micronesia

Kosrae, Pohnpei, Truk and Yap are the four states of the Federated States of Micronesia. The FSM's estimated 1986 population was 94,534. Truk had more than half the people – 47,724.

All four states are part of the Caroline Islands and all have similar colonial histories under Spain, Germany, Japan and the US, but their cultures, traditions and identities are distinctly separate.

While the people are all Carolinians they have eight major indigenous languages between them and no two states have the same native tongue. They communicate in English, the language of their latest colonial administrator.

More than anything else, what now ties them together is their new political affiliation as the FSM.

Geography
The FSM has 607 islands sprinkled across more than a million square miles of the Pacific. About 65 islands are inhabited.

The total land area is 271 square miles (436 square km). Pohnpei has nearly half the land area, with the rest almost equally divided among the other three states.

Political Beginnings
In July 1978, the Trust Territory districts of Pohnpei, Kosrae, Truk, Yap, the Marshalls and Palau voted on a common constitution. The Marshalls and Palau rejected it, along with the concept of a single unified Micronesian nation. They went on to establish separate political futures.

What was left became, by default, the FSM.

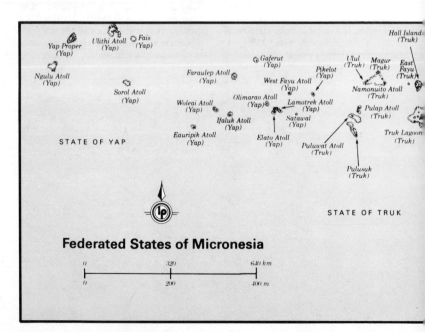

Federated States of Micronesia

National and state governments were then elected. Tosiwo Nakayama of Truk became the first FSM president under the new FSM constitution which took effect in May 1979.

In October 1982 the FSM signed its Compact of Free Association with the USA. After being signed into law in the US, the compact was officially implemented in November 1986. Although the United Nations has not yet approved it, for all practical purposes the compact is in effect. Islanders now have their own FSM passports.

One of the key aspects of the compact is an agreement by the FSM to refrain from any action which the US would determine to be incompatible with its obligations to defend the area. This pretty much gives the US military carte blanche to do anything it wants in the FSM. Not all islanders were keen on this provision, but having grown dependent on US handouts they needed the money that comes with the compact. More than ever, the US relationship with Micronesia remains forged in greenbacks.

Government

The FSM has three levels of government: national, state and municipal. The national government is divided into executive, legislative and judicial branches. The FSM Congress is unicameral, with 14 senators. Four senators are elected at-large and 10 are elected based on population apportionment. The president and vice president, who cannot be from the same state, are elected by Congress from among its members. The national capital is the town of Kolonia, which is in Pohnpei.

Each state has an elected governor, elected legislature (30 legislators in Truk, 23 in Pohnpei, 14 in Kosrae and nine in Yap) and a state court.

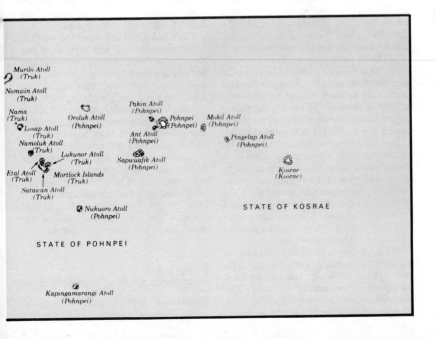

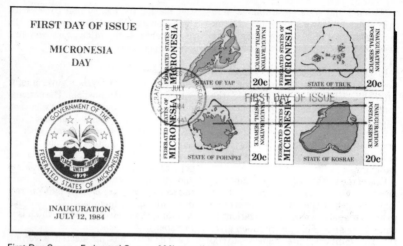

First Day Cover – Federated States of Micronesia

Economy

Over the 15 years of its new compact with the US, the FSM will receive direct grant assistance of $60 million annually for the first five years, tapering down to $40 million annually for the last five.

In theory the grants are heavier in the early years to allow the FSM to build the infrastructure needed for economic development and as seed money to stimulate private businesses. In reality, offering a bigger chunk of money right off may have been a way for the US to sweeten the deal.

Particularly in the district centres, US-funded capital improvement projects have recently been buzzing along constructing water and sewerage systems, hospitals, roads, docks, power plants and airfields. The conspicuously posted signs and plaques with Ronald Reagan's best wishes just keep coming – 30 years and a number of cholera epidemics too late.

Many people in the FSM still rely on subsistence farming and fishing, with only about 30% of the work force employed in the money economy. The government employs over half of those directly. Most government jobs are based in social services and with the exception of a handful of small projects such as soap factories and fisheries they contribute little of substance to the economy.

The FSM imports $50 million worth of goods annually but has exports of less than $2 million. New business ventures include seaweed farming, processing of solar-dried fish and raising of sea cucumbers and trochus shells.

After US aid, the largest current single source of income comes from fishing rights fees collected from tuna boats who fish within the FSM's 200-mile limits.

Land in the FSM can be sold only to Micronesians, although non-Micronesians can lease land. The FSM requires new businesses to have a minimum of 51% local interest. One obvious effect of that ruling is the total absence of Japanese resort hotels à la Guam and Saipan.

Kosrae

Kosrae is a casual, unpretentious back-water, where people consistently return a smile. This is one of the least spoiled and least developed areas in Micronesia, an unhurried place that retains a certain air of innocence.

Although not as well known as Pohnpei's Nan Madol ruins, Kosrae's Leluh Ruins are equally impressive and more easily accessible. Kosrae has lush, tropical forests throughout the interior and its coast is a mix of sandy beaches and mangrove swamps. The island is known for its citrus fruit, especially oranges, tangerines and limes.

Until 1987 the main way to get to Kosrae was on a nine-seater missionary airline flight. Having more than half a dozen visitors on the island at any one time was quite unusual so, in a friendly way, people took note when someone new was in town.

Now that Air Mike has added it onto its island hopper route Kosrae might be in for some changes, though strangely no one seems to be preparing for more visitors.

Geography

Kosrae is a high volcanic island with a rugged interior of mountain ridges and river valleys. Mt Finkol, the highest point, rises to 2064 feet (619 metres). The island is roughly triangular and covers an area of 42 square miles (107 square km). It's one third the size of Pohnpei, an island it resembles in shape and topography.

Leluh, Utwe and Okat are the main deepwater harbours and all villages are along the coast.

Climate

Temperatures on Kosrae average 80°F year-round. Rainfall averages 185 to 250 inches per year (470 to 635 cm) and is heaviest in summer, with more falling on the west coast than on the east. Trade winds come mainly from the north-east and are weakest from May to November.

History

Kosrae once had the most stratified society in Micronesia. By the year 1400 Kosrae was unified under one paramount chief, or *tokosra*, who ruled from the island of Leluh. Essentially a handful of high chiefs owned the land, low chiefs managed it and the mass of commoners worked it. It was a feudalistic system with each group passing a percentage of their produce up the ladder.

While the commoners lived on the main island, which was then called Ualang, the royalty and their retainers lived inside more than hundred basalt-walled compounds on Leluh and the nearby islets of Pisin, Yenyen and Yenasr. With its canal system and coral streets the fortressed island of Leluh would have rivaled its medieval counterparts in Europe.

Pohnpeian legend says that around the 14th century Kosraean warriors sailed to Pohnpei and overthrew the oppressive *saudeleur* rulers there. Trukese legends also suggest cultural influences from Kosrae around the same time.

Western Contact Kosrae was sighted by Europeans at least as early as 1801. It became known to sailors as Strong's Island, named in 1804 by the captain of the American ship *Nancy* after the governor of Massachusetts.

It wasn't until 1824, however, that a western ship finally pulled into harbour. It was just one of many stops in the Pacific for the sailors of the French ship *Coquille*, captained by Louis Duperrey, but for the Kosraeans it was their first contact with westerners.

Duperrey and his crew stayed on Kosrae for 10 days and provided the outside world with an excellent account of the island. They estimated the population to be about 5000, with about 1500 living on Leluh, the ruling centre. They said the Kosraeans seemed to be a peace-loving people and had no weapons. They were awed by the foreigners who gave them iron hatchets and other presents.

In 1827 the Russian ship *Senyavin*, captained by Fedor Lutke, docked at Kosrae and also received a hospitable welcome.

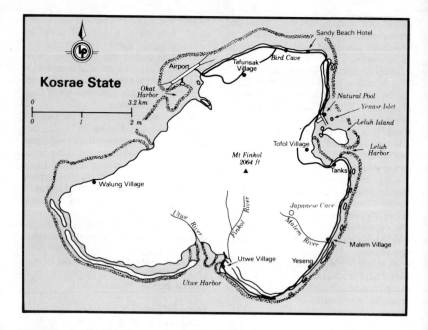

Lutke noted that although the Kosraeans had dugout canoes as long as 30 feet, they had no need to go outside their own island and did not own boats for the open ocean.

Whalers and traders started calling at Kosrae in the early 1830s, attracted by deepwater harbours and reports of plentiful supplies of food, water, wood and women.

Not all early confrontations were peaceful ones however. In 1835 Kosraeans torched the Hawaiian ship *Waverly* and massacred the entire crew, apparently to punish the sailors who had boldly bedded island women without first getting permission from Kosraean men. The Boston trading ship *Honduras* was similarly attacked the same year and only two of the crew managed to escape.

In the early 1840s relations again became harmonious under the reign of chief Awane Lapalik I, who was known as 'Good King George' by visiting westerners. From then until the decline of whaling in

the Pacific in the mid-1860s, whaleships visited Kosrae by the dozens each year.

Missionaries In 1852, when the first missionaries arrived from Hawaii, the diseases introduced by foreign sailors had already begun taking their disastrous toll on the islanders. The Kosraean people were in serious danger of being completely wiped out.

Ironically this made the missionaries' goal of total conversion considerably easier, not only by lessening organised resistance but by lowering the number of souls which needed saving. When the population hit an all-time low of about 300, virtually every remaining Kosraean was converted to Christianity.

The conversion was thorough. Traditional songs, dances, myths and other oral histories were frowned upon, discouraged or banned and ultimately forgotten. Tatooing went out of fashion, alcohol was forbidden and the ceremonial use of *seka*, a narcotic drink like Pohnpei's sakau, was no longer allowed.

Traders Traders started arriving in full force in the 1870s. One of Kosrae's most famous visitors during this time was the American 'Bully' Hayes, a notorious swindler and trader who roamed the Pacific after years of involvement in the China opium trade. He was a frequent visitor to Kosrae where he traded in beche-de-mer, copra and coconut oil.

In March 1874 Hayes' 218-ton brigantine *Leonora* sank in Utwe Harbor during a sudden storm, becoming Kosrae's most famous shipwreck. Hayes was murdered at sea three years later in a brawl with his Dutch cook.

The Japanese Period The Japanese, who arrived in 1914, exploited Kosrae's natural resources and took over three of the island's four coastal villages, forcing the Kosraeans to move inland.

Developments in agriculture, forestry, fishing and copra helped support the Japanese war effort during WW II and provided for the 7000 Japanese who moved there. Kosrae was never invaded by allied forces during the war.

Post WW II After the war, when the United States took over and the Trust Territory was set up, Kosrae was included in the Pohnpei district. For decades Kosrae played only a secondary role as development was centred on Pohnpei, 350 miles to the north-west.

In 1977 Kosrae broke away from Pohnpei, becoming a separate district within the Trust Territory and later a separate FSM state. Kosrae gets more money this way than it would as an appendage of Pohnpei State, though a desire for a bigger slice of the pie was not the only motive. Kosraeans and Pohnpeians had never before considered themselves one political unit until lumped together at the whim of the US administration.

Economy
Less than 15% of the population works in the money economy and 80% of those work for the government. Much of the population still relies on subsistence farming and fishing for their livelihood.

Citrus is exported but on a very small scale. A small experimental agricultural farm behind the tourist office is part of a plan to help farmers increase production.

Kosrae is one of the cleanest islands in Micronesia. At first the large piles of beer cans lying beneath certain trees appears to be littering on a massive scale, but they are actually community deposit spots for an aluminum recycling project. Garbage is regularly collected from metal drums placed along the roadsides.

In the past few years Kosrae has acquired two banks, a water treatment plant and there is electricity in most villages.

People & Culture
In Kosrae when you talk about the culture, you talk about religion – the most essential part of modern Kosraean society.

Kosrae's estimated 1986 population was 6668 and about 95% of the islanders are Congregationalists.

The religious beliefs and practices of the late 1800s, that so totally overtook these people, have changed little over the years though today the ministers are Kosraean.

The church has a firm grip on most aspects of Kosraean life and while it no doubt helps to make Kosrae a homogenous society of law-abiding people it also fosters intolerance. It has also most certainly contributed to the disintegration of the indigenous culture. Under church influences, Kosrae's traditional matrilineal society has developed into a western-style patrilineal system.

Conversion to another faith, even another Protestant faith, is seen as a disgrace to the rest of the family. The convert is commonly disinherited and cut off from family land.

It is against the law to go fishing or for

stores to be open on Sundays. Many leisure activities are also frowned upon on the sabbath. US Civic Action Team soldiers building roads on the island caused quite a sensation not too long ago by water skiing in the harbour on Sunday.

An information board at the airport reads:

Sunday is reserved as the day of rest, so you'll find all businesses are closed. Restaurants are open in the evening. All visitors are invited to join in our church services, which begin at 10 am in each village. Come and listen to our church choirs, to witness an important aspect of our culture.

Language

English is the language of the government and is widely spoken but Kosraean is still the native language.

'Good morning' or 'hello' is *lotu mwo* and 'thank you (very much)' is *kulo (na maluhlap)*.

Early whalers used the expression 'ah shit' so often that the natives picked up on it and identified the whalers as *ahset*. This is still the common word for 'foreigner' today. Kosrae, pronounced kosh-RYE, was formerly called Kusaie.

First Day Cover – Kosrae

Holidays

Kosrae celebrates Kosrae Constitution Day on 11 January, Kosrae Liberation Day on 6 September, Thanksgiving on the 4th Thursday in November and Christmas.

Orientation

The state is divided into the districts of Leluh (including Tofol), Malem, Utwe and Tafunsak (including Walung).

The airport is off the north-west side of the island near Okat Harbor. From the airport, the main road runs clockwise around the coast ending in Utwe. Its's paved at first, but once you hit dirt it's very rough. Walung village on the west coast can only be reached by boat.

The administration centre for the new state of Kosrae is in Tofol, two miles south of the causeway to Leluh. New construction going on in Tofol represents a shift in business activities from Leluh.

TOFOL

Tofol is the state administrative centre. It's so small, however, that it seems odd to think of it as the centre of anything. It's just a few buildings scattered here and there along a couple of dusty roads.

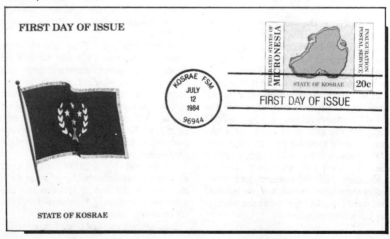

The short walk up to the radio station offers a good view.

Information

The Bank of Hawaii, Bank of the FSM, Air Mike office, hospital, high school (with the state's only library, such as it is) and the post office are all in Tofol. All mail to Kosrae uses the zip code 96944.

International telephone calls can be made at the communications building in Tofol and the tourist office (tel 3044) in Tofol has maps and brochures.

LELUH ISLAND

Leluh (also 'Lela' or 'Lelu') is connected to the main island by a causeway. Just off the causeway there's a natural saltwater swimming pool that's full of water even when the tide is low and the flats surrounding it are exposed. At low tide the area between Leluh Island and the northeast point of Kosrae is good for shell collecting.

The low part of Leluh was artificially extended by early Kosraeans who then used the land to build a massive walled city for their rulers. The original piece of land, now called Leluh Hill, and the flat extension together form Leluh Island.

Leluh Hill has a scattering of caves and tunnels used and fortified by the Japanese during WW II. A trail up the hill starts diagonally opposite Legal Services, but as it crosses private land it's best to find a local guide. There's a good view of the harbour from the top.

If you look across the bay toward Tofol you'll see the rugged ridgeline of the mountain range that forms the profile of the 'Sleeping Lady'. According to legend the gods were angry with a woman so they laid her in the sea in a sleeping position and turned her into the island of Kosrae. Try to imagine a woman lying on her back with her hair spread out behind her head. The pointy breasts are easy to spot.

The state museum is housed in the oldest non-traditional building on the island – a cement building built in the 1890s. It's open from 9 am to 3 pm Monday to Friday and has artefacts from the Leluh ruins, including detailed charts of archaeological work done there, and other exhibits.

The museum staff can provide guide service through the ruins. Ask if the interpretive guidebook *Leluh Ruins Historical Park* is back in stock.

Leluh Ruins

In its heyday this royal city and feudal capital covered the entire lowland area of Leluh Island. The building of Leluh dates back at least as far as 1400 AD, and probably as early as 1250 AD. Though the outskirts of this massive urban complex have been torn down the ruins still comprise much of the island.

A ride around Leluh's perimeter road however, reveals only a sleepy waterfront village and a smattering of homes and businesses; but this place is deceptive. The ruins are just behind these homes, beyond their backyards and almost completely concealed by vegetation.

Once inside the complex it's the sort of isolated setting you might imagine trekking hours through dense jungle to find. The ruins seem so extraordinarily vast and encompassing that the outside world feels far away.

Still extant are the dwelling compounds of some of the high chiefs, two royal burial mounds, a few sacred compounds and numerous large walls built of stacked hexagonal basalt logs. Pounding stones used for food preparation or making *seka* are easily identifiable.

The Kosrae Historic Preservation Office has begun to renovate the ruins, repairing walls and walkways and building footbridges over the canals.

You can stroll along wide coral paths through a large part of the ruins. A good place to start is at the museum where a trail, directly across the street, leads to the best preserved section. Some of the property you cross going in and coming out is private, so if you see anyone in the area, smile and ask permission to proceed.

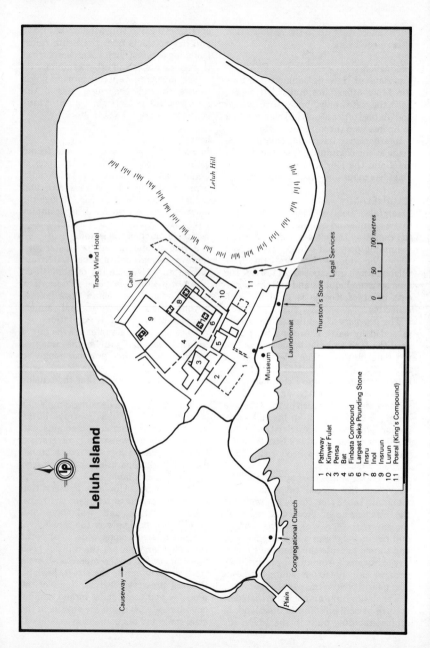

Leluh Island

Leluh Hill

Trade Wind Hotel

Canal

Legal Services

Thurston's Store

Laundromat

Museum

Congregational Church

Causeway

Pisin

100 metres

50

0

1 Pathway
2 Kinyeir Fulat
3 Pensa
4 Bat
5 Finbata Compound
6 Largest Seka Pounding Stone
7 Insru
8 Inol
9 Insruun
10 Lurun
11 Posral (King's Compound)

Kinyeir Fulat, to the left as you enter the ruins opposite the museum, has walls reaching 20 feet high. It's believed to have served as both a dwelling compound and meeting house.

The compounds beyond are called *Pensa* and you'll notice that the ancient builders incorporated brain coral in the wall construction. The high chief's feast house occupied the south-east compound and the adjacent areas of Pensa were used for food preparation and contain pounding stones.

Bat is the large dwelling compound across the canal from Pensa. Its high basalt walls are thought to be among the newest in town, dating from around 1600 AD.

Insru and *Inol* contain mounded tombs which served as temporary resting places for deceased royalty. It was a sacred area, closed to commoners except for a group of female mourners. The king's body would be placed in a tomb until the flesh decayed. From the time the king was laid in the crypt the mourners kept a continuous watch over his tomb and decaying body. After his flesh decomposed, the bones were ceremoniously carried to the reef off Yenasr Islet and dropped into a deep hole.

In 1910 a German excavation of the most recent tomb found a male skeleton. It was presumed he was the last king to be buried on Luluh Island and that in the whirlwind of Christian conversion his bones, and with them Kosraean traditions, were quickly abandoned.

SOUTH OF TOFOL
Sansrik
In Sansrik, about 1½ miles south-east of Tofol, the rusted remains of Japanese tanks and parts of a small sawmill are scattered in front yards at the water's edge.

From there you can look across to Leluh Island which, according to legend, was formed when a whale got trapped inside the reef. The hill is the humped body, the flat part the tail.

Mutunlik
Not far ahead, partly hidden behind a small house in the village of Mutunlik (on the right side coming from Tofol), are 115 concrete steps heading skyward. It's a climb to nowhere these days, but a Japanese weather station and lookout tower were once on top. Local basketball teams train by running up and down the stairs.

Malem
Behind the municipal building in Malem, which is 4½ miles from Tofol, is a nondescript plaque put up by the Kosraean-Japanese friendship society.

To get to one of the caves where the Japanese hid, take the first road to the right past the municipal building, continue on by the Malem Congregational Church on the left and keep going. When the vehicle road ends take the washed-out road, staying to the right of the river. Depending on the road's condition, you may have to walk across a couple of small streams. When you get to a small dam, climb up a few steps onto the bank to the right and continue on for about two minutes. Look carefully for a cave opening on the right. It was a Japanese bunker with the general's house just above it.

Surfers take to the waves off Malem Village. Yeseng, the next village, has several concrete WW II bunkers scattered along the beaches behind people's homes.

Utwe
Utwe (also called Utwa) is 4½ miles from Malem. This is a pleasant village to stroll around. The villagers often sit outside their homes weaving coconut fronds or cooking over an open fire while semi-naked children play nearby. Half-carved canoes sit by the roadsides covered with coconut fronds to protect them from the elements.

It's a pretty walk from Utwe up the Finkol River to the Sipyen Waterfall. You can do the first section on your own, just ask anyone in Utwe how to get started. After about 45 minutes or so you'll come to some nice pools.

With a guide you could continue walking upriver for about three hours to some man-made pyramid tiers. They're overgrown with vegetation but you can still see a basalt altar built to honour the ancient Kosraean deity *Sinlaka* who was goddess of breadfruit harvests, famines, diseases and typhoons.

East of Utwe, turn inland at the pole marked 'X 7' to get onto the new road being constructed along the south and west sides of the island that will eventually complete the island circle route.

Go about 3½ miles along the new road to get to Sipyen Waterfall on the Finkol River. The waterfall should be just after the second bridge; you'll probably be able to see it from the road.

WALUNG

The new circle road will eventually connect Walung on the west coast with the rest of the island. Not everyone in Walung is happy about ending their isolation.

For now it's a quiet place with few visitors. Mangrove trees extend along most of the shoreline and on rainy days, craggy green peaks poke their heads up above the mist. There's a church and school as well as foundations of an old missionary school.

Sections of the village, where the tide washes in, are connected by footbridges made of long logs, and channels have been dug to let saltwater into a number of fresh-water areas that once bred mosquitoes.

The only way of getting to Walung, until the road is finished, is by canoe or speed-boat. There are no scheduled boat services so arrangements must be negotiated with people heading in that direction.

Private canoes operate between Utwe and Walung, either outside the reef or along small channels through mangrove swamps. Speedboats from Okat Dock take 15 minutes.

TAFUNSAK

There's a steep-walled gorge in the Tafunsak area which is a good place to explore on sunny days. Don't go there when it's raining though because it's extremely narrow and has the potential to fill up with water quickly. The walls rise 70 to 80 feet in some places and some sections are just eight to 10 feet wide, so it could be very dangerous during a downpour.

No guide is necessary to get to the canyon. Just take the road inland behind JJ's store and bakery in Tafunsak Village. It's a 45-minute walk up the gorge, following an old steel water pipe. There are a couple of waterfalls and pools along the way.

Behind the high school in Tafunsak there was once a good waterfall, but the water has been diverted and it's now very small.

Bird Cave

A large swampy cave west of the rock quarry in Wiya Village is home to a colony of swiftlets who cling onto the rocks by their claws and build nests of dried saliva and moss. When flying they look like small bats.

Islanders collect the bird droppings in the cave bottom to use as a rich fertiliser. Like lots of other places in Kosrae, this big swampy cave is thought to be haunted. In this case the belief is spurred on by rumours of Kosraean bodies left in the back of the cave by the Japanese.

If you're not really interested in caves and swiftlets, this is a good site to bypass. If you do visit, tread gently. These birds are vulnerable to disruption by humans and may abandon a cave that is visited too often.

Off the Beaten Track

A sign at the airport announces:

All lands (with the exception of the government center of Tofol) and all beaches are private. Therefore it is polite to ask the landowner if he is present to visit. The answer will undoubtedly be 'of course!'

Take heed if you plan to explore this island.

Killin Killin at the Kosrae Community

Action Program (tel 3217) in Tofol may be able to arrange a guide for serious hikers. KCAP runs a youth training programme and a Micronesia Bound course, aimed mostly at high school drop-outs who are taught wilderness survival techniques.

One of the nicest trails is from Tofol up to a plateau that looks down on Leluh and Okat harbours, the reefs and the airport. It takes about 1½ hours one way. If you're in good physical condition you could climb from there up to the right breast of the Sleeping Lady, an additional 1½ hours.

If not it's a moderate 4 hour walk from the plateau down the other side to Okat Harbor. Part of the way the trail goes through a *ka* forest. The wood from these trees is used to make racing canoes. If you're descending to Okat, arrange to arrive at the harbour at low tide as the last part of this walk is over sand bars and through mangroves.

Diving

As Kosrae really has no dive facilities or formal guide or boat services, diving here becomes an arrange-it-yourself operation. The Marine Resources Division Office on the causeway to Leluh might be able to provide filled tanks ($5 each) for a few divers, but all other equipment would need to be brought in. Write in advance to check if their compressor is operational.

For those who manage the logistics (as some residents do), Kosrae has unspoiled coral reefs close to shore and both walk-in and boat diving. The confluence of two currents makes for prolific and varied marine life.

There are two American PBY search planes in about 60 feet of water. The best one is at the mouth of Leluh Harbor on the right shoal side. The place where the guns used to be is visible and a glove still stuck to the co-pilot's wheel looks eerily like a hand floating underwater.

Two Japanese boats, a 300-foot freighter and a fishing ship, which were both skip-bombed and blown apart, are popular dives. A more recent wreck, a medi-vac

plane that crashed into the sea immediately after take-off, is broken in three pieces and crumpled like an accordion on the ocean floor.

Bully Hayes' ship, the *Leonora*, remained untouched in Utwe Harbor for more than 90 years. After a diving team from the Scripps Oceanographic Institute and a private group from Kwajalein stripped artefacts from the wreck, the site was officially designated off-limits to sport divers. Now all wrecks are protected under law and can only be visited with advance notice and when accompanied by an authorised guide arranged through Teddy John of the Historic Preservation Office.

There's good diving between Utwe Harbor and Walung, where large groupers, barracuda and hump-headed parrotfish can be seen. At several places you can just step into the water at high tide, swim out 50 or 100 feet and start diving.

The most shark activity, including tiger sharks and small docile whitetips, is around the reefs from Walung to Okat. Kosraeans say there hasn't been a shark attack in three generations.

Snorkelling & Swimming

The best spots for snorkelling and swimming change with the seasons and the trade winds, so it's best to ask. It's said to be good between Malem and Utwe in the winter, though there are riptides and larger waves around Malem. The areas near Tafunsak Village, around the bridge to the airport and off Kosrae's north-east point are said to be good in the summer, but rough from December to February.

Local woman go swimming in clothes that cover their knees. Swimsuits and shorts are not acceptable in public buildings or around town.

Places To Stay

The *Sandy Beach Hotel* (tel 3239; Box 6) has 10 thatched-roof cottages right on Tafunsak beach. The verandas face the ocean and there's good snorkelling, during high tide, just outside the front doors. The

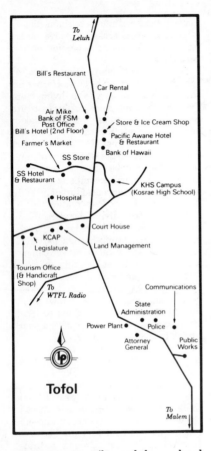

To
Leluh

Bill's Restaurant

Car Rental

Air Mike
Bank of FSM
Post Office
Bill's Hotel (2nd Floor)
Store & Ice Cream Shop
Farmer's Market
Pacific Awane Hotel
& Restaurant
SS Store
Bank of Hawaii
SS Hotel
& Restaurant
KHS Campus
(Kosrae High School)
Hospital

KCAP
Court House
Legislature
Land Management

Tourism Office
(& Handicraft
Shop)
To
WTFL Radio
Communications

State
Administration
Power Plant
Police
Attorney
General
Public
Works

Tofol

To
Malem

rooms are on stilts and have closed ceilings and screens so mosquitoes are not a problem unless you let them in from the bathroom which has some open thatch. Rooms with small electric fans cost $25 a single or $40 or double. Couples may stay in a single room with one double bed for $35. With air-con it's $35 single, $45 double. All rooms have private bathrooms and refrigerators and there's free bottled water on request. The showers are a pipe with cold water. This is Kosrae's most popular hotel, though it's not walking distance to Tofol or Leluh. They're

planning a restaurant and more rooms and say they'll provide free airport transfers.

The *Tradewind Hotel* (tel 3047; Box TE) is on Leluh Island. There are four units with refrigerators, private bathrooms and air-con for $25 a single or $45 a double. Check to be sure the ventilation is adequate and the air-con works, as there are reports of rooms being hot and stuffy.

The *SS Hotel* (tel 3172; c/o Lucien Robert, Box 62) in Tofol has four rooms, each with two comfortable double beds and a ceiling fan. All rooms share one bathroom. There's free coffee and oranges in a large common lounge. Rates start at $20 a single.

A new place across from Bill's Restaurant (tel 3181; Box 87) in Tofol will have Kosrae's most modern hotel rooms if they don't end up fully booked with monthly tenants. Rates may start at $25 for singles.

The *Pacific Awane Hotel* (Box KHC), now government-owned, is the former Skilling Hotel which was once the only hotel in Tofol. The prices there are higher than the rooms deserve, as government workers with expense accounts have artificially inflated the room rates. There are five rooms with air-con and shared bathroom for $20 a single or $28 a double. The roof upstairs leaks and one room downstairs has a louvered glass window that opens directly onto one of the restaurant tables. Even with the louvers closed, you can't help but hear the dinner conversation. Other rooms have their own peculiar characteristics.

Camping Camping seems to be a fairly foreign concept in Kosrae. If you want to set up a tent, consult with the chief of the village that you want to camp in.

Places To Eat

All three of Kosrae's restaurants are in Tofol, a few minutes walk apart.

The *Pacific Awane Restaurant* is a popular place to eat, both for the food and for the video movies that play day and night. It's a bit of a jolt the first time you walk in and find a small crowd staring straight at you, until you realise they're really gaping at a TV near the door. It's a good place to eat if you can stomach watching Chuck Norris karate a Vietnamese to death as you cut into your dinner. The grilled tuna plate ($3.25) is a large serving of fresh tuna, rice, breadfruit and salad. Fried breadfruit (rarely seen on Micronesian menus) costs 75 cents. When it's offered, mangrove crab dinner is a real bargain for $4. Be sure to try the banana pie. The Awane is one of the main hangouts for Kosrae's foreign community.

There's an ice cream shop next door to Pacific Awane.

Bill's Restaurant is quiet and cool. There's no video and after a few meals at the Pacific Awane this may be quite an attraction in itself. For the most part, the prices and menu are similar to the Awane's, though you can also get breakfast for $2 to $3.

Lucien's, below the SS Hotel, has local food and the cheapest prices. Fish tempura is just $2. It's a popular eating spot for Peace Corps volunteers.

There's a farmer's market on the driveway leading up to the SS Hotel which has fresh fruit.

Entertainment

Entertainment in the conventional sense is limited on Kosrae. There are no bars, discos or staged cultural shows and even the movie theatres closed down when video rentals came in. Beer and other liquor can be bought at restaurants and local stores.

Things To Buy

A few local handicrafts are on sale downstairs from the tourist office in Tofol. Typical crafts include wooden taro pounders, carved wooden canoes and woven bags and purses.

It's also possible to buy directly from craftspeople in their homes. You could check with Steve or Pam Leathley at the Calgary Baptist Church in Malem. They can direct you to some of the parish women who make handicrafts.

Getting There

Air Air Mike lands on Kosrae only on Mondays going east and Fridays going west on its island hopper route. It costs $212 from Majuro to Kosrae or $107 from Pohnpei to Kosrae.

Pacific Missionary Aviation (tel 3038, agent Rodney Albert) flies a nine-passenger twin-engine Beechcraft between Pohnpei and Kosrae. The flight takes about two hours and operates in the morning from Monday to Friday. If the weather is clear there's a good view of Pingelap on the way and Mokil can sometimes be seen off in the distance. The one-way fare is $95 or a return flight is double. Customs officers sometimes meet the PMA flights and check luggage; and sometimes they don't.

Boat When it's in service, the field trip ship *M/V Frysna* makes about one trip a month to Pingelap, Mokil, Pohnpei and Majuro. The one-way deck class fares from Kosrae are: $9.30 to Pingelap, $13.50 to Mokil, $18.30 to Pohnpei and $30 to Majuro. Cabin class is $31.20, $45, $61 and $100 respectively and return fares are double. There are 12 cabins. The Stevedoring and Terminal Company (tel 3083) on Leluh will have updated information.

Yachts sometimes dock at Leluh Harbor but the word is that yachties who don't get advance permission to enter the state are often asked to leave soon after arrival.

Getting Around

Airport Transport People commonly leave their rental cars at the airport when catching a flight. Although there aren't any booths, if you ask around you might find a rental car available. Otherwise, getting a ride from someone going into Leluh or Tofol shouldn't be a problem. After all, the road only goes in one direction. People won't be put out if you ask to join them for a ride into town. Check with the airline agent if you need help.

Hitching It's very easy to get rides around Kosrae and there's no need to stick out a thumb. Just start walking along the road and someone will stop and give you a ride, usually in the back of a pick-up truck.

No one thinks of charging for the lift and an offer of money would probably be considered an insult, especially for short rides. There are no taxis on Kosrae.

Car Rentals TE's Car Rental (tel 3045) is opposite Bill's Restaurant in Tofol. Cars can also be rented through the hotels or from Thurston's Store (tel 3047) on Leluh. Rates officially start at about $25, but you might not find anything for less than $30.

Pohnpei

Pohnpei, with its lush vegetation, jungle hillsides and flowering hibiscus fits the typical South Sea island image, albeit a wet one. The abundant rainfall feeds a multitude of streams, rivers and tumbling waterfalls and the damp rainforest interior which is uninhabited and difficult to reach has soft, spongy ground and moss-covered trees.

Pohnpei's boldest landmark is the scenic Sokehs Rock, a steep cliff face often compared to Honolulu's Diamond Head. The ancient city of Nan Madol, abandoned on nearly a hundred artificial islets off the south-east coast, is Micronesia's best known archaeological site.

The capital town of Kolonia is relatively large by island standards, yet it retains an uncrowded small town character. Outside the capital it's largely unspoiled and undeveloped. Men carry machetes as they walk along the dirt roads. Pohnpeians are fond of wearing and giving *mwaramwars*, head wreaths of fragrant leaves and flowers.

Pohnpei was spelled 'Ponape' until 1984 and many schools and businesses still retain the old spelling.

Geography

Pohnpei Island is high, volcanic and roughly circular, edged with coves and jutting peninsulas. The interior has rugged mountain ridges and deep valleys. Averaging 15 miles (24 km) in diameter and with a land mass of 129 square miles (330 square km), it's the third largest island in Micronesia.

The centre of Pohnpei Island is Mt Nahna Laud but the highest peak is the 2595-foot (778.5-metre) Mt Ngihneni. The coastline, devoid of natural sandy beaches, is mainly tidal flats and mangrove swamps. In between the island and its surrounding circular reef is a lagoon covering 70 square miles (179 square km), containing dozens of small islands.

Pohnpei State also includes eight outlying atolls, each covering less than one square mile of land.

To the south-east, almost like stepping stones down to Kosrae, are the atolls of Mokil and Pingelap – 80 and 140 miles (129 and 225 km), from Pohnpei Island. To the south-west are Sapwuafik (formerly Ngatik), 90 miles (145 km) away; Nukuoro – 250 miles (402 km); and Kapingamarangi – 445 miles (716 km). Oroluk is 180 miles (290 km) to the north-west and Pakin and Ant are just a few miles west of Pohnpei Island.

Climate

While the town of Kolonia has an average annual rainfall of 192 inches (487 cm), Pohnpei's interior gets 400 inches (1016 cm), making it one of the rainiest places on earth. The lowest rainfall occurs between January and March and the wettest months are April and May. A typical Pohnpei day is cloudy with intermittent showers and the sun breaking through every now and then. Catching a good sunset is a treat to be relished.

Temperatures average 81°F and most of the year there are north-easterly trade winds. From July to November however the winds die down, the humidity inches up and the nights especially can be oppressive.

Pohnpei is within typhoon spawning grounds, although outside the major tracks. Interestingly, two of the most destructive typhoons to hit Pohnpei in the past 30 years, one in 1957 and the other in May 1986, were both named Lola! The latest Lola, centred 85 miles north of Pohnpei, caused an estimated $5 million in damages. Kolonia's Kapingamarangi Village and the thatched huts of the Hotel Pohnpei and The Village hotel were particularly hard hit.

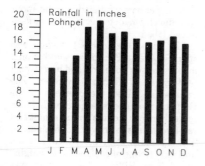

Rainfall in Inches Pohnpei

History

Though Pohnpei was inhabited at least as early as 200 AD, virtually nothing is known of Pohnpeians prior to the *saudeleurs*, a tyrannical royal dynasty of unclear origins. The saudeleurs ruled from Nan Madol, an elaborate city of fortresses and temples that probably reached its peak of power in the 13th century.

The most common story of the demise of the saudeleurs tells of conquests from Kosrae. The *Thunder God*, who had been severely punished for having an affair with the wife of a saudeleur on Pohnpei, set out for Kosrae in his canoe. The canoe sank, but the *Thunder God* was able to continue on when a taro flower changed into a needlefish and guided the god to the island. On Kosrae he made a woman of his

own clan pregnant and the child, *Isokelekel*, was raised on the stories about the cruel saudeleur back on Pohnpei. After reaching adulthood Isokelekel gathered an army of 333 men and went to Nan Madol. He conquered the saudeleur and established a new system of royalty.

Pohnpei was divided into districts, each with two separate families of nobles. The senior man of the highest ranking family was the *nahnmwarki*, or district chief. The head of the other royal line was the *nahnken*, or secondary leader. The victorious Isokelekel became *nahnmwarki* of the region called Madolenihmw, the highest ranked district on Pohnpei and the one which included Nan Madol.

Sometime before the arrival of westerners in the 1820s, Pohnpei Island was divided into the five districts of Madolenihmw, Uh, Kitti, Sokehs and Nett. These districts are the same municipalities in existence today, with the addition of the town of Kolonia, which previously was part of Nett. Each municipality still has its own *nahnmwarki* and the system of ranked titles remains largely intact.

Western Contact In 1528 a Spaniard, Alvaro de Saavedra, became the first known European to sight Pohnpei but it wasn't until 1595 that the island was actually claimed for Spain by Pedro Fernandez de Quiros. Even then, like most of the Carolines, it was virtually ignored by the Spanish who were concentrating their efforts in the Marianas.

In 1828 Fedor Lutke, of the Russian sloop *Senyavin*, christened the island of Pohnpei and the atolls of Ant and Pakin 'the Senyavin Islands' and for quite a while the name stuck.

One of Pohnpei's more colourful visitors was James O'Connell, probably an ex-convict from Australia, who became known as 'The Tattooed Irishman' after enduring Pohnpeian tattooing rites. O'Connell was shipwrecked on Pohnpei around 1830 and was captured by Pohnpeian islanders whom he thought were cannibals. In order to save his life he entertained the natives by dancing an Irish jig – over and over again apparently, as the Pohnpeians were quite impressed with his antics. He not only managed to save his own life but he earned the respect of one of the chiefs and gained a 14-year-old wife as well. When the American ship *Spy* pulled into port in 1833, O'Connell escaped.

Whalers, Traders & Missionaries Whalers, traders and Protestant missionaries began arriving in Pohnpei around the mid-1800s. During each of the peak whaling years of 1855 and 1856 more than 50 whaleships dropped anchor in the island's lagoon.

One bizarre event took place in 1865 during the American Civil War. The Confederate ship *Shenandoah*, on a mission to destroy the Union whaling business in the Pacific, pulled into Madolenihmw Harbor alongside four Yankee whaleships, took the officers as prisoners and set the ships on fire. The news, just one week later, that the Confederate South had surrendered to the Union did not reach the crew of the *Shenandoah*, who managed to destroy almost 40 Union whaleships before returning home.

As in other Micronesian islands, the diseases spread by visiting westerners took their toll but the worst was the smallpox epidemic of 1854 which was introduced by the crew of the American whaleship *Delta*. It killed between 2000 and 3000 Pohnpeians. The native population dropped from an estimated 10,000 in the early 1800s to less than 5000 by the end of the century.

In 1870 the naval cruiser *USS Jamestown* pulled into Pohnpei and forced the island chiefs to sign a treaty which, among other things, allowed foreigners to buy Pohnpeian land. Kolonia was then named Jamestown.

The Spanish Period The Spanish began to occupy Pohnpei in 1886, following the papal arbitration that gave Spain authority over the Caroline Islands. Just three months after his arrival, however, the island's first Spanish governor was killed in a rebellion in which Pohnpeians protested the use of forced native labour in building a fort in Kolonia. Spain's occupation of Pohnpei continued to be plagued by a series of uprisings, quite a few of which concerned the Catholic missions that the Spanish were trying to introduce into the staunchly Protestant communities.

The German Period The Germans arrived in 1899 after buying the Carolines from the Spanish. Their interest was in copra and other commercial products and they were rather heavy-handed in going about their development projects. They too used forced labour.

The 1910-1911 Sokehs Rebellion was sparked when a Pohnpeian working on a labour gang on Sokehs Island was given a beating by a German overseer. The Pohnpeians killed the overseer so the Germans promised revenge, though it took more than four months for their ships and reinforcements to arrive from Melanesia. The Germans then blockaded Kolonia and sent troops of Melanesians charging up Sokehs Ridge. The uprising was suppressed and 17 rebel leaders were executed and thrown into a mass grave. Not wanting to see the incident repeated, the Germans exiled 426 Sokehs residents to Palau and then brought in islanders from the Mortlocks, Pingelap, Molik and Ngatik to settle on Sokehs Island.

The Japanese Period The Japanese took over in 1914. As elsewhere in Micronesia, Pohnpei became a site of intense commercial and agricultural development. The Japanese cultivated trochus shells and set up a sugar plantation to make alcohol.

At the beginning of WW II there were nearly 14,000 Japanese, Okinawans and Koreans living on Pohnpei and only about 5000 natives.

Although Japanese military fortifications

on Pohnpei were hit by air bombings throughout 1944 and Kolonia experienced massive destruction, Pohnpei was not invaded.

Economy

The majority of workers in the moneyed economy work for the government. The area of agriculture is the next largest employer while subsistence farming is still widespread. Pohnpei is home to PATS, Micronesia's only agricultural trade school.

As is common throughout Micronesia, packages that at first appear to be aid often turn out to be ill-conceived financial burdens. A new 170-ton capacity ice and cold storage plant was recently built and paid for by the Japanese but the monthly operating expense of over $25,000 has turned out to be too costly for the Pohnpeians to handle.

Pohnpei also has a sprinkling of pepper plantations. Pepper grows on climbing vines which in the wild sometimes reach to the top of full-grown trees. When cultivated, the vines are usually trained up posts six to eight feet high for easy

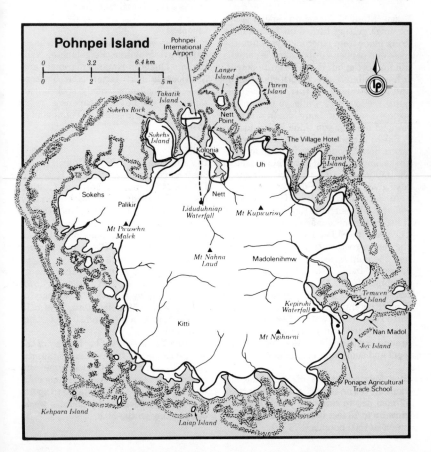

Pohnpei Island

picking. After copra, Pohnpei pepper is the leading export and a hot item in American gourmet shops.

People & Culture

The state population is 28,902 (1985 census). About 90% of the people live on Pohnpei Island and of those, 20% are Kapingamarangis, Mortlockese, Pingelapese, Mokilese and, in smaller numbers, Kosraeans, Palauans and Americans.

The people of the remote Pohnpeian islands of Nukuoro and Kapingamarangi are the only Polynesians in Micronesia.

Sakau Many Pohnpeians spend their evenings getting turned-on by sakau, a drink made from *piper methysticum*, the roots of a pepper shrub. Sakau is called a mild narcotic, but it can be quite potent. It has a sedative effect, with your tongue and lips numbing out first. You then feel quite mellow and while your thinking seems clear your body doesn't always respond quite as you think it should.

Sakau is a bit slippery and slimy going down. Some people liken it to a mud milkshake, and whether it's the sakau itself or the impure water used to rinse the roots, it may give the novice a case of the runs.

In Micronesia sakau is unique to Pohnpei, although the Kosraeans enjoyed it before the missionaries came along. In Polynesia it's called 'kava'. Traditionally the pepper roots were pounded on a stone and the pulp squeezed by hand through hibiscus bark. Nowadays there are machines to do the work though connoisseurs claim the hand-squeezed sakau is more potent. Either way, the juices are mixed with a little water and poured into a coconut shell which is usually passed around communally. Sakau is perfectly legal and somewhat ceremonial.

Food Pohnpeians are big on yams and yams are big on them. Sometimes it takes 12 men just to carry one yam! They can grow up to 10 feet in length and weigh as much as 1500 pounds (675 kg).

Yams take on almost mystical qualities in Pohnpean society and there's a lot of prestige attached to growing the biggest yam in the village. You've heard of the Eskimos having dozens of words for 'snow' – well the Pohnpeians have more than 100 words for yams.

Pohnpeians can eat yams day after day after day. Oddly (or is it?), yams are rare on restaurant menus. Breadfruit and seafood are other island staples.

Funeral feasts are important social events that can last three days and everyone brings gifts of food and sakau. Dog is a traditional feast food.

Language

Pohnpeian is the main native language. Others are Mokilese, Pingelapese, Ngatikese, Nukuoro-Kapingamarangi and Mortlockese (the latter is a Trukese dialect). English is widely spoken and some older people speak Japanese.

The common greeting in Pohnpeian is *kaselehlia*.

Holidays

In addition to US holidays, local observances include Sokehs Rebellion Day on 24 February, Traditional Culture Day on 31 March, FSM Constitution Day on 10 May, Kolonia Independence Day on 17 May, Micronesian Day on 12 July, Liberation Day on 11 September, United Nations Day on 24 October and state Constitution Day on 8 November.

In Pohnpei, each municipality has its own constitution and thus its own constitution day holiday: 27 February in Kitti, 1 May in Madolenihmw, 26 May in Uh, 25 August in Nett and 20 September in Kolonia.

Liberation Day is the big holiday of the year, with people from different municipalities competing in canoe races and traditional events such as coconut husking as well as all the standard sports events. Festivities run for about a week, culminating on the 11th.

KOLONIA

Kolonia is often likened to an American frontier town. Ramshackle shops line the broad main street running the length of the downtown area, most people drive pick-up trucks and the occasional pig wanders onto the road.

About halfway down Main St, beside the tourist office, is a small Japanese tank painted in pastel camouflage splotches. A few blocks south, the state legislature buildings sit on the highest hill in Kolonia.

Along the waterfront road on the east side of town you'll find warehouse-style businesses, including a large co-op and farmer's market. The Protestant church there was built in the early 1930s.

There's a popular swimming spot just before the airport. Sand dredged from the lagoon was brought in to create Pohnpei's first beach a few years back and to the surprise of island skeptics, the sand hasn't yet washed back into the lagoon. A swarm of kids spend hot afternoons jumping from the side of a rusting ship into the water and then climbing the anchor chain back up to the deck.

With a population of 6313 (1985 census), Kolonia is the largest town in the FSM. Despite Pohnpei's heavy rainfall, Kolonia has water rationing.

Information

Pohnpei's only post office is on Main St in central Kolonia. All mail should be addressed to Kolonia, Pohnpei, FSM 96941.

The tourist office, next door to the post office, is open from 7.30 am to 4.30 pm, Monday to Friday. In addition to the standard tourist handouts, they have reference materials, magazines and a sitting area where you can read them.

There's a busy coin-op laundromat across the street, but at times the water pressure is so low that it takes half an hour just for the washing machine to fill.

The Air Mike office and the Bank of Guam are together in a small complex on the intersection opposite the Namiki Restaurant, a block south of the tourist office.

Long distance telephone calls can be made from the communications building or from the Palm Terrace Hotel. The Palm Terrace also sells Guam's *Pacific Daily News*.

The hospital is a mile south-east of Kolonia, on the road heading down the east coast.

North Kolonia

At the north end of Main St is the German bell tower, all that's left of the Catholic mission built in 1907 by the Germans and torn down by the Japanese during WW II. A new Catholic church is nearby.

Also in this area are the moss-covered remains of Spanish stone walls, built around 1887. The walls once enclosed Fort Alphonse and large sections of the Spanish colony.

Cemeteries

The cemeteries of the casualties from the Sokehs Rebellion are in the north-west part of Kolonia. The German cemetery, near South Park Hotel, holds the remains of sailors from the German cruiser *Emden* who died fighting the Sokehs rebels. The overgrown mass grave site of the executed Pohnpeian rebels is in a residential area to the north-east of the German cemetery.

Kapingamarangi Village

This village, on the west side of town in an area called Porakiet, is now home to the Polynesians who moved to Pohnpei from Kapingamarangi and Nukuoro atolls following typhoon and famine disasters. Their breezy thatched homes with partially open-air sides are on raised platforms a couple of feet off the ground. They live a more open and outdoor lifestyle than other Kolonia residents.

The Kapingamarangi people are friendly and don't seem to mind you strolling around the village. Men make wood carvings and women do weavings which are sold in the village gift shops. You

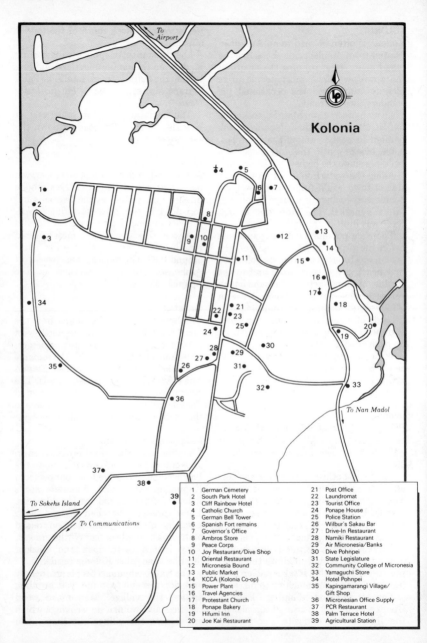

Kolonia

To Airport

To Nan Madol

To Sokehs Island

To Communications

1	German Cemetery	21	Post Office
2	South Park Hotel	22	Laundromat
3	Cliff Rainbow Hotel	23	Tourist Office
4	Catholic Church	24	Ponape House
5	German Bell Tower	25	Police Station
6	Spanish Fort remains	26	Wilbur's Sakau Bar
7	Governor's Office	27	Drive-In Restaurant
8	Ambros Store	28	Namiki Restaurant
9	Peace Corps	29	Air Micronesia/Banks
10	Joy Restaurant/Dive Shop	30	Dive Pohnpei
11	Oriental Restaurant	31	State Legislature
12	Micronesia Bound	32	Community College of Micronesia
13	Public Market	33	Yamaguchi Store
14	KCCA (Kolonia Co-op)	34	Hotel Pohnpei
15	Power Plant	35	Kapingamarangi Village/ Gift Shop
16	Travel Agencies	36	Micronesian Office Supply
17	Protestant Church	37	PCR Restaurant
18	Ponape Bakery	38	Palm Terrace Hotel
19	Hifumi Inn	39	Agricultural Station
20	Joe Kai Restaurant		

might be able to purchase things directly from the craftspeople, but it's not a come-on scene and you'll probably have to ask if you're interested.

Agricultural Station

There is an agricultural station, started by the Germans and expanded by the Japanese, in the southern part of town. A three-story building on the grounds once had a weather station on top. It was one of the few structures left standing in Kolonia after WW II but the building now stands abandoned and condemned.

Communications & Sunsets

Just outside town is the communications building, where you can make long distance phone calls, and the Sunset View Bar. Both places are up on a hill and offer some excellent views along the way.

To get there head past the PCR Restaurant and where the road forks, take the left branch. After one mile turn right onto a road which is paved as far as the communications building.

A little over half a mile from that turn-off is a three-way fork. Take the road to the far right and you'll see the sign for Sunset View Bar.

SOKEHS ISLAND

The road heading to the right at the fork past the PCR Restaurant leads to Sokehs Island.

Once you cross the causeway onto the island the road divides, skirting the coast in both directions. Both ways dead-end as the island road doesn't connect around the northern tip.

The walk around Sokehs takes half a day. The northern part, where there's no driveable road, is made up of large rough rocks so you'll need sturdy shoes. This is the road the Germans ordered to be built with forced labour in 1910, prompting the labourers to resist and turning the incident into the armed Sokehs Rebellion.

Sokehs Ridge

The trail to Sokehs Ridge starts behind the municipal office, just to the right after coming over the causeway. The ridge, about 900 feet high, is loaded with anti-aircraft guns, naval guns, pillboxes and tunnels. There's a good view of Kolonia from the top. It's about a 45-minute walk up the path on a switchback trail with reinforced walls. The path isn't difficult but it starts out grassy and overgrown. If you have any problems finding the start of the trail ask someone to show you. If you come by car, you can park behind the municipal office. The trail doesn't cross private property and you can do this walk on your own.

Sokehs Rock

The steep 498-foot Sokehs Rock can be climbed by those who like a challenge. After crossing the causeway, take the road to the right. The trail starts about ¼ of a mile before the end of the road. If you have a problem finding the start of the trail, ask local kids for directions. Part way up there's a wrapped cable you can use to pull yourself along. It's very slippery when wet. There's a good view of Kolonia and the reef from the top.

NETT MUNICIPALITY

Lidduduhniap Waterfall on the Nanpil River is a half-hour drive from Kolonia. It's at the end of a rough dirt road leading inland off the circle-island road down by the hospital. If there have been recent heavy rains, you may need a four-wheel-drive vehicle to get there. The waterfall is actually twin cascades and the pools are quite good for swimming. A family up at the top charges $1 to get in. There are thatched shelters and cooking facilities in the area though there's sometimes a small fee to use them. A new multi-million dollar hydroelectric plant is being built on the Nanpil River.

Nett Point is another popular place for swimming and barbecues. As in most places, it should be safe if there are families around, but you might want to avoid the area if just drinkers are hanging out.

AROUND THE ISLAND

A 54-mile road goes around the main island but it's a rough and rutted one and a lot of the travelling can only be done at about 10 miles per hour. If you're a glutton for punishment you can drive the whole thing in a day. Try to avoid renting a low-riding sedan though.

A less strenuous route would be to go down the west coast as far as PATS, take in Kepirohi Waterfall, Nan Madol and perhaps a few hours on the beach at Joy Island and return the same way. It would still be a full day but it'd be a lot more relaxed.

Pwusehn Malek

Legend says the volcanic cone formation in the Palikir area was created during the defeat of Pohnpei's saudeleur dynasty. The independent ruler of Palikir apparently changed himself into a giant rooster to fly to Nan Madol and along the way he left a huge pile of droppings.

Pohnpeians call the hill *Pwusehn Malek*. The English translation so stumped Pohnpei's tourist office that their brochure simply lists it as 'Mount' followed by a long blank space. The literal translation is 'Chickenshit Mountain'.

Just before the causeway to Sokehs Island a road heads uphill to the left. This is the start of the circle-island road, heading anti-clockwise, from where you can start marking the following distances.

The road to Palikir has small farms, rolling hills and good views. Stop after 3¼ miles. On the right side of the road, there are steps molded out of the red clay going up to the top of a low hill perhaps a hundred feet high. It only takes a minute to run up to the top for scenic views of Sokehs and the north-west coast.

Pwusehn Malek is ahead on the right at the 5½-mile point. A trail starts there, by the telephone pole on the right side of the road, and it's about a 10-minute walk on a grassy and overgrown trail up to the first ridge. It's an easy trail but when it's wet it can be muddy and slippery.

Palikir is the designated area for the construction of the new FSM capital complex. Until it's completed, government offices remain in Kolonia.

East Coast

To get to Kepirohi Waterfall and Nan Madol take the circle-island road clockwise from Kolonia toward Ponape Agriculture and Trade School (PATS). The route passes through villages in Nett, Uh and Madolenihmw municipalities and it generally takes two to three hours to get there, depending on the road conditions.

Take the road south from Yamaguchi Store in Kolonia and count mileage from there. The turn-off to The Village hotel is to the left just before the five-mile mark.

Shortly after, you'll cross a bridge and enter Awak Village in Uh. The church on the right, with the mountain behind, is definitely picture postcard material. The public elementary school is across the road.

At 21½ miles you'll cross a bridge over a river where women and children bathe and do laundry. Another ¼ mile past that is an unmarked trail to the right leading up to Kepirohi Waterfall. This impressive 70-foot cascade is the one commonly pictured on tourist brochures. There's a nice pool underneath for swimming. It usually costs $1 to visit the falls.

A ¼ of a mile along from the turn-off to the falls is another road junction. This time you get three choices and as usual nothing's marked.

If you want to continue on around the whole island then you veer right and follow the main road through Kitti and Sokehs municipalities and back to Kolonia. If you're planning to visit PATS, Nan Madol or Joy Island then go straight ahead at this intersection rather than taking the sharp left or veering right. Either way, you'll have had enough potholes to last a lifetime.

PATS, 22½ miles from Kolonia, is a private Jesuit-run high school that offers four-year courses in agriculture, construction and mechanics to students from all over Micronesia. The school is surrounded by about 200 acres of land, some of which has been developed as an experimental farm. If you want to tour the PATS complex you should try to arrange it in advance by writing to the school, c/o Box 39.

To get to the dock for boats to Joy Island or Nan Madol, drive straight through the PATS complex and down to the Madolenihmw Municipal Office. If pre-arranged, the boats will pull up in front of the office, to the right of the Temwen Island walkway.

NAN MADOL

Nan Madol was an important political, social and religious centre built during the saudeleur dynasty. It was a place for ritual activity and the homes of royalty and their servants.

Ninety-two artificial islets, stretching out nearly a mile in length and a half-mile in width, were built on the tidal flats and reef off the south-east side of Pohnpei, near Temwen Island.

Basalt which had cooled naturally into hexagonal columns, some of them 25 feet in length and 50 tons in weight, were quarried on Pohnpei Island and hauled to the site by raft.

The columns were stacked horizontally around the edges of the islets as retaining walls and filled with coral rubble and rock. In this manner the islets were eventually raised and the twisting canals shaped into what is sometimes referred to as the 'Venice of Micronesia'. On the level surfaces were built temples, burial vaults, meeting houses, bathing areas and pools for turtles, fish and eels.

The eastern half, Madol Powe (upper town), was the section for priests and rituals. The western half, Madol Pah (lower town), was the administration centre.

The construction of Nan Madol began in force between 1100 and 1200 AD and continued for another two to three hundred years. Nan Madol was uninhabited when the first westerners came ashore in the 1820s, but it was a recent abandonment. In 1852 missionaries recorded that elderly Pohnpeians could still remember when Nan Madol was densely populated.

The best time to visit is at high tide when small boats can easily navigate the twisting mangrove-lined channels which wind through the complex.

Though many of the ruins have collapsed it just adds to the impact, especially as you round a sharp corner in the canal and suddenly find yourself in the shadow of the massive Nan Dowas. This is the largest structure still standing and the most impressive sight.

The outer walls of the Nan Dowas (Nandauwas) compound stand 25 feet high. The inner compound contains four crypts which were burial places for the saudeleurs and later the nahnmwarkis. The largest crypt is rectangular and is in the centre of two sets of enclosing walls, covered by basalt stones about 18 feet long and weighing a ton each.

The islet of Karian also has high walls surrounding a tomb.

Pahn Kadira was probably the administrative centre of Nan Madol and also featured the temple of the *Thunder God*. A large, low platform is all that remains of the temple.

The islet of Idehd has a six-foot wall inside which cooked turtle innards were fed annually to the 'holy eel'. This was part of a two-week religious ceremony which included canoe building competitions, feasting, singing, dancing and sakau drinking.

Dorong, also an important ritual area, has a natural reef pool in its centre, which may have been used for raising clams. Near one wall is a large stone once used for pounding sakau.

Though Nan Madol is Pohnpei's premier sightseeing spot for foreigners, not all Pohnpeians feel comfortable there and the local belief that people shouldn't disturb the ruins may be more than mere superstition. In 1907 the German governor died of a mysterious ailment immediately after excavating a burial tomb on Nan Madol. The German administration claimed it was heat exhaustion but a lot of older Pohnpeians still don't buy it.

Nan Madol holds its mysteries well. Some believe that the legendary lost continent of Mu, or Lemuria, may lie off its waters and that Nan Madol was built as a mirror image of a sunken city that at the time of construction could still be seen lying beneath the water's surface.

JOY ISLAND

If you're looking to get away from it all, Joy Island is the place. Joy is a quiet little island with a white sand beach and 11 unfurnished rough wood cottages with thatched roofs, back-to-basics style. It's easy to get in some snorkelling and a visit to Nan Madol in one day. Or you could play Robinson Crusoe and hide out there for a while.

For $13 one of the caretakers on Joy will pick you up by motorboat at the municipal building near PATS and take you out to Joy Island for a swim. When you've had your fill he'll then take you for a cruise through Nan Madol and eventually return you to the municipal building.

Everything must be pre-arranged at the Joy Restaurant (tel 336) in Kolonia where you buy your vouchers. The manager radios down to make the arrangements and it all works quite smoothly. The cost breakdown is $5 for the boat ride from PATS to Joy and back, $5 for the boat to Nan Madol and $3 for Nan Madol's sightseeing fee.

You can also stay overnight on Joy. Lodging costs $5 per person if you bring your own bedding or $7 if they provide a futon, blanket, sheet and pillow set. Bring your own food and use Joy's covered outdoor cooking facilities. There's an electric generator and lights in the huts. You can borrow the island's outrigger canoe to paddle around the lagoon.

Joy Island does get some small groups of Tokyoites who book up the place for R&R,

so if you want more privacy check ahead. Pohnpeians sometimes come over on weekends for picnics, but otherwise it's usually deserted except for the grounds-keeper and boatsman.

To get there take a taxi or drive to PATS to connect with the motorboat. It might be difficult to get a taxi back to Kolonia late in the day so an alternative is to take a boat from Kolonia to Joy Island. It's $70 round trip for a boat carrying up to five passengers arranged through the Joy Restaurant. Or you could try negotiating with someone down by the docks.

Diving & Snorkelling

Pohnpei has pretty coral reefs, manta rays, shark action and lots of fish. If the sea is rough divers may have to stay inside the barrier reef, which lies one to five miles offshore, and be content to explore the lagoon waters. Visibility is much better outside the reef. Night diving is available and it's also possible to dive Nan Madol.

Snorkellers usually stay inside the barrier reef. Joy Island has good snorkelling, particularly near the floating piers.

Pakin and Ant atolls are considered better for diving than the main island. The one-way boat ride takes one hour to Ant and 2½ hours to Pakin. Spring, summer and autumn are the best months for diving. From December to February the waters between Pohnpei and Pakin are rough. There are three dive companies to choose from, but no dive instructors.

Dive Shops *Dive Pohnpei* (tel 314; Box Drawer 1090) offers full-day boat trips with two tanks and two dives for minimum of four people. This costs $55 for dives around Pohnpei or $65 to Pakin or Ant. Snorkelling trips around Pohnpei cost $50 for one person or $25 to $30 each for two or more people. Prices include all gear. Dive Pohnpei sells, rents and services a wide range of diving equipment and offers dive/hotel packages.

Joy Ocean Service (tel 336; Box 484) is across the street from the Joy Restaurant.

Top: Couple in outrigger canoe – Truk
Left: Yapese boy
Right: Japanese war ruins, Eten – Truk

Top: Trukese kids
Left: Bathing in Wichon River – Moen
Right: Majuro High School mural

Two-tank dive tours by boat around Pohnpei cost $80 for individuals or $45 each for three or more people. It costs an extra $10 to go to Ant. Snorkellers pay about $30 each, for a minimum of two people. Joy sells snorkelling equipment.

Both places rent filled tanks for $3.50, full dive sets for $15 and a set of mask, snorkel and fins for $3 to $4.

For two-tank dive tours around Pohnpei Island, *The Village* (Box 339) charges $80 for one person or $50 each for two people. Divers must bring their own regulator and buoyancy compensator. Other equipment is supplied on a rental basis but only for divers on Village tours. Snorkelling costs $25 for a full day or $15 for a half day, with a minimum of four people.

Hiking

Micronesia Bound might be able to arrange guides for serious hikers who want to hike into the interior and stay overnight, climb Sokehs Rock or undertake similar hikes. If you're interested see the director, Seder Obed. Their office is in the same building as the government offices down by the old Spanish wall.

Places To Stay

Hotel Pohnpei (tel 329; Box 430) near Kapingamarangi Village, is a real find. Nineteen thatch and wood cottages, with walls of woven split bamboo, are built in native Pohnpeian style. It's in a garden setting with tropical flowers and views across the water to Sokehs Rock. The tightly fitted cottages are screened all the way round and all rooms have fans, refrigerators and bottled spring water. The bathroom showers are sun-lit and draped with ferns and hanging plants. The hotel's outrigger canoe is available to guests free of charge. To top it off, this is one of Pohnpei's cheapest hotels at $20/$28 a single/double.

The Village (Box 339) has 21 thatched cottages in a natural setting five miles south of Kolonia. The rooms have waterbeds and ceiling fans. This is the trendy place to stay for Kwajalein contract workers on R&R and for other tourists with American Express cards. The Village is perched on a hillside and the open-air restaurant/bar has a panoramic overview of the lagoon and Sokehs Rock. Rates are $50 to $70 for singles and $55 to $75 for doubles.

The *Palm Terrace Hotel* (tel 393; Box 300) is the best value of Pohnpei's modern hotels. The 11 large rooms, which overlook the landscaped agricultural station grounds, have air-con, ceiling fans and bathrooms with tubs. The TVs can play video movies that you can rent for $2 at the grocery store downstairs. The management is very helpful and the rooms cost $35 for singles or $40 for doubles. Couples can opt for a single room as they have one double bed.

The *Cliff Rainbow Hotel* (tel 415; Box 96) has 45 rooms with prices ranging from $24 to $60 a single or $40 to $66 a double. The cheaper rooms are very basic but all have air-con and private bathrooms. If you're on foot, it's a bit more out of the way than the other Kolonia hotels.

The *Hifumi Inn* (tel 382) has 10 rooms with shared bathroom for $9.50 to $18.50 a single or $12.50 to $22.50 a double. Some rooms have air-con, some have fans. There are a lot of couples at this place – apparently lower rates may apply for those who just want to use the rooms for a few hours.

If the *South Park Hotel* (tel 255, Box 829) has reopened it might be worth checking out. It's up the road from Cliff Rainbow, on a hilltop overlooking the bay and Sokehs Rock.

Hotel Pohnpei, the Palm Terrace and The Village have free airport transfers and sometimes run their mini-vans up to meet incoming flights to see if there are any potential customers. Add 6% tax to all room rates.

Places To Eat

Only the hotel restaurants are open on Sundays. The rest of Pohnpei's eating places take the day off.

The *Joy Restaurant*, a popular place

with Peace Corps volunteers and other westerners, has excellent food. A Joy Lunch is fried fish, rice, sashimi and salad for $4. Fried fish burgers cost $1 and beef tofu with rice is $5. It's open from 11 am to 2 pm and 5.30 to 8.30 pm from Monday to Friday, and for lunch only on Saturdays. As is common with oriental food worldwide, MSG is added. At least at Joy they don't mind holding the MSG upon request. If MSG doesn't register with the waiter just say: no *aji-no-moto*.

Hotel Pohnpei's thatched open-air dining room, looking across the water to Sokehs Rock, is one of the least expensive places to have breakfast. It is actually the only meal served and the menu is limited but what a setting to start your day! French toast and coffee is $1.50 and two eggs, toast and coffee costs $1.75. If there's someone around to climb a tree, drinking coconuts are 50 cents.

The *Palm Terrace Restaurant* is next to the hotel of the same name. It has a simple, $3 a serve salad bar, which sometimes also has papaya or other fresh fruit. Some meal specials also include a selection from the salad bar. Mexican-style tacos cost $1 each and the Palm Terrace's reasonably priced pizza is the best in town. The chef, who previously got rave reviews at The Village, is now running the kitchen here.

The *Oriental Restaurant* has meals similar to Joy's as well as Korean specialties. The Oriental's lunch special is fried fish, rice, sashimi, soup, green salad and kimchi for $4.50. Lunch specials are served at dinnertime too and the restaurant is open Saturday evenings.

The *PCR Restaurant* is just up from the Palm Terrace Hotel toward Sokehs. Their Napolitan spaghetti is loaded with fish, octopus, green peppers and tomato sauce and comes with garlic bread for $5. This is one of the classier places in town to eat.

Joe Kai Restaurant, near the Hifumi Inn, has moderately priced food. They have meals such as sweet and sour fish or chicken adobo from $2.75.

The Village Restaurant has Pohnpei's most expensive menu and features such dishes as mahi-mahi almondine for $10.95 and rack of lamb for two for $32.50. This is a good place to stop for breakfast, which is reasonably priced, if you're on your way around the island. If you have a sweet tooth, try their Pohnpei hot cakes.

The *Cliff Rainbow Restaurant* beside the hotel is a bit pricey, the air-con is usually up too high and the food sometimes takes a slow route from the kitchen. The nicest thing about breakfast is that they sometimes have slices of papaya and other fruit.

The *Island Buffet*, on the 2nd floor of Yamaguchi Store, has ribs, fried chicken and fried fish. At the *Namiki Restaurant* you can get lunch for $2 to $3; and the *Drive-In Restaurant*, behind the Namiki, is another cheap place to grab a meal.

Entertainment

Several of the hotels have bars in or alongside their restaurants.

The *Palm Terrace Bar* is a popular watering hole favoured by American expatriates who glance up from Micronesia's longest bar to check out whoever walks through the door. The parking lot is especially lively on weekends. Young women looking to meet men are referred to as 'wanteds' and this is a gathering spot.

When there's a good sunset, the *Sunset View Bar* is the place to be. For directions on how to get there, refer to the Communications & Sunsets section.

Kolonia residents have to pay $10 annually to drink alcohol in town but visitors staying less than 30 days don't need a permit. The law, enacted in 1971 after two unarmed policemen were shot in a bar, has resulted in a proliferation of small bars being set up just outside Kolonia's town limits. They're generally open until the wee hours of the morning and can get a bit rough and rowdy.

Several sakau bars in town serve up sakau in the evenings. At *Wilbur's* it's pounded by hand, at *Namiki* by machine.

Unlike alcohol drinkers who tend to be temperamental, sakau drinkers are quieter and relaxed.

The Micronesia Cultural Center in Nett has cultural shows with dances, singing, chanting and demonstrations of traditional arts. You might be able to sample local food and sakau as well. The cost is $12.50 per person, for a minimum of five people, but you need to arrange it through the tourist office or tour companies. They need at least 24 hours notice.

Things To Buy

Packages of gourmet Pohnpei pepper make good lightweight presents for folks back home. A three-ounce pack of black or white peppercorns costs about $1.50 or you can buy it packaged in woven coconut frond gift boxes for about $3.50.

Oils, lotions and shampoos made from coconut oil are sold separately in small stores for local use or gift-packaged at the handicraft shops.

Handicrafts include wooden outrigger canoe models, shellwork, coconut graters, mobiles, woven wall hangings and wood carvings of dolphins, fish and sharks. There are several gift shops in Kolonia but try Ponape House on Main St, the Joy Restaurant or the shops in the public market.

The Kapingamarangi Village in Kolonia has handicraft shops with mangrove wood carvings at reasonable prices. They're closed Sundays but even then someone will probably get the manager to open up for you if you ask. People from Kapingamarangi Village also sell their handicrafts at the airport during flight departures.

Friends of the Pohnpei Public Library (Box 284) sell calendars with drawings of local legends for $3.50. For $4.50, they'll send you one airmail. Proceeds will help build a library at Kolonia's agricultural station.

Getting There

Air Mike flies to Pohnpei on its island hopper route, connecting it with Truk,

Kosrae (once a week) and Majuro (on the flights which skip Kosrae). The regular Truk-Pohnpei fare is $149, though there's a Sunday night flight for $75. The fare between Kosrae and Pohnpei is $107, and between Majuro and Pohnpei is $280.

Pacific Missionary Aviation (tel 796; Box 517), which is based in Pohnpei, flies a nine-seater plane to and from Kosrae every morning from Monday to Friday. The one-way fare is $95.

PMA flights between Pohnpei and Pingelap were halted after Typhoon Lola damaged Pingelap's airstrip in 1986. The company plans to re-start that route and add a flight between Pohnpei and Mokil in the near future. PMA also offers charter flights and flying lessons. Flights leave Pohnpei from a two-storey cement building on the west side of the main terminal. Refreshments are for sale around flight time.

The Airport The airport is on Takatik islet, connected to Kolonia by a causeway. The small open-air terminal building was built in a traditional manner using coconut cord tied according to ancient meeting house requirements. Unfortunately it will all be torn down under plans to build a new terminal and expanded runway by the early 1990s. As with other modernisation projects in Micronesia, with each new stage of development another level of native island influence is lost.

Getting Around

Taxi Pohnpei's taxis are shared pick-up trucks or large vans. They're sometimes hard to distinguish from private vehicles but you can always try waving one down to see if it stops. From Kolonia it costs 50 cents to Sokehs Island, $1 to The Village hotel and $2 to PATS. Taxis aren't recommended after dark.

Hitching Hitching is fairly easy, although if you've got your thumb out it will often be one of the unmarked taxis that stops to pick you up – and they expect payment.

On the other hand, when you're just walking along the road, people who have had some passing contact with you, even a customs officer, will often stop and offer you a ride.

Car Rentals Hervis Rent-A-Car (tel 866) rents cars at the airport for $30 a day. Make sure you agree with the check-out time and petrol level marked on your rental agreement before you drive away.

The Palm Terrace Hotel rents cars for $27 a day and is the only place on Pohnpei with optional insurance. There are more than a dozen other rental dealers, mostly mom-and-pop places, with cars for $25 to $30 a day.

Tours In addition to taking the Joy Island route to Nan Madol, there are several tour companies offering package tours to Nan Madol and Kepirohi Waterfall as well as land tours, fishing excursions, picnic trips and so on.

The Village hotel's Nan Madol tour, which includes snorkelling time and a visit to Kepirohi Waterfall, costs about $25 per person, for a minimum of four people.

Other tour companies include Joe Henry Sea Taxi Service (Box 151), Heritage Tours (Box 646) and Pohnpei Island Transportation Co (Box 750). You can also ask at the hotels.

ISLANDS IN POHNPEI LAGOON

The number of islands in Pohnpei's lagoon depends on the tide and how you make the count. Not including the artificial islets of Nan Madol, there are about 24 basalt islands, 30 coral islets on the barrier reef and some islands of alluvial sands.

The basaltic island of Langer figures in colonial history. German traders had copra operations there and the Japanese built a seaplane base on the island which survived US bombings in 1944. After WW II the seaplane ramp was used as Pohnpei's only runway, with all air travel by Grumman SA-16 amphibian, until 1970 when the current airport was built on Takatik.

ANT & PAKIN ATOLLS

Ant and Pakin atolls are off Pohnpei Island's west coast. Uninhabited Pakin is to the north and Ant, which is sometimes inhabited, is to the south. Both have good

First Day Cover – Pohnpei

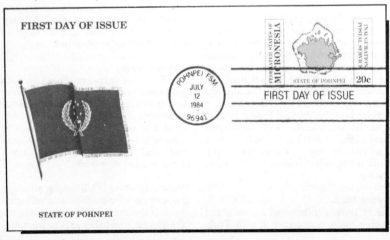

beaches and are popular diving and snorkelling spots. Ant also has a large seabird colony, including black noddys, great crested terns, sooty terns and great frigate birds.

OROLUK ATOLL

Oroluk has a sizable population of hawksbill and Pacific green turtles, as well as a dozen people. Although its 19 islands total less than ¼ of a square mile of land it has a large lagoon. The luxury cruise ship *SS Thorfinn* stops at Oroluk for snorkelling and diving.

MOKIL ATOLL

Mokil is a tidy little place that was once often visited by Marshallese and Gilbertese and later became a popular stop with whalers.

Mokil Atoll's three islets total about ½ a square mile. Fewer than 300 people live on Kahlap, the largest and only inhabited islet. The other two, Urak and Mwandohn are farmed. Mokil has a partially completed airstrip.

PINGELAP ATOLL

Pingelap has three islands but all of the atoll's 738 people (1985 census) live on Pingelap Island. Sukoru and Deke islands are visited for gathering coconuts and crabs.

Early foreigners did not find a ready welcome in Pingelap until about the 1850s when whaling ships became accepted and then commonplace. In the 1870s, Congregationalist missionaries trained two Pingelapese teachers on Pohnpei and sent them back to their home islands. In just two years they had not only converted practically the entire population, but had adults and children alike all wearing western clothing.

Pingelap is known for *kahlek*, a special kind of night fishing which uses burning torches to attract flying fish into handheld nets. Kahlek means 'dancing' and refers to the way the men holding the torches have to sway to keep their balance

when they're standing up. This sort of fishing is done from January to April.

SAPWUAFIK ATOLL (NGATIK)

With the drawing up of its municipal constitution in 1986, Ngatik Atoll renamed itself Sapwuafik Atoll, correcting an inaccuracy it had been carrying for 150 years. The name Ngatik now, as in pre-European times, refers solely to the largest and only populated island in the atoll.

A massacre in 1837 changed the island society forever. Charles 'Bloody' Hart, an Australian captain aboard the British ship *Lambton*, was after fine pieces of tortoise shell he had seen on an earlier excursion to the atoll. But the shells had religious significance to the Ngatikese and they refused to trade. In fact during the first visit, trading negotiations were halted by a group of armed islanders who attacked the crew and forced them to run for their lives back to the ship. Hart however was a swindler, accustomed to getting his own way and although his crew had escaped unharmed, they went back for revenge. The Ngatikese, armed only with clubs and slings, had little defence against the muskets of the *Lambton's* crew, and the sailors massacred all the island men.

The 566 people (1985 census) of Sapwuafik are largely descended from a mix of Ngatikese women and American, British, Pohnpeian and Gilbertese men, many of them crew members of the *Lambton*.

NUKUORO & KAPINGAMARANGI ATOLLS

The people of Nukuoro and Kapingamarangi atolls are physically, linguistically and culturally Polynesian.

Nukuoro has 42 tiny islets. Most of the population of about 400 live on the largest island which is one-third covered by taro. Subsistence comes largely from taro farming and fishing.

Kapingamarangi Atoll is just one degree, or 65 miles (104 km), north of the equator. Its 33 islets total just over ½ a square mile, with a lagoon seven miles across at its widest point. The population is about 500. Kapingamarangi is having an outbreak of leprosy, with about 10% of the population currently affected.

Taro Patch Day, celebrated annually on 15 March in Kapingamarangi, honours the completion of a huge community taro patch in the 1940s. Feasts of roasted eel are a speciality of the day. Kapingamarangi islanders are said to catch sharks by pulling them up by a rope from their canoes and clubbing them to death.

Getting There

The *Micro Glory* makes about 24 field trips a year with various routings to Pohnpei's outer islands. The ship holds 125 passengers and has eight cabins. Deck passengers pay three cents per mile. Cabin passengers pay 10 cents per mile plus $2 per night for the bed.

The mileage fare from Pohnpei to Mokil is $2.85 on deck or $9.50 for a cabin. Between Pohnpei and Kapingamarangi it costs $13.35 on deck and $44.50 in a cabin. You can take along your own food or pay $2.50 for breakfast, $3.50 for lunch and $4 for dinner. The ship leaves from the commercial dock on Takatik Island. Contact the Pohnpei State Transportation (c/o Office of the Governor) for more information on the ship. If you want information on the outer islands try the Office of Island Affairs (tel 710).

Truk

Truk is colourful, lively and rough around the edges. Houses are commonly painted in several bright contrasting colours. On hot days village women sit bare-breasted in streams doing laundry and young children run around naked. Speedboats zip back and forth across the lagoon and from Moen you can watch the sun set behind the Faichuk Islands, often with a brilliant light show.

Truk's biggest draw card is its sunken wrecks, and its most enthusiastic visitors are divers. A whole Japanese fleet rests on the lagoon floor – a moment in time captured in an underwater museum. Most of the wrecks lie off Dublon, Eten, Fefan and Uman islands and represent the largest naval loss in history.

The waters of Truk Lagoon are clear and calm and you don't have to be an experienced diver to take a look at its underwater attractions. Some of the shipwrecks are only a few feet under the water's surface and can be snorkelled.

Truk is the most populated Micronesian island group outside Guam, with more than 46,000 people. In response to political pressures from Trukese women, some tired of alcohol-related domestic violence, Moen and several other islands are now officially dry. Government employees can lose their jobs if they're caught drinking on Moen. Still, alcohol is readily available at black market prices and nearby uninhabited islands are hot weekend picnic spots. Budweiser cans are a major litter problem on these picnic islands.

Geography

Truk State includes 192 outer islands in addition to the 15 main islands and more than 80 islets that make up Truk Lagoon. All in all, about 40 of Truk's islands are inhabited.

Truk Lagoon The whole lagoon area was once one large volcanic island but over the millennia most of the island has sunk. The 15 high lagoon islands are the tallest peaks of that original island. The lagoon formation is similar to an atoll although, strictly defined, an atoll no longer contains high volcanic islands.

There are also numerous low coral islands inside Truk's enormous lagoon, which is enclosed by 140 miles (225 km) of barrier reef. At its widest point, the 822-square-mile lagoon (2104 square kms) is almost 40 miles (64 km) from one reef to another. It has five main passages.

Oceanic View of Truk Lagoon

The major islands in the lagoon are Moen, Dublon, Fefan, Uman, Eten, Param, Udot, Pata, Polle and Tol, all mostly mountainous and wooded. The islands in Truk Lagoon total about 46 square miles (118 square km) of land.

Climate

The most pleasant time of year is the dry season from January to March. Annual rainfall averages 143 inches (363 cm) in the lagoon. The rainiest time is from June to September when the humidity is always high and the mosquitoes are most evident. It can also get uncomfortable between July and November when the north-easterly trade winds die down and tropical disturbances are most frequent.

History

Legend says that at a time estimated to be about the 14th century the great leader Sowukachaw came by canoe to Truk with his son Sowooniiras. Where they really came from is anybody's guess but most people put their money on Kosrae since in Truk (as in Pohnpei) there are many legends relating to Kosrae.

The two men are credited with introducing new varieties of breadfruit and a method of fermentation used to preserve breadfruit. That's important because at the time breadfruit was about it as far as food went. The arrival of Sowukachaw also represented the beginning of clan history and some sort of social ranking system. When the Trukese trace their ancestry they go back as far as that time and never any further.

European Contact The first Europeans to sight Truk Lagoon were with the Spanish ship *San Lucas*, captained by Alonso de Arellano, in 1565. The Trukese came after them with hundreds of canoes filled with armed warriors. The Spaniards stayed only long enough to fire a few cannon shots and make their way across the lagoon and out another passage.

When Manuel Dublon, captaining the *San Antonio*, came to Truk in 1814 to collect beche-de-mer he became the first European in 250 years to enter the lagoon.

The Germans took possession of Truk in 1899 and developed a copra trade, with their headquarters on Dublon Island.

The Japanese & WW II The Japanese Navy began building bases on Dublon immediately after occupying the islands in 1914. The islands were thought to be so impenatrable that the lagoon earned the title of the 'Gibraltar of the Pacific'.

Truk Lagoon became the Imperial Fleet's most important central Pacific base. The huge sheltered lagoon with only a few passageways in and out made for a perfect, calm anchorage. Unfortunately for the Japanese, it also made it easy to seal them in.

On 17 February 1944, the US Navy launched an air-bomb attack code-named 'Operation Hailstone' against the Japanese Fourth Fleet docked in the lagoon. Like sitting ducks, they were bombed non-stop for two days and by the finish some 60 ships had sunk to the bottom. The islands of Truk, however, were never invaded.

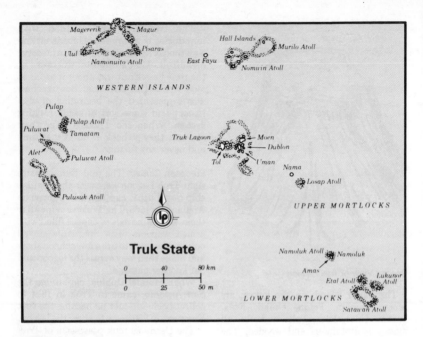

When the US military moved in after the war, Dublon was crowded with the 30,000 Japanese soldiers who had survived the air raids but had no way off the island. Since it was easiest to keep them on Dublon until they could be repatriated to Japan, the US established its headquarters on Moen.

People & Culture

Each island has a predominant clan, the members of which are generally the descendants of the first people to settle that island. While the head clan no longer owns all the island's land, the members still enjoy limited privileges. For instance other people on the island are often obliged to present the clan with some token of respect, such as the fruits from the first harvest.

The chief of the predominant clan is still called on to mediate in disputes between other island clans. He does not initiate this process, but waits until disputes are brought to him and is otherwise not in a position to tell people from other clans what to do. Today the chief's actual power over those outside his own clan is only nominal.

Love Sticks In the days of thatched houses, love sticks were used by courting males to get a date for the evening. These slender sticks of mangrove wood were each intricately notched and carved in a design unique to its owner.

A young man would show his love stick to the object of his desire, so she would be able to recognise the carving at the appropriate time.

If all went well the suitor would wait until the young woman had gone to bed and then push the love stick in through the side of the thatched house and entangle it in her long hair. She would be woken by his gentle pulling, feel the carving to determine who was outside and, if tempted, would sneak out into the night for a secret rendezvous.

It seems like a system with a built-in potential for disaster, like poking the loved one in the eye or tangling the stick in her mother's hair, but perhaps there was more to it than is usually told. When thatched houses went out of fashion, so did love sticks. Replicas make popular souvenirs.

Magic Believers say Trukese magic is powerful and they take it very seriously. It takes many forms – as a curse, a love potion, a way to remove evil spirits or a form of protection. Satawan Atoll is said to have the strongest magic.

Perfumed love potions, called *omung*, may contain such exotica as centipede teeth and stingray tail mixed with coconut oil. If a beautiful woman falls in love with a plain-looking man, people will joke and say he used omung. Trukese say that nowadays money is a more effective way to win someone's heart.

Clothing Many Trukese women wear *nikautang*, a dress with puffed sleeves, a dropped waist with lace trim and a gathered skirt that hangs below the knee. Also popular are *uros*, which are brilliantly coloured appliqued skirts. Sometimes around Moen you see men from Truk's Western Islands wearing the bright cotton loincloths that are also worn in Yap.

Preserved Breadfruit One Trukese food specialty is *oppot*. It's made by filling a pit with ripe cut breadfruit and alternating layers of banana leaves, then covering the top with rocks and leaving it for months, or even years. Uninitiated noses might think it rotten, but this is Trukese preserved breadfruit, a staple on long canoe journeys or during months when fresh breadfruit is not in season.

Language

'Good day' is *ran annim* for Trukese from the lagoon, or *ran allim* for outer islanders. 'Thank you' is *kili so*. Add *chapur* for 'very much'.

Trukese call the islands in the lagoon *chuk* (pronounced 'chook'), which means 'mountain'. The outer islands are *fanabi - fanu* is island, *bi* is sand.

Itang, a specialised and highly metaphorical language taught only to chiefs and people of high rank, has been in use

First Day Cover – Truk

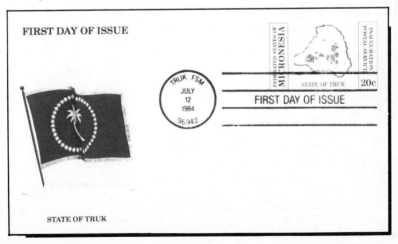

FIRST DAY OF ISSUE

TRUK FSM
JULY
12
1984
96942

FEDERATED STATES OF MICRONESIA

STATE OF TRUK 20c

FIRST DAY OF ISSUE

STATE OF TRUK

since the 14th century. It is used to pass down secret knowledge and to call on supernatural powers.

Holidays
Truk celebrates many of the standard US holidays, as well as FSM Constitution Day on 10 May, Micronesian Day on 12 July and United Nations Day on 24 October.

MOEN ISLAND
Moen is the capital and commercial centre of Truk. At just over seven square miles (18 square km), it's the second largest island in the lagoon. Dense tropical forests fill the interior with the highest point, 1214 foot (364 metre) Mt Teroken nearly in the centre. Villages circle the outer edges of Moen and the main road extends four fifths of the way around the island, with a gap between Sapuk and Neauwo on the south-east side. There are plans to complete the road.

The district centre and government offices are on the north-west side of the island and the airport is on the coast nearby. Trukese call Moen's harbour the 'boat pool'. Moen is in the midst of a small construction boom, with stores, apartments and office buildings springing up all around the place.

Information
The tourist office is in the Department of Resources & Development office directly opposite the hospital.

Truk's only post office is in central Moen. It's open 9 am to 3.30 pm on Mondays, 8 am to 3.30 pm from Tuesday to Friday and from 10 am to noon on Saturdays. All mail to Truk uses the zip code 96942.

Long distance telephone calls can be made 24 hours a day from a tin building just south of the COMSAT station.

Air Mike's office is at the airport.

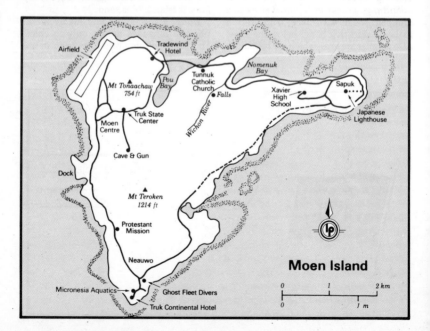

Moen Island

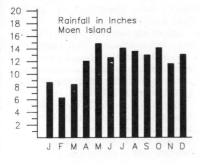

Rainfall in Inches
Moen Island

The Bank of Guam is next to the Seaside Restaurant and the Bank of the FSM is north of there, also on the main road. Banking hours are 10 am to 3 pm Monday to Friday, and 10 am to 5 pm on Saturdays. On payday Fridays you'll have a long wait.

Truk has a new local newspaper called *Eni Ke Fen Sinei*, which translates something like 'I Think You Knew It All Along'.

Mt Tonaachaw

When the legendary Sowukachaw came to Truk he brought a lump of basalt rock with him and stuck it on top of Mt Tonaachaw. There he built a meeting house from where he ruled all of Truk Lagoon.

The steep-sided 754-foot (226-metre) mountain, with its lone tree on the knobby top, is the backdrop for the airport and harbour. Trukese are wary of climbing this mountain because Neawacha, the ghost of an old woman who lives there, has the power of curses.

Truk Museum

The Truk Ethnographic Exhibition Center at the airport has interesting displays of traditional clothing, war clubs, masks, fish traps, baskets, tools and love sticks. It also has artefacts from the lagoon shipwrecks, including the compass and binoculars from the bridge of the *Fujikawa Maru*. There's a good photo display of pictures taken during the two-day bombing assault on the Japanese fleet and Dublon Island.

The museum is supposed to be open 8 am to 4 pm from Monday to Friday. It's definitely worth a visit and there's no admission charge.

Japanese Gun & Cave

A large Japanese naval gun overlooks Moen centre. To get there, head east from downtown Moen and take the first paved road to the right after the hospital. Go up the steep hill until the road ends at a big water tank.

Between the last two houses, but on the right side of the street, are steps leading up the hill. It's a two-minute walk to the cave. You go straight through the cave to get to the gun and a view of the town.

Japanese Memorial

A Japanese memorial to war dead stands along the coast, north of the docks. It looks like a big black marble. The Japanese character for peace, *wa*, is carved into the pedestal. There's a sunken barge in the waters behind.

South Field

The Truk Coconut Processing Plant is in the southern part of Moen in a white metal building to the left before the gate to the Truk Continental Hotel. If you want to see how soap is made from copra, go on in.

This area was South Field, where the Japanese had a seaplane base and fighter strip. The plane ramp is beyond the soap factory as is a ferro-concrete boat, the result of a failed government-funded small industries project.

The Truk Continental has the only easily accessible sandy beach on Moen. There's a grass-covered Japanese bunker on the hotel grounds.

East of the Airport

From the airport heading east, the road edges along the coast and passes through small villages. After the Bethesda church on the right, the road goes across Pou Bay. The Tunnuk Catholic Church is up a hill to the right.

Micronesian Seminar
Tunnuk Church is headquarters of the Micronesian Seminar, directed by Father Fran Hezel. The seminar's library is an excellent resource centre, with an extensive collection of books, microfilms, magazines, maps, reports and theses on all parts of Micronesia. If you're doing research on Micronesia, the reading room is a pleasant place to be. It's open to the public daily, with no formal hours.

Wichon Falls
The falls are not very big but you'll see an interesting cross-section of village life on the 10-minute walk there.

Start from JS Enterprises, a small store at the end of the paved road east of the airport, and head up the rough vehicle road to the right of the store. After about five minutes turn onto the road that joins it, walk behind a small house and up Wichon River. It's a friendly village, but you are walking across private land so it's polite to ask at the store for one of the kids to guide you or ask permission to cross as you go along.

Village women sit in the stream washing their clothes and children are eager to pose for photos. Under the falls there's a cool water hole deep enough for swimming.

Xavier High School
The Jesuit-run Xavier High School opened in 1953 as the first four-year high school in Micronesia and maintains a reputation as the region's best.

Originally the site of a German chapel, the land was taken by the Japanese in 1940. They constructed a fortified radio communications centre, the main building of which survived two direct hits by US bombers amazingly requiring only a patch job on the roof. The rooms, with two-foot-thick concrete walls and vault-like steel doors and windows, now serve as the school's main classrooms. Go up and check it out.

Visitors are welcome to climb the roof for a panoramic view of Truk Lagoon and to walk around the grounds, providing they don't disturb classes. Cars should be parked under the big mango tree at the far right of the main building.

Go quietly through the centre doorway of the main building, past the study hall and up the stairs on the left. At the top of the stairs go through the door on the left, then turn right to get outside, where there are stairs up to the roof. A display cabinet at the top of the stairs on the 2nd floor holds objects from sunken ships, including dishes, sake bottles, a phonograph record and a porthole.

The windmill on the grounds runs the school's computers and there are tunnels burrowed into the hill alongside the driveway leading up to the school.

Japanese Lighthouse
The view from the old Japanese lighthouse in Sapuk is one of the best on the island. However it's a hit and miss affair whether you'll be able to hike up to the top without various people along the way claiming to be landowners and demanding anything from $1 to $10. It should make things easier if you first seek out the local policeman, Rively Wanter. He is the rightful owner and can give you a permission note prior to the climb.

To get to the lighthouse, after leaving Xavier High School, you take the road going down along the water. After passing a long thin wharf the road will loop a bit inland and come to a 90 degree corner. Stop at the corner and look for the driveway straight ahead. The lighthouse is a 30-minute walk up that trail.

Diving & Snorkelling
Truk Lagoon is a wreck diver's dream. On its bottom rest almost 60 Japanese ships, including oil tankers, submarines, tugboats cargo and passenger ships, as well as scores of US and Japanese planes.

The ships lie just as they sank in 1944 – some upright, some intact, some in pieces spread across the lagoon floor. Each is a separate time capsule. The holds are full of guns and trucks and fighter planes, the dining areas are littered with dishes, silverware and sake bottles and the skeletal remains of the perished crews lie 'buried' at sea.

The wrecks have become artificial reefs for hundreds of species of vividly coloured corals, sponges and anemones that have attached themselves to the metal. These shelters also attract large schools of fish. The water is warm, about 85°F, and visibility is 50 to 100 feet. For the most part, divers don't have to be especially experienced.

The largest wreck in the lagoon is the *Heian Maru*, a 535-foot (160 metre) passenger and cargo ship lying on its port side at 40 to 110 feet. Divers can see the ship's name and telegraph mount on the bow and also visible are large propellers, periscopes and a torpedo.

The *Fujikawa Maru* landed upright in 40 to 90 feet of water and is a popular dive. The stern mast of this aircraft ferry sticks up out of the water but it's another 60 feet down to the main deck. The hold contains four Zero fighters at 90 feet.

Underwater photographers like the *Sankisan Maru* for its excellent soft coral formations. It's a munitions freighter more than half destroyed and lying at 50 to 100 feet with a cargo of trucks, machine guns and ammunition.

Although it's the wrecks that make Truk special, there are also some interesting and colourful reefs.

Though strictly illegal, some local fishermen have been tearing the wrecks apart looking for stores of explosives, which they then use to dynamite the reefs for an easy catch of fish. Unfortunately there's a ready market for fish caught this way.

Dive Shops To keep souvenir hunters at bay, the wrecks have been declared an underwater historical park and can't be visited without an official guide. Diving permits and complete rental services are available through the three dive shops on Moen.

The *Blue Lagoon Dive Shop* (tel 796; Box 429), Truk's first dive shop, is 1¼ miles south of the airport on the right. Rates start at $65 for two tank dives plus a picnic excursion to an uninhabited island or a land tour of Dublon.

Micronesia Aquatics (Box 57), run by former Peace Corps volunteer Clark Graham and his Trukese wife Chineina, is just inside the gate of the Truk Continental Hotel. Graham specialises in underwater photography and insists that divers be conservation oriented.

The newest diving business is the *Ghost Fleet Dive Shop* (tel 724; Box 295), on the left just before the Truk Continental. The rate for a full day with two tank dives is $55. In between dives they'll take you to visit a nearby island at no extra charge.

Places To Stay

The *Christopher Inn* (tel 652; Box 37), in central Moen opposite the airport, has two rooms with fans for $28/$34 a single/double, and 19 air-con rooms for $32 a single or $38 a double. All rooms have refrigerators and private bathrooms. Supposedly there's a free bus service to and from the airport – a two-minute walk away.

The *Tradewind Hotel* (tel 781; Box 520) has four air-con studio apartments, with balconies, that cost $42 a single or $52 a double. Each has a full kitchen, with oven and refrigerator, and a private bathroom. They're building four more units which will probably be without kitchens and therefore less expensive. The Tradewind is in a quiet residential area above the JS Enterprises store, one mile east of the airport on the road to Xavier. Look for a yellow building with red trim on the inland side of the road. The Tradewind also rents two-bedroom apartments by the month and there are plans for a coin-operated washer and dryer downstairs. Airport transfers are free.

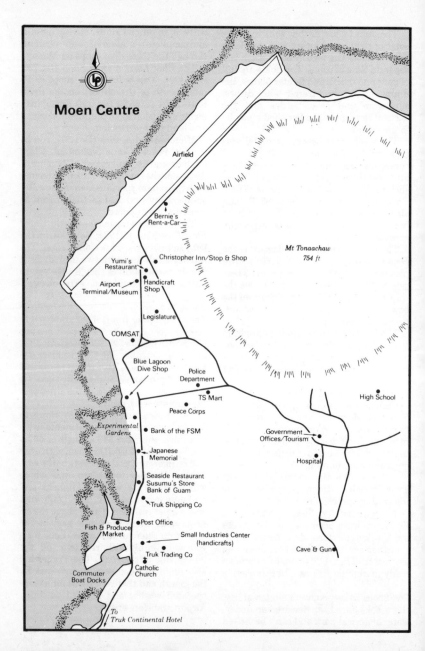

The *Truk Continental Hotel* (tel 727; Box 340) is Moen's up-market hotel. It has 56 air-con rooms in several two-storey buildings, each with bathrooms, balconies and a view of the lagoon. There's a dining room, white sand beach and a gift shop. Room rates start at $69 for singles or doubles. Airport transfer costs $7 return.

All three hotels add a 10% tax to the room charge. Moen has a housing shortage so smaller places that start out as hotels often end up renting to long-term residents.

Places To Eat

The *Seaside Restaurant*, across from Susumu's store, has good Japanese and western food at moderate prices. Try their huge special *teishoku* (fixed lunch), of pork, chicken and a whole reef fish with rice, miso soup and small salad for $4.

The *Christopher Inn* has two restaurants which are both OK but nothing special. Breakfast is better upstairs in the Roof Garden where egg, toast and coffee costs $1. You can get sandwiches downstairs in the Rainbow Coffee Shop starting at $1.75 and occasionally there's a lunch special. Most Trukese don't bother to climb up to the 2nd floor, so there's more local atmosphere downstairs.

Yumi's Cafe is popular for its big hamburgers which are meals in themselves and cost $1.60. Onion rings cost $1, chicken adobo with rice is $3.75 and all portions are large.

The *Truk Continental* has the fanciest setting and prices although the food isn't particularly special. The reef fish dinner costs $9.95 and breakfasts start around $5. The air-con seems to be stuck on 'frozen'.

The fruit stalls opposite the post office sell drinking coconuts for 25 to 50 cents. Other treats include cooked and pounded breadfruit wrapped in taro leaves, and limes, mangoes, cucumbers and other fresh produce, most of which comes from Fefan.

Stay clear of unboiled tap water. Stop & Shop (at the Christopher Inn) sells the cheapest bottled water in Moen.

Things To Buy

A good place to find handicrafts is the government-run Small Industries Center. They have grass skirts, weavings, wall hangings, carvings of wood and coral, baskets, love sticks, masks and sea shells. There are also a couple of small shops near the airport.

Getting There

Air Mike is the only airline which flies to Truk, connecting Moen Island with Pohnpei and Guam on the island hopper route. The full-fare between Guam and Truk is $201 one way; and between Pohnpei and Truk is $149. Sunday evening flights are half price.

Getting Around

Taxis Shared taxis, which are usually pick-up trucks, can be identified by signs in their front windows and will stop when flagged down. It costs 25 cents to go anywhere around the downtown area, and 50 cents to either the Truk Continental or Xavier.

Car Rentals VJ Car Rental (tel 653) at the airport has cars without air-con for $20 and with air-con for $25 to $27. Truk Travel Unlimited (tel 701) has cars from $25 to $27 and you can also try Bernie's Rent-a-Car (tel 677).

Tours Mr Yasumori (tel 629) runs half-day land tours of Moen for $16 per person. Boat tours, for up to five people, cost $20 per hour and usually take in Dublon, Eten, Moen and some snorkelling time at a shallow shipwreck.

ISLANDS IN TRUK LAGOON

The most easily accessible main lagoon islands outside Moen are Dublon, Eten and Fefan. Uman and Param are not particularly receptive to visitors and the Tol islanders have a reputation for being a bit rough and rowdy. Many of these islanders commute by boat to jobs on Moen while others have subsistence farms or earn money through fishing or copra.

It's a more traditional Trukese lifestyle on the islands in the outer lagoon where the roads are scarce and the vehicles are few. On some islands people still live under thatched roofs and cook outdoors over open fires.

DUBLON ISLAND

Dublon is also called Toloas, which was the island's original name until 1814 when Manuel Dublon landed there and humbly renamed it.

It's a peaceful island today, but there are signs of its former importance under occupying powers. Both the Germans and Japanese made Dublon their administrative centres and the Japanese military headquarters there included submarine, seaplane and coastal defence bases. US bombings left them in ruins.

After the war Dublon became sleepy and overgrown but it's now in line for redevelopment, and electricity is on its way. In the meantime Dublon still provides a good glimpse of rural Trukese life.

There are docks at Sapou, in the northeast corner of the island, and in the south at the new fisheries plant. A road runs around the island and there are a few private pick-up trucks, but no taxis. Most visitors go over with a guide, but you could try winging it on your own.

Sapou

Overgrown vegetation in Sapou Village partly conceals the remains of what was once a good-sized city. The wooden buildings are long gone, but the cement footings they were built upon are still there. Broad cement sidewalks, once covered with tin roofs to shelter the Japanese against sun and rain, are now shaded by breadfruit trees. The remains of the Japanese naval hospital are up the hill above the new Youth Center.

The colourful village church, which is dark grey trimmed with bright primary colours, sports a sign in Old English lettering reading: *kinamue* – which means 'peace'.

South Dublon

If you drive anti-clockwise from Sapou to the south side of Dublon, you'll see a large Japanese dome-like concrete bunker on the right side of the road. An iron pipe protruding from the top served as an air vent.

Ahead, where the road splits, you can take the right fork to see a fortified Japanese building with heavy metal doors and windows. It's now a village hangout.

A little further on is the junior high school, built on the paved grounds of the Japanese seaplane base. A seaplane ramp goes down into the water. The former base for the US Air Force Civic Action Team is ahead along the shore.

Back on the main road there's the remains of a collapsed Japanese oil storage tank on the left, which is now used by a local family as a garage. Ahead, up a grade to the left, a new aluminium geodesic dome covers a large freshwater reservoir. The concrete water tank was built by the Japanese who secretly placed a steel fuel tank in the centre to serve as a hidden reserve.

Turn right at the next road to get to Dublon's deepwater dock and the new multi-million dollar fisheries complex and freezer built by the Japanese.

East-central Dublon

Continuing on the main road, there are more burned-out oil storage tanks on the right. At the crossroads, turn left and you'll pass a small Japanese memorial. Just past the municipal building turn left, then keep an eye out to the left for the entrance to a massive cement tunnel built under the mountain. The tunnel looks big enough to run a subway through and did in fact hold a fleet of military vehicles. It ran under the Japanese governor's residence and still has a rusted electric generator inside.

Further down on the left, a sign in Japanese announces a naval cemetery. Steep stairs lead up to the site but this is

Top: Airai Bai – Palau
Left: Old Age Centre – Koror
Right: Breeding giant clams at MMDC – Palau

Top: Nan Madol – Pohnpei
Left: Community meeting house – Yap
Right: Traditional meal of taro & pork cooked in blood – Yap

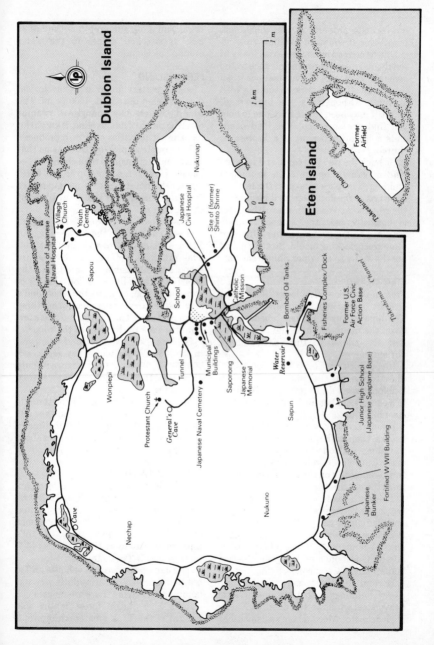

now private property so you should ask permission if you want to climb up.

Down the road on the left look closely to see the narrow overgrown entrance to the general's cave, one of five openings to an interconnecting network of tunnels with air vents. Although it's close to the road, you still may need to ask someone to help you find the entrance. The road dead-ends a little further on at a Protestant church.

Go back the way you came and take the road diagonally opposite the municipal building. There's a school on the left and the ruins of the Japanese civil hospital at the crossroads. What remains of the latter is basically just the arched concrete entrance hall, now covered in graffiti and some grotty looking mould. Straight ahead are the stairs to a former Shinto shrine.

ETEN ISLAND

From a distance Eten looks like a huge aircraft carrier which, in effect, it was. The Japanese used Trukese labour to tear down the mountain tops and carry away half the island to turn Eten into a airfield.

If you dock on Eten's north-west side, directly opposite the fisheries complex on Dublon, then it's a 10-minute walk inland to a complex of bombed-out concrete and steel buildings.

From the dock you pass a couple of houses, then walk up to the right through the village and follow the path to the right of the Catholic church. It's a well-defined trail, sometimes on the pavement still left from the old airstrip.

The path leads directly to a massive two-storey concrete structure. The roof and 2nd floor are partly caved-in with twisted steel reinforcement rods hanging down. Islanders say it was hit by 15 to 20 bombs. One room is amazingly still intact and apparently someone's living in it.

Beyond are three more similar two-storey buildings with the same style of heavy steel windows and doors as Xavier High School on Moen. There's a demolished

tower and a big gun on top of the hill as well as wrecked planes in the water around the island.

FEFAN ISLAND

Pieces of pottery found in archaeological digs on Fefan date back 1500 years. The island, which has mangrove swamps covering much of its shoreline, is known for its farming activities and fresh produce.

The couple of pick-up truck taxis that circle the rough, island road charge $2 per person. However, as the trip around takes about 1½ hours there's no guarantee there'll be one on your side of the island at the right time.

Mesa Wharf is on the east side of Fefan and you can take in the whole village of Mesa, such as it is, in a 10-minute stroll. The municipal office and elementary school are both visible, to the left, from the wharf. There's a little tea house, made of corrugated iron, opposite the school and a small store carrying not much of anything down past that. The village church is a few minutes walk to the right of the wharf.

On Fefan, kids come up and touch you to see if you're for real. They smile, ask your name, follow you around for a minute or two and then go back to whatever they were doing.

Most war relics are inland or on the hills and difficult to reach. Some anti-aircraft guns are spread out on top of a hill directly up from Mesa Wharf. The hike takes about 30 minutes but there's no real trail.

TOL & THE FAICHUKS

The Faichuk Islands, in the western part of Truk Lagoon, include Tol, Polle and Pata. Tol is the largest and most populated of the Faichuks and is about a one-hour boat ride from Moen. One of Tol's mountains rises more than 1400 feet (420 metres) and is Truk's tallest.

The Japanese once had vehicles on Tol but the roads took a beating during the war bombing and today there are no cars.

Tol's high jungle forest is the sole habitat of the Truk greater white-eye, a

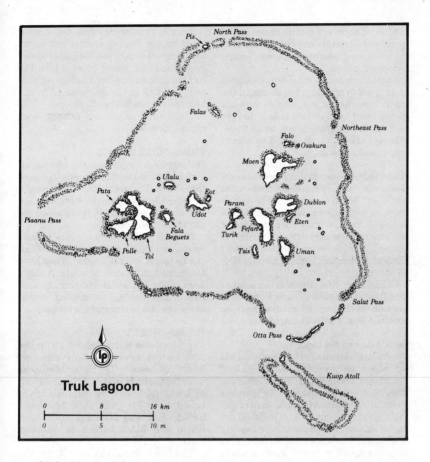

Truk Lagoon

```
0           8          16 km
|-----------|-----------|
0           5          10 m
```

rare bird with one of the most restricted ranges of any in Micronesia.

The Faichuk islanders wanted Truk to opt for commonwealth status, so when the majority of Trukese voted instead to become a state in the FSM the Faichuks started statehood attempts of their own.

Basically the islanders are looking for their fair share of the new development which is now centred on Moen. With one-third of Truk's population, they feel they're entitled to one-third of the state budget. They want electricity and paved roads. Perhaps more importantly they want a water system as they sometimes run out completely and have to rely on drinking coconuts.

The FSM Congress actually approved the Faichuks as a new FSM state after 98% of Faichuk voters chose by referendum to break away from the rest of Truk. The movement failed with a veto by the FSM president.

PICNIC ISLANDS
Trukese make good use of the low coral islands scattered around the lagoon as fishing, picnic or drinking grounds.

Most of them are classic desert island specimens – crystal clear waters surrounding white sand beaches and a small stand of coconut palms.

Snorkelling can be excellent, though in some spots dynamiting has damaged the coral. Deserted or not, the islands are owned and you're supposed to get permission from the owners to go there. Whoever takes you out should be able to help you arrange it.

Places To Stay *Fanos Beach Resort* is a new place on a picnic island about three miles north of Moen's airport. The small cottages, with *futon* mattresses, cost from $7 to $30. You can bring your own food or eat in their small kitchen. Alcohol is allowed. For more information contact Vincent & Brothers Enterprises (tel 606) on Moen.

Other than this, there is no accommodation on the outer islands. Permission to camp on the populated islands can be obtained from the local magistrate.

Getting Around the Lagoon

Commuter boats leave the lagoon islands for Moen on weekday mornings and return from Moen in the early afternoons. They're obviously convenient for islanders commuting to Moen to work, shop or sell their produce, but the schedules are backwards for anyone planning a day trip from Moen. The boats are often referred to as *yamma*, after their Japanese-made Yanmar diesel motors.

Boats from Fefan tie up at the Moen dock, on the side opposite the post office, where the Fefan women market their vegetables. Boats from Dublon, Tol and the Mortlocks are usually moored on the other side of the dock.

The *Truk Queen* boats go to Tol for $1.50 one way, leaving Tol at 7.30 am and Moen at 2 pm. Boats to Uman, Fefan and Dublon cost $1 one way, leave for Moen between 6.30 and 7 am and return between 2 and 4.30 pm. Boats from Udot may run only a couple of times a week.

Private speedboats cross the lagoon every day. If you ask around you might find someone to take you to another island in exchange for petrol money. Like the commuter boats however, most speedboats come to Moen in the morning and return to home islands in the afternoon.

The tourist office can arrange boat rentals from $60.

TRUK'S OUTER ISLANDS

Outside Truk Lagoon are the Mortlocks, Hall Islands and Western Islands. Together they have 11 atolls and three single islands. All are flat coral formations, some just wisps of sand barely rising above the surface of the ocean.

In their isolation, the outer islands maintain a more traditional lifestyle than can be found in Truk central. They have footpaths but no cars or roads. A day's work might include cultivating the taro patch and fishing or making copra, sleeping mats or coconut fibre ropes.

THE MORTLOCKS

The Mortlocks stretch about 180 miles (290 km) in a south-easterly direction from Truk Lagoon. The Upper Mortlocks include the single island of Nama as well as Losap Atoll with its main islands of Losap and Pis. The Mid-Mortlocks include Etal and Namoluk atolls, and Kuttu and Moch islands in Satawan Atoll.

The Lower Mortlocks incorporate the other Satawan Atoll islands of Satawan and Ta as well as Lukunor Atoll. The Japanese have donated a large freezing facility for the fishing co-op on Oneop Island in Lukunor Atoll.

The largest of all Truk's outer island groups is Satawan Atoll, with its four main islands and 45 islets covering a total of only 1.8 square miles (4.6 square km).

The Mortlockese are an easy-going people and tend to be very gentle. Outer islanders in general are a more religious bunch overall than the people of Truk Lagoon, perhaps because the Christian missionaries were in the Mortlocks long before they were in the lagoon. Despite the stricter Christian following, religious prohibitions such as those against building fires on Sunday have recently been abandoned.

The Mortlockese make traditional masks of hibiscus wood. Once worn by men during battle and to ward off evil spirits, they are now just carved for Truk's tourist trade.

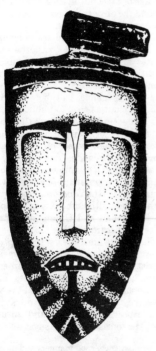

Dance Mask of the Mortlock Islands

THE HALL ISLANDS
The Halls, north of Truk Lagoon, include the single island of Fayu and the atolls of Murilo and Nomwin. Fananu Island in Nomwin Atoll is said to be the most attractive of all the Halls.

These islands are, in a sense, a satellite community of Truk Lagoon. They were once allied with Moen and with islands on the Truk Lagoon reef, with whom they share a common dialect.

THE WESTERN ISLANDS
The Western Islands, Truk's most remote and traditional, share close ties with the outer islands of Yap. Though political distinctions divvy them up into two separate states, outer islanders in the central Carolines have more in common with each other than they do with the high islands of Yap or Truk Lagoon to which they belong.

On these islands the men still often wear bright loincloths and the women wear woven fibre or grass skirts. Houses are made of thatch, subsistence comes from the sea and men still sail single-hulled outrigger canoes carved from breadfruit logs, relying on centuries-old navigational methods.

Young women from the Western Islands who attend the University of Guam, at first enter classrooms crawling on their knees if there are any of their male relatives in the room. This would be expected in their home islands but university teachers, not too keen on the custom, eventually get them to make some concessions to western culture.

The Westerns include Namonuito, Pulap, Pulusuk and Puluwat atolls. Namonuito is a huge triangular atoll, the people of Pulap are said to be Truk's best navigators and Pulusuk has Truk's only freshwater pond.

Puluwat's five islands almost surround its small lagoon, leaving just one passageway and an excellent anchorage with a safe refuge from storms. The Japanese had an airstrip and lighthouse on one of the now uninhabited islets.

Outer islanders used to have a reputation for being tough fighters and the people of Puluwat were probably once the most feared people in all the central Carolines. Around the late 1800s however, they got religion and have since become as gentle as lambs.

Places To Stay

There are no guest houses on any of the outer islands, but the governor's office on Moen can sometimes make arrangements with island magistrates to help accommodate visitors. Food is always a good gift.

Getting There

Field Trip Ship Two field trip ships, the *Micro Trader* and the *Micro Dawn*, make a total of about 30 trips a year, each an average of one week long. The ships, which can carry 150 people, might go to the Westerns one trip, to Namonuito and the Halls on another and to the Mortlocks on yet another. It costs three cents per mile on deck or 10 cents per mile plus $2 per night for a cabin. From Moen it's 170 miles to Satawan, 160 miles to Pulusuk and 80 miles to Murilo.

It is recommended that you take your own food although you can buy breakfast for $3.50, lunch for $4.50 and dinner for $5.50. You can get more information from the Office of Transportation (tel 592) or from the Truk Shipping Company (tel 455, Box 669) in the former Kristy's Hotel, in central Moen.

Boats to the Mortlocks The Mortlocks have two new government boats. The *Miss Moch* runs between Moen and the mid-Mortlocks about once a week for $4.65 one way.

The *Miss Lukeisel* goes to the Upper Mortlocks about twice a week. It makes extra trips between May and August, when the water is calmest, and at Christmas. Nama Island, 48 miles (77 km) and two hours from the lagoon, costs $2 one way. Losap and Pis, about 60 miles (96 km) away, cost $2.50.

Yap

Yap, the land of giant stone money, remains Micronesia's most traditional stronghold.

You know you're in a unique place as you catch your first glimpses of Yap while waiting in line for immigration. A cross-section of islanders come to meet the flights at the ramshackle open-air terminal. Most people dress in western clothes but a fair number of the men and boys wear the bright coloured loincloths and many women wear grass or woven hibiscus skirts. Everyone, including the very official-looking customs officers, has a bulge of betel nut in their cheek and all around the airport's wooden benches, red stains spot the dirt floor.

Out in the villages, which are connected by centuries-old stone footpaths, men's houses are still built in the elaborate, traditional style of wood, thatch, rope and bamboo. The caste system still survives and village chiefs still hold as much political clout as elected public officials.

It's a deceptive place. Even though you can fly in by jet, Yap still isn't any more developed than some of Micronesia's remote outer islands. Yap has only two small hotels and seldom sees more than a handful of visitors at any one time – which is just the pace the Yapese are comfortable with. And although it's a stopover between Palau and Guam, it's a world quite distinct from either.

The Yapese are a shy yet proud people. They are offended by the occasional tourist who brazenly points a camera at them as if they were subjects in an anthropological museum, yet at the same time they're very receptive to travellers who respect their customs and culture.

As the tourist brochure says:

It takes patience, good manners and plenty of understanding to see Yap and observe some of its traditions. Yap is not a world built for tourists, but a world that welcomes visitors.

If you visit Yap on its own terms you won't be disappointed. For the traveller who treads gently, it's still a rare place to see.

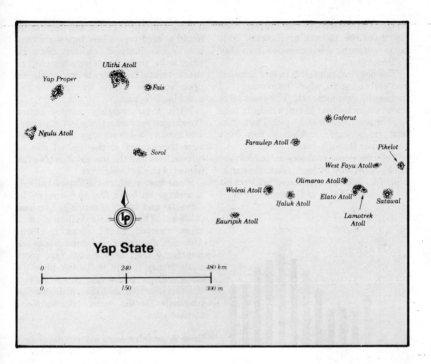

Yap State

Geography

Yap Proper, which consists of four main and 10 small islands within a coral reef, is 515 miles (829 km) south-west of Guam. The major islands are Yap, Tamil-Gagil, Map and Rumung. These islands are unusual for Micronesia, as they were formed by land upheavals of the Asian continental shelf. About 65% of the population lives on the 38.7 square miles (99 square km) of Yap Proper, which comprises 84% of Yap State's total land mass.

The three small islands that sit in the channel between Tamil and Yap islands – Pekel, Bi and Tarang (O'Keefe's) – total only about 10 acres combined. Garim (Bird Island), off the south-east tip of Yap Island, is an uplifted 300-foot-long (90 metre) chunk of coral undercut by the ocean. The other small islands are even tinier chunks of rock.

Strung out some 600 miles (966 kms) to the east are 134 outer islands, with a combined land area of 7.26 square miles (18.5 square kms). Most are mere strands of coral and sand precariously emerging from the water. A major typhoon can easily sweep one of these islands clean of its vegetation of coconut trees and occasionally wash an entire island into the ocean.

Trade winds blow into the north and east sides of the islands, leaving the south and west shores with good sandy beaches.

Climate

Yap has a consistent year-round temperature of about 81°F with about an approximate 10° variance between noon and night. Humidity is higher during the night and early morning.

Mornings tend to be sunny with a gradual build-up of fair-weather clouds, whose accumulation during the rest of the day gives rise to evening showers. This pattern is particularly common from May to December.

The heaviest rainfall is in late summer and early autumn, when the average is 13 inches (33 cm) a month. The least rain, about seven inches (18 cm) a month, falls in February, March and April. The north-east trade winds influence Yap from November through June.

Fully developed typhoons are uncommon near Yap, as most of them pass to the north. Ulithi Atoll, however, received a direct hit by Typhoon Marge in December 1986.

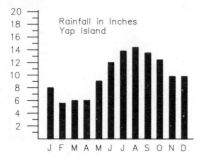

History

Studies of pottery and other archaeological finds on Map Island dates the earliest known Yapese settlement at around 200 AD.

The Yapese once reigned over a scattered island empire, extending from the Marianas in the north to deep into the eastern Carolines. Lengthy ocean-going voyages were not uncommon but the Yapese empire was built upon magic, rather than conquest. The high chiefs of Yap Proper employed sorcerers who had powers to cause famine, sickness and typhoons. In fear of this sorcery the outer islanders offered an annual tribute to remain in good favour.

Stone Money Legend has it, that the ancient navigator Anagumang set sail for Palau in search of the right stone for

Yapese currency. To his satisfaction he found a hard crystalline limestone that the Yapese quarried into flat discs. In order to lug them, holes were punched in the centre and the stones were then placed upon barges and towed by canoe the 250 miles back to Yap.

With their weighty cargo, entire expeditions were sometimes lost in storms. The most valuable stones were those that were transported at the highest cost of human lives and the stones often bore the names of the lost mariners.

Stone money, which the Yapese call *rai*, can range up to 12 feet (3.6 metres) in diameter and weigh as much as five tons (4535 kg). The Japanese civilian government counted 13,281 coins in 1929. Although single pieces of stone money are commonly seen throughout Yap, most stone money is kept in 'banks' lined up along village pathways. Stone money remains in active use today, although the US dollar settles most commonplace transactions.

Caste A complex caste system developed over a period of time as a consequence of warfare between Yapese villages. The victors would demand land ownership rights and patronage of the defeated village. The people of that village retained rights to use the land but were compelled to perform menial tasks, such as road construction and burial of the dead, for their landlords.

A village is inhabited by members of the same caste. Every plot of land in the village has a name and rank with the highest ranked plot belonging to the village chief. Even today, the village in which one is born still determines one's name and caste.

Depending on how you differentiate them, there are either seven or nine castes in Yapese society today. Each village has its own chief with the paramount chiefs of Yap coming from the three highest caste villages.

It's not really obvious where a village

stands in the caste hierarchy just by looking at it. Caste has a more profound effect on people's status rather than upon their standard of living.

Western Contact According to one story, when early explorers first reached Yap the Yapese paddled out to meet them. The explorers pointed and asked the name of the island. The Yapese, with their backs to the shore, misunderstood the point and holding up their paddles they replied *yap* – which was their word for paddle. Ever since, the islands that the natives call *Wa'ab* have been known to those outside its shores as Yap.

The first contact with westerners was in 1526 when the Portuguese explorer Dioga da Rocha landed on Ulithi. The islanders were 'without malice, fear or cautiousness' and da Rocha and his crew remained on the island for four months. Over the next 300 years the rest of Yap's islands were discovered and added to the charts.

Early attempts to settle Yap however, were half-hearted at best. In 1731 a Spanish mission was established on Ulithi but when a supply ship returned a year later they found that the 13 people of the colony had been killed by the natives.

Apparently Europeans got the hint because for the next 100 years visits to Yap were few and far between. What little contact there was took place mainly with British merchants. Strangely however, Dumont d'Urville, the only European known to have visited the main Yap islands in the early 1800s, found a people who spoke enough Spanish to request cigars and brandy. It's largely thought their knowledge of Spanish was the result of their own inter-island commerce with places as distant as the Marianas.

In the 1830s two Spanish ships came to gather beche-de-mer in Yap but at some point during the operation the crews were attacked and brutally murdered. In 1843 the English captain Andrew Cheyne made a similar attempt for a cargo of beche-de-mer. The chiefs seemed cooperative at first, but a brush with would-be assassins and contact with a survivor of the Spanish massacre convinced Cheyne to drop the venture before suffering a similar fate. It wasn't until the 1860s that regular trade with the west was gradually established. The Germans opened the first permanent trading station in 1869.

O'Keefe David O'Keefe, a shipwrecked Irish-American, washed ashore in 1871. He was to spend the next 30 years of his life with the Yapese who nursed him back to health. Where Germans had failed in

ISLAND OF STONE MONEY

getting the Yapese to produce copra in quantity, O'Keefe saw an opportunity to succeed.

He had noted that the colourful cloth and trinkets that traders used to entice other islanders raised little curiosity among the Yapese, who stubbornly preferred traditional hibiscus clothing and grass skirts. Realising that the enormous stone money the Yapese quarried in distant Palau offered more leverage as a medium of exchange, O'Keefe decided to use his ship to develop the transporting of stone money into a trade. Yapese chiefs paid for the stone money with copra and O'Keefe soon came to dominate the copra trade in Yap. O'Keefe's Irish temper and penchant for feuding with colonial administrators made him legendary among the Yapese.

The Spanish & German Periods Although Spain had long held claim to Yap, it wasn't until the Germans attempted to annex the islands in 1885 that the Spanish established a permanent garrison. Formal colonial occupation of Yap was to continue for the next 100 years.

In 1899, in the aftermath of the Spanish-American War, Spain sold Yap to Germany whose interest in the islands was primarily commercial. Concerned about the shortage of labourers to work their plantations and mines, they developed health and sanitation services in hopes of stemming the rapid depopulation. The Germans were the first to use forced Yapese labour, both in Yap and in the phosphate mines on Angaur in Palau.

The Japanese Period The Japanese took over in 1914 when the outbreak of WW I forced the Germans to withdraw.

Concern over Yap's transpacific cable station, on line between the US and Shanghai, led the US to demand access to Yap as a precondition to recognising Japan's League of Nations mandate over Micronesia. The two countries signed such a treaty in 1921.

The Japanese then began to arrive in Yap and set up stores, farms and sea-based industries. Their numbers were not as great as in other parts of Micronesia but they nonetheless came to vastly outnumber the dwindling Yapese population.

As WW II approached, the Yapese were forced to build airfields and military fortifications. As punishment for non-cooperation the Japanese would smash pieces of Yap's highly valued stone money, sometimes using the broken pieces as road fill.

American forces decided not to invade Yap Proper, although it was bombed during US air raids, but Ulithi Atoll was captured and developed into a major Allied support base in 1944.

Government

Yap's state constitution establishes two councils of traditional leaders. The Council of Pilung has chiefs from Yap Proper and the Council of Tamol has chiefs from the outer islands. If the governor is from Yap Proper, then the lieutenant governor must be from the outer islands, and vice versa.

The chiefs pretty much decide who runs and who wins. Although the Yapese can vote for whomever they like for political office, people still generally follow the advice and leadership of their chiefs. The councils have the right to veto any legislation that affects traditional customs.

Known for his poetry and wit, Yap's first governor, John Mangefel, was progressive yet culturally conservative. He was adamant that Yap retain its traditions and reject inappropriate western values. His own official attire was zories (thongs), short pants and an unbuttoned shirt and one of his more colourful actions was an attempt to pass legislation that would make wearing ties illegal.

Economy

Yap's moneyed economy is reliant upon US funding. Government jobs account for 70% of Yap's 1300 wage earners.

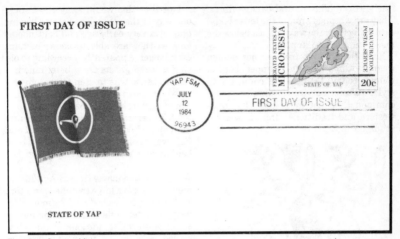

FIRST DAY OF ISSUE

STATE OF YAP

FEDERATED STATES OF MICRONESIA

STATE OF YAP 20c

INAUGURATION POSTAL SERVICE

YAP FSM
JULY
12
1984
96943

FIRST DAY OF ISSUE

First Day Cover – Yap

Most people of working age maintain traditional roles in the village subsistence economy. The Yapese grow taro, yams, sweet potatoes, bananas, Polynesian chestnuts, breadfruit, tapioca, papaya and coconuts. They are skilled fishermen, using hook and line, nets, spears and traps.

Most of Yap's locally produced income comes from the export of copra, trochus and handicrafts. Tourism is of minor importance. In 1984, there were only 868 tourists.

People

The physical characteristics of the Yapese are of purely western Pacific origin. There are traits that indicate Philippine, Palauan and Indonesian influences. There was little intermarriage with Europeans or Japanese, which makes the Yapese unique among Micronesians.

Attempts by the Japanese to assimilate the Micronesian peoples by offering privileges to the offspring of mixed Japanese-Micronesian parents had no impact on the Yapese. They continued to marry traditionally in accordance with their caste system and foreigners remained excluded.

For reasons still unknown, the Yapese population dropped by half under the Japanese administration. The population in 1945 was only 2582. With the birth rate among the world's lowest there was serious concern that the Yapese were on the verge of extinction.

The Americans reacted by sending medical teams and a slew of anthropologists. Fortunately the latter needn't have made such haste, for the population slowly edged upwards and the 1980 census recorded a population of 10,284.

Culture

The Yapese, more than any other Micronesian peoples, have been reluctant to adopt western ways. Despite four colonial administrations, their culture remains largely undiluted by outside influences and they still proudly retain their own customs and traditions.

Traditional Dress The loincloth worn by men and boys is called a *thu* and is usually of bright, red or blue cotton cloth.

Women have two kinds of traditional dress – grass skirts or *lava-lavas*. The latter are wide strips of cloth made from finely woven hibiscus and banana fibres. They are wrapped around the lower body, extending from the waist to just below the knee, and are tied in place.

Traditionally, neither men nor women wear clothing on their upper bodies, though today T-shirts are coming into style. Western-style clothing is more common than not in Colonia, but both western and traditional dress is seen all around Yap.

Betel Nut Everyone, but everyone chews *buw*, or betel nut. Small stores do a good business selling zip-lock sandwich bags of betel nuts and pepper leaves for about $1.25 for 'a plastic'. Yapese betel nut is sold to outgoing passengers at the airport, packed in gift boxes made from Budweiser cases. If you're flying to Palau it's the equivalent of the duty-free bottle of Johnny Walker – the perfect gift for the betel nut connoisseur.

Betel nut is split open while green, sprinkled with dry lime made from coral, wrapped in pepper leaves and chewed. It produces a mild high that lasts about 10 minutes. Sometimes tobacco, or tobacco soaked in vodka, is added.

Betel nut turns the saliva bright red and stains the teeth red and then black. It's the lime that stimulates the flow of saliva. Once called 'a dentist's nightmare' by westerners, it's been discovered that chewing betel nut may actually help prevent cavities.

Not that this would sway the Yapese one way or the other. They start chewing *buw* at a very early age and continue as long as they are able to chew; perhaps even longer. Apparently, according to old stories, even ghosts chew betel nut. If a sailing canoe was to stop for no obvious reason in the middle of a lagoon the sailor would prepare a special betel nut mixture, wrap it in extra leaves and tie it up tightly with many knots, throw it overboard and sail away easily while the ghost who'd been holding his canoe was untying the knots.

Traditional Community Houses A *faluw*, or men's house, is a large thatched structure with a sharply pitched roof, supported by heavy wooden pillars and resting atop a stone platform. Traditionally the faluw served as a school for young boys, as quarters for bachelors and as a meeting place for the village leaders.

Pebai are community meeting houses. They often look much like men's houses, only larger with open-air sides. Pebai are mostly built inland whereas faluw are usually by the water.

Once common throughout Yap, women's houses or *dapal* are now only found on the outer islands. When a girl reached puberty she was ushered off to a dapal for initiation and all women in the village went to women's houses to wait out their menstrual periods, using the time to weave, bathe and relax.

Women's Roles Traditionally women have had subservient roles in Yapese society. They did the cooking and tended the fields, harvesting from one plot for male family members and from another for the females. The food then had to be prepared in separate pots over separate fires. Not only could men and women not eat together but neither could members of different castes share the same food or eat together.

Although such restrictions are not so strictly adhered to today, this still may have some bearing on why there are so few restaurants in Yap.

Language

The native languages are Yapese, Ulithian, Woleaian and Satawalese. The last three are the languages of outer islanders.

In Yapese, 'hello' is *mogethin*, 'excuse me' is *siro*, 'thank you' is *kam magar* and 'good-bye' is *kafel*.

Holidays & Special Events

Mitmits are Yap's big traditional celebrations. One village gives a mitmit for another village in return for the one they received years before. It's an all-out feast accompanied by gift-giving and traditional singing and dancing. The completion of a major village project such as a new community house is also a time for major festivities.

Sporting events, ceremonial dancing and feasts take place on Yap Day on 1 March and United Nations Day on 24 October.

High school graduations are important events and Yap also recognises US public holidays, FSM Constitution Day on 10 May and Micronesian Day on 12 July.

Exploring Yap

Exploring Yap requires a grasp of Yapese etiquette. Once you step off the road anywhere in Yap, you're on private property. Even some of the stone pathways through villages are private and walking along them is somewhat similar to cutting across someone's backyard. Some villages have areas that women are not allowed to enter.

The official line is that you need to get permission and sometimes a guide to visit each beach, pebai or village. Unofficially the word is that because you're a foreigner and don't know the rules, the Yapese will understand as long as you're considerate and don't overstep the bounds.

The catch-22 is that if you have a guide with you, there are certain things you won't be able to see or do, because the guide knows precisely where he is and isn't allowed to take you.

One couple said they'd missed out on lots of photographs because the guide they'd gone out with said he'd get into trouble if they took certain pictures. In Yap this is understandable with photos of people, but he also prevented them from taking more routine photos, including a landscape view because there was a grass shack in the foreground that he said was owned by 'bad people'.

In reality it's not that difficult to go off on your own, asking people along the way for directions and permission when appropriate. Smiles go a long way in Yap. In a village you should greet everyone you see so it doesn't look as if you're sneaking around. Be prepared to back off when it's obvious you're intruding, and always ask before snapping someone's picture.

To the Yapese, not asking permission is an insult. But they're a very generous people and if you do ask, they'll probably let you go nearly anywhere and see almost anything you want.

YAP PROPER

The major islands of Yap, Map and Tamil-Gagil are all connected by bridges and easily explored. Rumung is separated from the rest of Yap Proper by Yinbinaew Passage and can only be reached by boat. Yap Proper has 10 municipalities with more than 100 villages.

The landscape of the main islands is mainly rolling hills with a green cover of grass interspersed with sparse pandanus and palm trees. In the south-west, the lowlands have thick growth and a marshlike jungle floor.

The most interesting sights by far are not WW II relics or scenic views, but the glimpses into Yapese culture.

The sparsely populated villages outside the capital of Colonia are quiet, peaceful and tidy. On weekdays, when the children are at school and adults are off fishing or at work either in Colonia or in their taro patches, the villages can look semideserted. In a way, it's not a bad time to explore. You'll still see some people, but with fewer folks around it's that many fewer whose permission you need seek out.

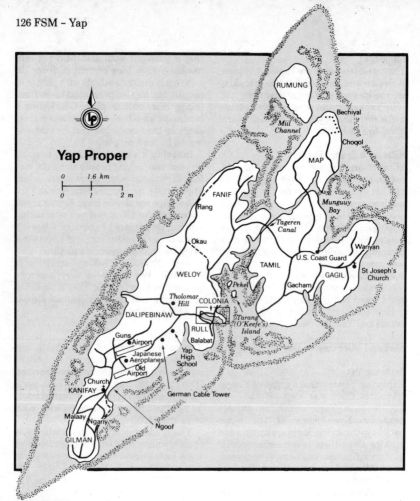

Yap Proper

0   1.6 km

0   1   2 m

RUMUNG

Bechiyal

Miil Channel

Choqol

MAP

FANIF

Rang

Munguuy Bay

Tageren Canal

Okau

Wanyan

U.S. Coast Guard

St Joseph's Church

WELOY

TAMIL

GAGIL

Pekel

Gacham

Tholomar Hill

COLONIA

DALIPEBINAW

Tarang (O'Keefe's) Island

RULL

Guns

Airport

Balabat

Japanese Aeroplanes

Yap High School

Old Airport

Church

KANIFAY

German Cable Tower

Malaay

Ngariy

Ngoof

GILMAN

YAP ISLAND
Colonia

Colonia is the state capital, the business and administrative centre and the only part of Yap that is the least bit modern. Even so the 'town' of Colonia, which the locals call Donguch, would be classed as a village almost anywhere else.

Colonia is built around Chamorro Bay, there are water views everywhere and two picturesque bridges over the bay.

The Yap Cooperative Association (YCA), a jumbled department store and snack shop, is sort of the town centre where Yapese gather to sit and chat.

The government administration building, previously the old hospital, is on the site of the old Spanish fort of which only remnants of a wall and the foundations remain. The first Spanish priest was headquartered at the site of St Mary's Catholic Church on the north side of the bay.

The 482-foot (144-metre) Medeqdeq Hill has a panoramic view of Colonia, the harbour and Yap's east coast. The top of the hill is about ¾ of a mile up from

Colonia on the road past the Catholic church. This is one of the few developed hiking opportunities in Yap.

There's a stone footpath just north of central Colonia. It starts just past the Catholic church, on the right side, and comes out between the Weloy Municipal Office and Ocean View Enterprises.

Information
The Tourist Office (tel 2184) has some basic maps and brochures and is the first place to contact if you're hoping to get to any out-of-the-way places.

The Land Management office sells USGS wall maps of Yap, the Trust Territory and Guam for $3 each and mailing tubes for $2. Ask for Harold.

The Bank of Hawaii in Colonia is Yap's only bank. It's open from 9.30 am to 2.30 pm Monday to Thursday and to 5 pm on Fridays.

Yap's only post office is in the western part of central Colonia. All mail should be addressed to Colonia, Yap, FSM 96943.

Long distance phone calls can be made from hotels or from the COMSAT station (open 24 hours) near the old airport.

There's a small modern hospital (tel 3444) north of Colonia. Yap has one radio station and one TV station.

Madrich Village
Outer islanders visiting Colonia usually stay in Madrich and live in the section of the village designated for their atoll. Most people in Madrich speak the Ulithian language and wear traditional dress. You can tell the outer island women by their lava-lavas because the only kind they wear have black and white stripes.

Madrich is on a point of land a ¼ of a mile south of central Colonia along the shore road. It was once the site of a Spanish trading station and is named after Madrid.

Rull Municipality
There are some fine stone money banks and a traditional faluw near Balabat Village in

Rull, just ½ a mile south of Colonia past Madrich along the coastal road.

German Cable Station
The paved road west of Colonia, heading towards the airport, passes the town's water reservoir on the right before a dirt road to the left leads up to Yap Proper's only high school.

Opposite the school's parking lot are the graffiti-decorated remains of the German communications station, which in 1905 completed a link to Shanghai through Guam and the Philippines via an undersea cable system.

Shelling from a British warship destroyed the station's 200-foot (60-metre) steel radio tower in August 1914, breaking Germany's communications link to its Pacific territories and marking the start of WW I activity in Micronesia.

Japanese Guns
The base camp of the Seabees, the US Navy's Construction Battalion established to build airstrips, is on the left just past the high school. The entrance to the new airport is about a mile farther down on the right.

If you want to see two Japanese WW II guns take the first right past the airport, drive around the end of the runway and turn right on the access road that skirts the airport's north side.

The guns, on the hill behind the airport fence, are visible from the road. You can get over the barbed wire fence by using the rungs of the nearest gun as steps. Continue up the hill to the right a short distance to the second and better-preserved gun. The tip of its barrel exploded open, presumably when it back-fired.

Japanese Zeros
The remains of a couple of Japanese Zero planes are easily visible behind the COMSAT and weather stations between the old and new airport runways. To get there, take the road to the left past the entrance to the new airport. The planes

were destroyed on the ground by US aerial bombings during WW II.

The road continues down to the old 5000-foot (1500-metre) airstrip built by the Japanese. There's no sign of the 727 that landed short of the runway in 1980, lost a wheel and skidded off into the brush. The plane caught fire but there were no fatalities. The airstrip is still used occasionally by PMA.

You can turn right, onto the runway to get back to the main road to Gilman.

Southern Tip of Yap

South of the old airport is the village of Ngoof with the St Ignatius of Loyola church on the right. About ½ a mile beyond that there's a turn-off to the left which takes you onto the coastal road south to Ngariy.

On the left side of the road in the village of Ngariy there's a faluw, pebai and a couple of *wunbey*, or meeting platforms. There in the open air the elder men of the village have their meetings, sitting against the stone backrests. A low platform in the centre is for holding food and betel nut which young men sitting around on the edges serve to the elders.

Gilman, at the southernmost tip of the island, used to boast a good beach but no longer – all the sand was removed for a landfill project.

The road going up the west side skirts the mangrove-studded coast where you can sometimes see edible mangrove crabs and large monitor lizards. The lizards, often several feet long, were introduced onto Yap and Ulithi by the Japanese to control the rat population and as a food source.

At Malaay village an extensive moss-covered Japanese stone wall, part of WW II defence fortifications, runs along the right side of the road.

Okau Village

The village of Okau in Weloy has one of Yap's best meeting houses and stone money banks at the end of a very pleasant walk down a stone footpath.

To get there from Colonia you take the road west, as if heading towards the airport, but instead of turning left with the main paved road take the right fork just after Clara's Hillside Restaurant. There are good views from Tholomar Hill along the way. When the road forks again, keep to the right.

The stone pathway is approximately three miles from Clara's and starts just before a small house on the right side of the road. It's easy to find as the road curves and goes over a bridge just beyond this point.

One section of the path meanders alongside taro patches, another part is lined with hibiscus and lush variegated plants and mosses grow in the cracks between the stones. It's very attractive and very peaceful, almost like walking through a Zen garden.

The large pebai, about 10 minutes down the pathway, is built on a raised stone platform. The supports are made of mahogany, the inside floor planks of betel nut and the roof is nipa palm lashed onto bamboo.

Yap's most valuable stone money is generally thickest in the middle and thinner at the edges, with circular gouge markings across the face. You can see this type of money in front of the pebai to the left.

Rang Beach

Rang Beach is a nice brown sand beach north of Okau. Swimming might be good at high tide, but at low tide it's all sea grass and sand flats. To get there continue on the main road about two miles past the stone pathway. The chief's house is on the left after a bamboo and thatch school bus shelter. Rang Beach is not far beyond this but it's proper to stop and ask the chief's permission to continue.

On the right, past the chief's house and immediately before going over a bridge, there's a small unmarked store at the end of a driveway where you can get soda or coconuts.

TAMIL-GAGIL ISLAND

Tamil-Gagil was once connected to Yap Island at the very upper end of Tamil Harbor by mangrove-covered swampland. During the German occupation the shallow Tageren Canal was dug to allow boat passage to Map and Rumung from Colonia. The US Coast Guard Loran Station and its 1000-foot (300-metre) tower are two miles east of the Tageren Canal but the station is being phased-out.

The centre of Yapese wisdom and the spot where Yap is said to have been formed, is in the middle of Tamil-Gagil at a sacred place called *Gacham*.

The largest piece of stone money is on the island of Rumung, but since the people of Rumung have decided they're not ready for foreign visitors, you may have to settle for Tamil-Gagil's No 2. The second largest piece of stone money is in the centre of Wanyan Village, past St Joseph's Catholic Church, where two huge rai flank a statue of the Virgin Mary. At the end of the road is a beach that's more or less public.

The Catholic church itself is interesting for the mural painted above its door showing Yapese men presenting gifts of stone money, lava-lavas, model houses, food and storyboards.

MAP ISLAND

The Map (pronounced 'mop') road is high enough in places to offer views of the ocean, channels and surrounding terrain. From two of the hills, Qapirgog and Tabiigaaw, you can see Miil Channel to the west and Munguuy Bay to the southeast. The hills are ½ a mile and 1¼ miles respectively from the Tamil-Map Bridge.

From Bechiyal Village, on the northern tip of Map, there's a pleasant 20-minute walk to a traditional faluw and pebai. The people of Map, being relatively receptive to visitors, decided a few years back to promote Bechiyal. Although listed as a cultural centre on tourist maps, the development never really took off, so it's still just a peaceful village on a nice beach.

If you've hired a car you can park it at the road's end, pulling off to the right, and cross the log bridge into the village on foot. The chief lives in the first house on the left and it's proper etiquette to ask his permission to continue. There's one main path through the village, so you won't get lost.

Diving & Swimming

There aren't many good beaches in Yap and even fewer open to use by non-villagers. The best beach is probably on the north-east coast of Map between Choqol Village and the Bechiyal men's house.

In Yap, although bare breasts are the norm, it's considered vulgar for women to show their thighs. Women may wear a swimsuit in the water but should wear a skirt on the beach.

Yap's waters are known for their sea grass meadows and there are also some good coral formations and a couple of shipwrecks not far offshore.

There are no dive shops in Yap. Diving services are limited but can be arranged through the hotels, the tourist office or the Yap Fishing Authority (tel 2185). With advance arrangements you should be able to get filled tanks, but you'll have to bring all other equipment.

Places To Stay

There are only two hotels in Yap Proper and both are in Colonia. Though seldom full, it's still advisable to make reservations in advance, since together they provide only 26 rooms. Yap has a 10% hotel tax.

The *Rai View Hotel* (tel 2279; Box 130) is the cheapest and costs $20/$27 singles/doubles with private bathroom or $23 a double with shared bathroom. It has 10 very basic rooms with air-con and TV.

The *ESA Hotel* (tel 2139; Box 141), run by a Palauan family, overlooks Chamorro Bay and is a little nicer than the Rai View. It costs $25 a single or $35 a double and has 16 clean, air-con rooms with private bathrooms. There's also an open-air lounge with TV.

Both hotels send minibuses to meet Air

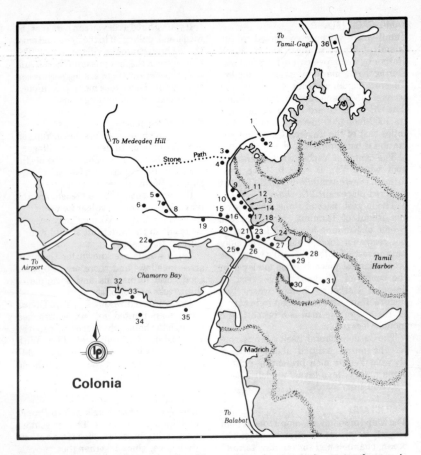

To Tamil-Gagil

36

To Medeqdeq Hill

Stone Path

1
2

3
4

9 11
5   10   12
6   7   13
8   15   14
19   16   17 18
20 21 23 24
22   27
25 26 28
29
30 31

To Airport

Chamorro Bay   Tamil Harbor

32
33
34   35

Madrich

Colonia

To Balabat

Mike flights and airport transfers cost $5 return.

The Protestant Mission (Yap Evangelical Church), opposite the ESA Hotel, has in the past provided accommodation in their guest room, for $5 or so, to visitors stranded when the hotels were full. The guest room is often occupied by church guests, however, and should not be counted on.

Guest Houses Some Yapese families have agreed to take travellers into their homes. This is arranged through the tourist office

and you have to write a month or so in advance to let them know when you're coming, how long you'd like to stay with a family and maybe a little about yourself.

You then contact the tourist office when you arrive, but plan to stay in a hotel for one or two nights first. The office will arrange for you to visit a few homes so you and the families can check each other out. The rates are negotiable, and the tourist office doesn't charge for the service.

This is a new idea in Yap and these are not established guest houses by any means, so this could be a terrific opportunity to

1	Family Chain Store
2	Island Flavor
3	Ocean View Enterprises
4	Weloy Municipal Office
5	Catholic Elementary School (St Mary's)
6	Museum (closed)
7	Catholic Church
8	Catholic Mission
9	Travel Agency
10	Yap Women's Association Handicraft Shop
11	Laundromat
12	Playground
13	Coconut Oil Soap Factory
14	Bambu Market
15	Land Management Office
16	Peace Corps
17	Fishing Authority
18	Petrol Station
19	Rai View Hotel & Restaurant
20	Police Station
21	Courthouse
22	Post Office
23	Laura's Store
24	Yap Co-Operative Association (YCA)
25	Bank of Hawaii
26	Legal Services
27	Air Micronesia
28	Commercial Dock/Waab Transportation
29	Government & Tourist Offices/Old Spanish Fort
30	Community Center
31	Legislature
32	ESA Hotel
33	Protestant Youth Center
34	Protestant Mission (Yap Evangelical Church)
35	Blue Lagoon Store
36	Hospital

experience Yapese home life while possibly saving a little on hotels.

Camping Camping is not recommended in Yap as every speck of land is privately owned. If you insist on communing with nature, however, you can probably get permission from a landowner, or the tourist office can help if you aren't successful on your own.

People for the most part think camping is a bit odd and may insist you pitch your tent in their backyard where they can keep an eye on you. They'll need to explain it all to the neighbours and will most probably breathe a sigh of relief once you've gone.

Places To Eat

Bambu Market sells passion fruit, bananas, papayas and other locally-grown fruits and vegetables in the front part of the store. They sometimes have *tuba* (coconut liquor) or coconut molasses. Refrigerated drinking coconuts cost 25 cents.

Lunch (only) is served on picnic tables at the rear of the Bambu Market, where breezes blow across from the bay. There are several different choices on the menu each day. Usual dishes are fried fish or chicken with taro for about $2.50 and ramen for $1.25, though sometimes they have a more exotic menu like trochus soup or banana pizza!

The main difference between the two hotel restaurants seems to be that people who want to either drink or avoid air-con go to the *Rai View*, while those who want air-con or don't need a bar go to the *ESA Restaurant*.

The Rai View has a breakfast special for $3, a lunch special for $4 and a dinner special for $5. Cheeseburgers cost $1.75, happy hour beer is 85 cents and cold coconuts served with a straw are 35 cents. The ESA has breakfast and lunch from $3.50 and dinner from $5.95, as well as a la carte items including reasonably priced sandwiches and ramen.

The *Protestant Youth Center* next to the ESA Hotel sells inexpensive sandwiches, noodles and soft drinks. It's open from 7.30 am to 4.30 pm Monday to Friday. The YCA also has a snack shop with cheap sandwiches, light lunches, hamburgers and home-baked goods.

Colonia's tap water is not safe to drink.

Entertainment

Island Flavor, at the rear of the Family

Chain Store, was the only club open on our last visit. On weekends live bands play popular American tunes with Yapese lyrics. The Seabees Camp shows free movies nightly except Thursdays.

Things To Buy
Yap has some of the finest handicrafts in Micronesia. The best place to go is the Yap Women's Association (YWA) handicraft shop, near Bambu Market. Woven lava-lavas (from about $15) are high quality and make good wall hangings and table mats. Other interesting crafts are betel nut pouches, bamboo combs, wood carvings and grass skirts.

The YCA has T-shirts and other stores sometimes carry lava-lavas and crafts.

The Yapese produce two kinds of soap using coconut oil, one for laundry and one for bathing. They overdose a little on the perfume in the bath soap – just one bar tucked inside your baggage will overwhelm even the rankest odours – but it does have a nifty 'Island of Stone Money' wrapper that makes it a good souvenir.

The Yap Institute of Natural Science (tel 3115; Box 215) puts out an interesting calendar and almanac with drawings and details of Yapese customs, tide charts, natural history and trivia. It's different each year and is readily available in Colonia for about $3 or you buy one by mail for $5 (including postage). The institute, a non-profit group 'engaged in the collection of ethnobiological knowledge, adaptive technology and ecodevelopment' also designs T-shirts with pictures of Yap's birds. These are sold around town.

Getting There
Air Mike is the only airline which flies to Yap. The full fare between Guam and Yap is $173. On Thursdays the flights are $100 either way.

The one-way fare between Palau and Yap is $103 but the one-way Guam-Palau fare for $251 allows a stop in Yap. The Thursday flight from Yap to Koror (but not vice versa) costs just $50.

Yap's immigration officials, unlike in some of the other FSM states, check for onward tickets. The number of days you tell them you're staying is what they stamp into your passport under 'period of permitted stay'. The airport is 2½ miles from town.

Getting Around
There are a few paved roads around Colonia, which is small enough to walk around, and most of the island's red dirt roads are in very good condition – by Micronesian standards.

Taxi Taxis are a new business in Yap. You'll probably have to negotiate with the driver but check with the hotels to see if any routes now have established rates.

Hitching There isn't enough traffic outside of town to really depend on hitching, though if you're walking along the road you might get offered a ride. Sticking out a thumb is not a custom here.

Car Rentals Pick-up trucks and sedans rent through the hotels for $25 to $30 per day.

Tours The ESA Hotel has bus or car tours for $15 per person if there are two or more people. They can provide a boat with operator for a full-day for $75 to $90.

The Rai View has bus tours for $16 to $25, depending on the number of people, and their boat tours cost from $20 to $45.

THE OUTER ISLANDS
The outer islands are made up of 10 atolls and five single islands. Of the 15 outer island groups, 11 are populated. Ulithi, the only one with an airstrip, is the largest and has the most people. Woleai is a very close second.

Ulithi and Woleai have about 750 people each, Satawal and Ifaluk have 400 each, Lamotrek and Fais have 250 each, Faraulep and Eauripik about 150 each and Elalu, Ngulu and Sorol have fewer than 60 people. Gaferut, West Fayu,

Pikelot and Olimarao are generally uninhabited.

Yap's outer islanders are some of the most isolated people on earth. Little is known of their origins although it's believed that their islands were settled quite independently of Yap Proper.

Yap's easternmost islanders and Truk's south-west outer islanders have more linguistic, physical and cultural similarities with each other than with either of their district centres.

Most outer islanders live the same way they have for centuries though some produce copra which they load onto the field trip ship when it stops by. Uninhabited islands are visited in outrigger canoes to gather turtles, turtle eggs and coconuts. On Lamotrek, for instance, turtle meat is the staple food between April and August.

Some of the smaller atolls have so little land that every spare bit is used for growing crops. During severe dry spells some islanders are forced to rely solely on drinking coconuts when they run out of catchment water.

ULITHI ATOLL

Ulithi Atoll, 100 miles (161 km) north-east of Yap, has 49 islands with a total land mass of 1.79 square miles (4.5 square km). Its lagoon is the world's fourth largest.

Traditional Ulithi, perched quietly on the outskirts of the Pacific, seems about as distant as one can get from 20th century influences. Only the scattering of rusting Quonset huts offer any evidence to the contrary.

The Japanese came in numbers that must have seemed enormous to the Ulithians, until the US moved in with temporary population densities rivaling major cities.

The Japanese had established a seaplane and naval base as well as a radio and weather station on Ulithi. When the Americans got close, the Japanese evacuated to Yap Proper taking most of the able-bodied Ulithians along with them.

In September 1944 the Americans landed on Ulithi unopposed. They quickly constructed an airstrip on Falalop Island and a 100-bed hospital and a recreation centre on Mogmog Island. The recreation centre eventually entertained as many as 20,000 soldiers a day.

Strategically located, Ulithi served as a major anchorage and supply and repair base for the final six months of the war. Its extensive lagoon held 617 naval vessels prior to the Okinawa invasion.

Somehow folks on Ulithi survived these brief encounters with uninvited visitors from the 'civilised' world. These days if you want to visit the atoll you have to obtain an invitation.

Other Outer Islands

Fais is a single island of raised limestone with a partial fringing reef. With an elevation of 60 feet (18 metres), it's the highest of Yap's outer islands and was once known for its agricultural production and phosphate mining.

Ifaluk has long white sandy beaches, lots of coconut palms and a lagoon in a near-perfect circle. There's a taboo area in the village where no one may enter and the chief reportedly won't allow motorboats into the lagoon.

Satawal is home to some of the world's most famous traditional navigators who still sail vast expanses of ocean in outrigger canoes without charts or compass.

Woleai is the population centre of the eastern outer islands and is slated to eventually become the next atoll to receive air service from PMA. It has remains of Japanese fortifications.

Permission & Accommodation

There's concern that the more isolated outer islands may be very vulnerable, should the 20th century suddenly appear upon their shores clad in a bikini and grasping a video camera. It's largely because of this that visitors are screened and sometimes discouraged.

In a recent government survey, outer islanders were adamant that visitors come only with prior permission and 99% thought visitors should be accompanied by a Yapese guide. The saving grace of all this is that 96% said they would like to share their knowledge of Yap's traditional culture and their present lifestyle with outsiders.

You can usually get off the field trip ship at each island to have a look around, but to stay longer you should get permission from the island chief through the governor's office in Colonia.

None of the outer islands have hotels. If you do get permission to visit, you'll probably end up staying at a men's house, with a family or camping. Where you stay will be the chief's decision. Gifts of coffee, bread or other food items unobtainable on the islands are welcome.

As far as Ulithi goes, it's not necessarily hard to get permission to visit, but it usually can't be done before arrival in Yap. They simply decide on the spur of the moment if they want to let you go. Usually the people are very friendly but they have never made provisions to accept tourists. They may charge you $50 a night just to use the beach and you'll have to take all your own food and water. If you make a good impression though you might fare better than that!

Getting There

Pacific Missionary Aviation (tel 2278; Box 460) flies an eight-passenger plane to Ulithi. Flights depart Colonia at 9 am on Mondays, Wednesdays and Fridays, and return from Ulithi at 10.30 am. If there are enough passengers, PMA might have two flights a day or add one on the off-days. The one-way fare is $40.

Field Trip Ship The WAAB Transportation Company (tel 2301/2302; Box 177) runs the field trip ship *Micro Spirit* between Yap Proper and all the populated outer islands. The full trip takes two weeks or more.

The deck fare costs three cents per mile and the cabin fare is 15 cents per mile. One-way deck fare from Yap is $3.10 to Ulithi and $10.95 to Woleai. It's $3 for breakfast, $4 for lunch and $4.50 for dinner but the food doesn't have the best reputation.

You can get a schedule from the company, and they're good about answering inquiries by mail, but as with most Micronesian ships it runs when the captain and crew are ready to go.

Resisting the Multinationals

Yap doesn't have, nor does it want, a Japanese resort hotel.

In an attempt to slip in the back door, Japan's multinational Nanyo Boeki Kaisha (NBK) began operations on the island of Map calling itself Yap Nature Life Garden Incorporated. They developed slowly, with the first Japanese guests staying in tents. Their long-range plans called for a resort development of 47 air-conditioned buildings, a dredging of the inner reef and a lengthy pier to the outer reef.

When the plans became known the chiefs of Map drew up a petition which read in part:

'Whereas we love our lands and the ways in which we live together there in peace, and yet live humbly and still cherish them above all other ways, and are not discontent to be the children of our fathers, it has become apparent to us that we have been persuaded to subscribe to processes that will quickly extinguish all that we hold dear.

'By . . . obscuring the nature and the extent of its ambitions and the inevitable and irreversible injury that these will cause to our customs and our pride, the company has far exceeded all pretense to legality and welcome to our land. It plans to make a dead sea of our lagoon, and thus a dead place of our shores.

'We, men and women on Map of majority age, now urgently and passionately unite to repudiate and refuse all association with that company and to ask the help of the people, customary leaders and district officers of Yap . . . in ridding us of this invasion and freeing us, that we do not become servants in our own land.'

The chiefs of Map went on to adopt a resolution stating:

'We, *pilungs* and *langanpagels*, elders and

elected officers, Chiefs in Council of and on behalf of all people of the Eighteen Villages and Fiefs of the Island of Map . . . declare our love of this place and of the ways passed down to us by the generations. We have inherited from our fathers a land that is lovely and provides for us with the fruits of the earth and of the sea. We are few in number but have a brave history and are strong in our resolve to preserve these things that are sweet to us.'

With a whole island against them the Nanyo Boeki Kaisha packed up and headed home. Ironically it wasn't the first time. The NBK, or South Seas Trading Company, spearheaded the commercial and economic exploitation of Micronesia during the Japanese era.

The Republic of Palau

Palau features Micronesia's richest flora and fauna, both on land and underwater. The islands are inhabited by exotic birds, crocodiles live in the mangrove swamps and orchids grow freely in people's yards.

Palau's waters contain an incredible spectrum of coral, fish and other marine life, including giant clams that weigh up to 1000 pounds (450 kg) and many rare sea creatures found in few other places.

The scenic Rock Islands have some of Micronesia's finest snorkelling and diving around their shores, and beyond them lie the sleepy southern islands of Peleliu and Angaur with their own special appeal to independent travellers.

The native name for the region is Belau but the new nation is called the Republic of Palau, and of all the political entities to come out of the Trust Territory it has the smallest population. Koror has the bulk of Palau's 14,000 people and by Micronesian standards it's a busy town.

Palau, however, is the one emerging nation that has not yet emerged. Until critical conflicts are resolved concerning Palau's anti-nuclear constitution and its pro-nuclear compact with the US, Palau remains the sole district still under Trust Territory administration.

Geography

The tightly clustered Palau archipelago consists of the high islands of Babeldaob, Koror, Peleliu and Angaur; the low coral atoll of Kayangel; and the Rock Islands, of which there are more than 200. The islands run roughly from north to south, covering about 125 miles (201 km). Except for Kayangel in the north and Angaur in the south all islands in the Palau group are inside a single barrier reef.

The state boundaries also encompass five other small islands, the isolated Sonsorol, Pulo Anna, Tobi, Merir and Helen. They are spread out south-west from the main Palau Islands almost as far as Indonesia.

Babeldaob, the largest island in Micronesia after Guam, is 27 miles long (43 km) and has a land area of 153 square miles (392 square km). All other Palauan islands together total 37 square miles (95 square km).

Palau is the westernmost part of Micronesia and is only 470 miles (757 km) east of the Philippines. It is part of the western Carolines.

Climate

In Koror, the average daily high is 87°F and the average daily low 75°F. The average annual rainfall is 147 inches (373 cm). February and March are the driest months, with about eight inches (20 cm) each; and from June to August is the wettest period with about 15 inches (38 cm) monthly. June is a month for thunderstorms which have been known to drop as much as an inch of rain in 15 minutes.

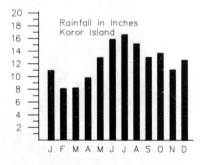

History

Carbon dating has established that the Rock Islands were settled around 1000 BC.

Traditionally the women of Palau tended the taro swamps and the men fished the reef and harvested breadfruit and betel nut. With a fairly vast land area

136

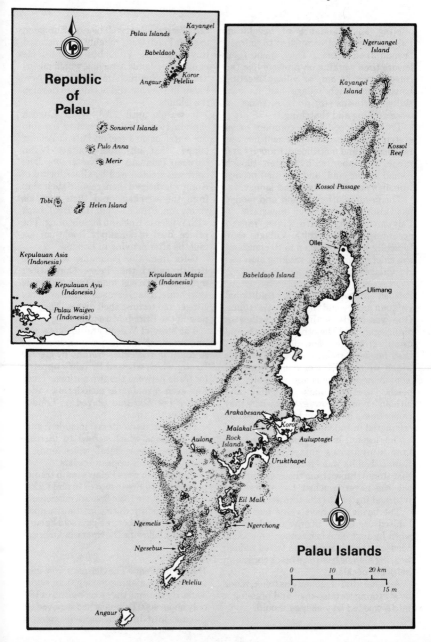

offering an abundance of vegetation Palauans were not compelled to journey beyond their shores. They spent their leisure time working on projects like the construction of *bai*, or village meeting houses, and each village had its own skilled artisans to do the tasks of woodworking and thatching.

They developed fairly complex social systems and the Palauan culture was matriarchal and matrilineal. Property and money was inherited by women, though owned by the clan, and the men needed women's permission to spend money.

The accumulation of land and money has always been very important in Palauan society, with clans ranked according to their wealth. Villages were typically settled by seven to 10 clans and the chief of the highest-ranking clan was the village leader.

Palauan Money *Udoud* is traditional Palauan money and there were two types. One was beads of fired red, yellow or orange clay and the other was glass and usually green. Common round beads were used for daily transactions, while beads which were oval, faceted or cylindrical were more prestigious and valuable. The beads were not made in Palau and although no one knows exactly where they came from, it is thought they possibly originated in Indonesia or Malaysia.

One legend, however, says they came from a mysterious Yapese island called Kablik. Kablik was said to be so magical that stones thrown from the island toward the sea never touched the water, but returned instead to the thrower.

The beads still have value but are in limited use today. Strings of udoud are worn by high-ranking women on special occasions and it's common to see women wearing a single bead on a black cord as an heirloom necklace.

Another kind of money was *toluk*, made by steaming tortoise shell and pressing it into a wooden tray-shaped mould.

Early Western Contact The first European to sight Palau was probably the Spaniard Ruy Lopez de Villalobos in 1543. He named the islands Arrecifos, which means 'the reefs'. Spain claimed authority over Palau in 1686 but did nothing to develop the islands.

It wasn't until 1783, when English captain Henry Wilson wrecked his ship the *Antelope* on a reef off Palau's Aulong Island, that any real contact began between Palauans and westerners. The crew was treated well by Chief Ibedul of Koror who helped them rebuild their ship from the wreckage and then sent his young son, Prince Lebuu (Lee Boo), back with Wilson to England for schooling. The prince died of smallpox less than six months after arriving in London.

Gifts from the Palauans, which the British called the 'Pelew Curiosities', included a bracelet made from a dugong vertebrae, a dagger made from a stingray stinger and tortoise shell dishes. They are now in the British Museum.

The story of Wilson and his crew was immortalised in the popular book *An Account of the Pelew Islands* by George Keate, which whetted Britain's appetite for trade between the two nations. There was even a romantic melodrama called *Prince Lee Boo* that played on London stages at the time.

Favoured trade items included guns and weapons which served to increase hostilities among local tribes and, at times, against European traders.

The English were Palau's main trading partners until Spain moved in and kicked the British out in 1885. Spanish missionaries managed to introduce Christianity and a written alphabet before Spain sold Palau to Germany following the Spanish-American War.

The German Period The Germans were more interested in making money than saving souls. By the time they took control in 1899 only about 4000 Palauans had survived the diseases introduced by western explorers, a drastic drop from the estimated pre-European contact population of 40,000. The Germans took steps to contain contagious diseases by instituting sanitary controls but at the same time they used forced Palauan labour to start coconut plantations and other business ventures.

The Japanese Period The Japanese occupied Palau from 1914 until the end of WW II. It was during this time that Palauan culture went through its most radical transformation, as the Japanese attempted to replace it with their own. Free schools taught the Japanese language, albeit a subservient dialect, and village chiefs lost power to Japanese bureaucrats.

Japan continued and expanded the commercial ventures started by the Germans and developed many more. Thousands of Japanese, Korean and Okinawan labourers were brought in to work in phosphate mines, rice fields, pineapple plantations and other lucrative businesses. Traditional inheritance patterns were shattered as Palauans lost their land, either through sale or confiscation.

From 1922 all of Japan's Pacific possessions were administered from Koror, which the Japanese developed into a bustling modern city complete with paved roads, electricity and piped-in water. Out of 30,000 residents only 20% were Palauan.

In the late 1930s, Japan closed Palau to the outside world and began concentrating on military fortifications.

World War II US air bombings of Malakal Island and Airai State in March and July 1944 destroyed a large number of Japanese ships, planes, fuel tanks and military facilities. However the real fighting in Palau took place in September of that year on the islands of Peleliu and Angaur.

Most Palauans were sent to central Babeldaob before the US invasion of the southern islands. As on other Micronesian islands, the reason for the forced relocation is not entirely clear. Some islanders insist that the Japanese had plans to kill the Palauans and even had ditches dug to use as mass graves. History books, however, tend to credit the Japanese for getting the people out of harm's way and undoubtedly the action did save many Palauan lives.

Koror and Babeldaob were never invaded and the 25,000 Japanese soldiers on those islands remained there until the war's end.

Government

A stalemate between Palau and the US has left Palau the only district officially remaining as part of the UN's Trust Territory.

In July 1978 Palauans voted against becoming part of the Federated States of Micronesia. In July 1980 they adopted their own constitution and their first president, Haruo Remeliik, took office in January 1981.

Palau's national congress, a two-house legislature, is called *Olbiil Era Kelulau* which means 'meeting place of whispers'.

The US did a good job of introducing its brand of democracy into this region. Palau has a similar political framework to both the US federal and state governments – except that its population is not 230 million but a mere 14,000. Some of the 16 states have fewer than 200 people, yet each has a governor and state office. It would be hard to find another nation where so few are governed by so many.

Koror is the provisional capital but Palau's constitution requires the capital be moved to Melekeok State in Babeldaob. The architectural renderings for the grandiose new capital complex are in the Melekeok State Office in Koror, next door to the Peace Corps. Many people doubt that the expensive complex will ever be built.

President Remeliik was assassinated in June 1985 but although there was important political posturing going on at that time, the exact motive for the killing has never been established.

Airai state governor Roman Tmetuchl, an outspoken critic of US policies in Palau, was considered a strong candidate for the suddenly vacant presidential office. That is, he was until his son and nephew were picked up and charged with Remeliik's murder. This move destroyed Tmetuchl's political career.

In a case investigated by American FBI agents and tried by an American prosecutor and an American judge, the defendants were found guilty in March 1986.

Palauan leaders who felt the trial was a sham, called for an immediate reopening of the case. With assistance from American Civil Liberties Union lawyers who shared their perspective, the case was appealed to territorial judges. In July 1987 the appeal judges, in a court opinion very critical of the original trial, overturned the verdict and ordered acquittals.

Nuclear Issues
Palauans wrote a provision declaring Palau nuclear-free into their constitution. Because of the nuclear ban Palau's constitution and its Compact of Free Association with the United States were legally incompatible. The compact would allow the US to operate nuclear-propelled ships within Palauan waters –the constitution would not.

If the US had accepted a nuclear-free compact, the compact would have only required 50% approval by voters. But with the US refusing to renegotiate, the only way to approve the compact was to override the anti-nuke provision in the constitution. For that, 75% of the popular vote was required. In five votes in as many years, they narrowly missed reaching the 75% margin.

As part of the compact, the US dangled a billion dollar aid package in front of the Palauans, but the Palauans held fast. US-sponsored 'voter education programmes', with free beer and barbecues on the eve of the elections, also failed to swing the vote.

The US reacted by tightening the financial screws on Palau, levelling off operational funding at $10.1 million for 1987. With Palau's new power plant alone siphoning-off $3 million annually, the money ran out early.

In the summer of 1987, after another election

failed to get the 75% approval, the government was no longer able to make its own payroll.

In July, 900 of Palau's 1300 government employees were laid off. Hundreds of those affected by the layoff camped outside the Palauan legislative building to demand a referendum to remove the nuclear ban.

The first referendum, on 4 August, was held to amend the constitution 'for the purpose of avoiding an inconsistency with the compact'. With 73.33% of the vote, it lifted the prohibition against nuclear technology in the islands. The second referendum, on 21 August, was on the compact and with only a simple majority required, it passed with 73% of the vote.

Voila! – anti-nuclear provision rescinded, US military gets Palau, Palauans get their money. In essence, Palauans voters felt they had little choice but to exchange their anti nuclear status for their economic survival.

The case may not yet be closed if the legality of the amendment is challenged. Equally important, other provisions in the compact may be in violation of the constitution.

Supertanker Port Proposal
In the mid-1970s there was a proposal to build the world's largest supertanker port at Kossol Reef, between Kayangel and Babeldaob, for the storing and transshipment of oil, mainly for Japan.

A US naval liaison officer in Micronesia at the time was quoted as saying:

You realise that there are millions of people in Japan and only 14,000 people in Palau: we may have to sacrifice those 14,000 people.

The Save Palau Organization, led by Ibedul (High Chief) Yutaka Gibbons, cited potential massive environmental damage and defeated the proposal.

Economy
Palau has major financial problems. On its massive new power plant alone it has over $35 million of unpaid debts and with the US cutting back on funding it may well be unpayable.

The power plant built in remote Aimeliik has been surrounded by controversy. Until 1982 Palau was getting its power from three diesel generators on loan from the US military. When the military abruptly decided the generators should be pulled out, the Palauan government found itself in need of a new source of power and signed a contract with the British company IPSECO. Palauans were told the huge plant would pay for itself with the power it would generate – a very unrealistic claim. The US State Department assured IPSECO's financial backers that funds would be available to pay for the plant through compact money, even though the compact hadn't been approved.

Those funds never became available and the loan on the power plant has been declared in default. The plant is now operational, although its continued use is in doubt because of its enormous over-capacity. In the end it just might be too expensive to operate.

Why such a large power plant was ever planned for such a small population is one still-unanswered question. The potential to utilise the power plant to its full capacity will probably never be realised, unless of course there is some large-scale development – such as a US military base!

A group of Palauan legislative leaders have drawn up legislation calling for Palau to sue the US for willfully contributing to a conspiracy to bankrupt Palau. They see the power plant as part of a plan aimed at forcing the republic to rescind its nuclear-free constitution in order to get desperately needed compact funding to pay for the power plant.

Palau, located in one of the richest fishing grounds in the western Pacific, is serious about its 200-mile fishing zone but does not have the capability of patrolling for illegal Taiwanese fishing boats in its waters.

Palau lost its tuna industry in the early 1980s when the world tuna industry went into a recession and its Van Camp Seafood plant closed. There are currently plans to resume operations.

In 1984 exports totalled half a million dollars, coming mainly from tourism, fish and crafts. Imports, including fuel oil, alcoholic beverages and canned fish, totalled $23 million.

People
Palauans have a reputation for being energetic, progressive and aggressive in terms of personal advancement. When it comes to education they are are in the forefront among Micronesians and a large percentage of high school graduates continue their education, often at overseas colleges and universities.

Palauans hold no qualms about travelling in search of economic opportunities and throughout Micronesia you'll find a scattering of those who have gone further afield.

Religion
Most Palauans are Christian. Both the Catholic and Protestant churches are well established and the Seventh Day Adventists have a noticeable stronghold.

Many Palauans still hold some form of traditional native beliefs, based on nature spirits, ghosts and village gods. *Modekngei* is a newer name for the traditional religion.

Language
Palauan is the native language, Sonsorolese is spoken by the south-west islanders and older Palauans often remember Japanese. Schools use both Palauan and English

In Palauan, 'hello' is *alii* and 'thanks' is *sulang*.

Many Palauan words begin with 'ng' – which is a nasal sound, pronounced like the ending of the word 'bring'. The 'ch' spelling is pronounced 'uh'.

Holidays
Legal holidays are New Year's Day, Youth Day on 14 March, Senior Citizen's Day on 15 May, Constitution Day on 9 July, Labor Day on the first Monday in September, UN Day on 24 October, Thanksgiving on the fourth Thursday in November and Christmas Day.

Koror

Koror is both the economic centre and capital of Palau and has more than two-thirds of the republic's population. Of the 9500 people who live there, most were drawn from their home villages by employment opportunities.

In pre-war days Koror was jammed not only with homes, restaurants, office buildings and military facilities, but also with geisha houses, Shinto shrines, kimono tailors and public baths.

It's a quieter and less crowded Koror one sees today, with a pace more typically Micronesian and no particular penchant for hustle and bustle. Koror is good for maybe a day of exploration, but it's best used as a base for trips to the Rock Islands, Peleliu, Angaur and other islands.

Orientation

The airport on Babeldaob is a 15-minute drive from central Koror. Koror is connected to neighbouring islands by an impressive array of bridges and causeways, including the aptly named K-B Bridge between Koror and Babeldaob. At the time of its construction the 1272-foot (381-metre) K-B Bridge was the longest single-span prestressed-concrete box girder bridge in the world. The east side of Koror, between the town centre and the K-B Bridge, is called Topside.

Information

All modern facilities, such as banks, travel agencies, laundromats, government offices and Palau's only post office, are in central Koror.

The tourist office is in a building near the Belau National Museum.

The mailing address for all box numbers in Palau is: Koror, Republic of Palau 96940. International phone calls can be made from the COMSAT station on Arakabesang Island.

Dr. Yano's Clinic (Belau Clinic), next to Air Mike's office on Lebuu St, is recommended if you need medical attention. Walk-in office visits cost from $10 to $12 and medicine prices are reasonable. There may be a fairly long wait. Koror's MacDonald Hospital is cheaper, but is referred to locally as 'the morgue'.

Belau National Museum

A good starting place for understanding Palauan history and culture is the Belau National Museum (tel 265). It has bead and tortoise shell money, a carved canoe, a model village and displays of artefacts and arts and crafts. There's also a stuffed crocodile which, at nearly 15 feet (4.5 metres) long, was the largest found in Palau since WW II.

To get there, turn off the main street by the sports ground, veer to the left past the hospital and continue on the main road to its end. The museum is open from 8 to 11 am and 1 to 4 pm Monday to Friday, and from 10 am to 3 pm on weekends. Admission is $2.

Next to the museum is a research library with a good collection of books on Palau and Micronesia, which museum officials will open upon request. The tourist office is in the building just below.

Malakal Island

Malakal Island, across a causeway from Koror, has the Fisheries Co-op, commercial port, small boat docks and other marine businesses.

The Micronesian Industrial Corporation, Palau's only copra processing plant, is north of the Carp Restaurant. The plant closed in 1980 after a ban in the Philippines on exporting coconuts, and a general drop in the world market price of copra.

The plant can crush 3500 tons of copra daily and employ 70 people, but Palau and the FSM together didn't produce enough coconuts to keep it in business. Now that Marcos is gone, coconuts are once again allowed out of the Philippines and there are plans to reopen the plant.

Ice Box Park, at the southern tip of the island, was once the site of an ice-making

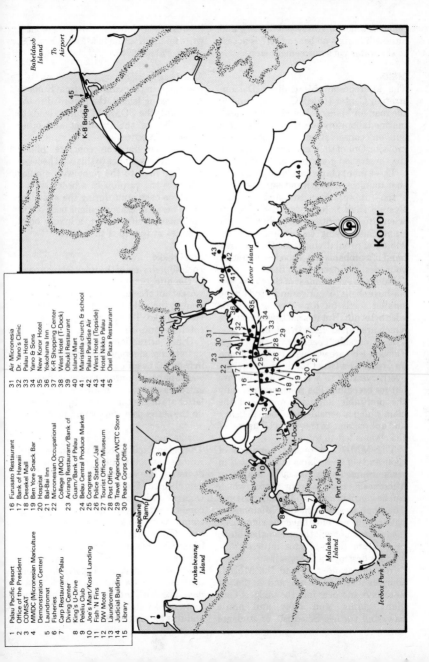

1   Palau Pacific Resort
2   Office of the President
3   COMSAT
4   MMDC (Micronesian Mariculture
    Demonstration Center)
5   Laundromat
6   Fisheries
7   Carp Restaurant/Palau
    Diving Center
8   King's U-Drive
9   Peleliu Club
10 Joe's Mart/Kosiil Landing
11 Fish N Fins
12 DW Motel
13 Laundromat
14 Judicial Building
15 Library

16 Furusato Restaurant
17 Bank of Hawaii
18 Desekel Mall
19 Ben Yore Snack Bar
20 Hospital
21 Bai-Bai Inn
22 Micronesian Occupational
    College (MOC)
23 Arirang Restaurant/Bank of
    Guam/Bank of Palau
24 Belau Central Produce Market
25 Congress
26 Police Station/Jail
27 Tourist Office/Museum
28 Post Office
29 Travel Agencies/WCTC Store
30 Peace Corps Office

31 Air Micronesia
32 Dr. Yano's Clinic
33 Palau Hotel
34 Desekel Mall
35 New Koror Hotel
36 Yano & Sons
37 K-R Shopping Center
38 West Hotel (T-Dock)
39 Olbuki Restaurant
40 Island Mart
41 Maristella church & school
42 Palau Paradise Air
43 West Hotel (Topside)
44 Hotel Nikko Palau
45 Osel Plaza Restaurant

plant. It's now a grassy public park and although there's no beach there is access to the water via some cement steps.

MMDC

The Micronesian Mariculture Demonstration Center (MMDC), at the end of the road on Malakal Island, is a research marine laboratory where work is carried out on conservation and commercial projects. One of their main projects is with the threatened giant tridacna clam.

These giant clams regularly grow more than four feet in length and can weigh half a ton (up to 1.5 metres and 450 kg). Despite their notoriety at the hands of science fiction writers, the probability of a giant clam trying to swallow your leg while you're out diving is nil. On the other hand it's probably not a good idea to stick your toes, or fingers, in to find out!

Palauans eat the meat of the clams, sell the huge shells to tourists and grind up the smaller shells for lime powder to chew with betel nut. But it is not these practices which are threatening the clams.

It is outside poachers, mainly from Taiwan, who are wiping out the tridacna on coral reefs around the Pacific, overharvesting to a point where few are left for breeding. The poachers take only the profitable adductor muscle of the clam which is considered to be a delicacy and aphrodisiac in the orient . The rest of the clam is left to rot.

The MMDC is raising hundreds of thousands of seed clams to be planted in reefs around Palau and other islands in Micronesia, especially in places which can be guarded against illegal harvesting. The hope is that someday Micronesian nations will not only have the clams as a food source, but will themselves be able to profit from the adductor muscle trade without destroying the species.

You can wander around the MMDC complex between 8 am and 4 pm on weekdays and peer into the tanks of fish, giant clams, and baby and adult hawksbill turtles. Scientists or students interested in doing research there may write for information to MMDC, Box 359, Koror, Palau 96940.

Arakabesang Island

After crossing the causeway from Koror to Arakabesang Island, the first road to the right after the COMSAT station leads to the Office of the President and other government offices.

Look out for the concrete pillars flanking the entrance to this road because the next road to the right with similar pillars is the turn-off to a beach with a seaplane base built during the Japanese era. There's another seaplane base out at the Palau Pacific Resort, a luxury hotel complex at the tip of the island.

Hotel Nikko

For a superb view of the Rock Islands head in the direction of the airport and when you get out of central Koror take the paved road to the right that winds down to the Hotel Nikko. This is also a great place to catch the sunrise.

Other attractions in the immediate vicinity include some live crocodiles caged in front of the office, the remains of a pre-war Japanese Shinto shrine near the hotel entrance and two anti-aircraft guns. The latter are at the top of the hill, all the way up the stairs past the swimming pool.

Snorkelling

The Palau Pacific Resort features some of Koror's best snorkelling, right on its own doorstep. The water is calm, shallow and very clear and there's a variety of colourful tropical fish, platter and mushroom corals. There's even lots of giant tridacna clams with their fleshy mantles in beautiful mottled designs of browns and iridescent greens and blues.

Breakfast in the open-air restaurant, followed by a morning of snorkelling from the beach, isn't a bad way to kick off the day. The NECO dive shop at the resort rents masks and snorkels for $3 per day and fins for another $3.

Top: Rock Islands from Hotel Nikko – Palau
Bottom: Former Japanese Headquarters, Airai – Palau

Top: Japanese cannon, Mt Taipingot – Rota
Left: Orange Beach monument – Peleliu
Right: Loading site for Hiroshima A-bomb – Tinian

Snorkelling is also good off Icebox Park or from inside the MMDC grounds. There are no beaches, but both have concrete retaining walls with steps leading into the water. The waters are deeper and the fish are larger than at the resort and several groups of clownfish hide in anemone shelters.

From the steps off Icebox Park, the best snorkelling is to the right. If you enter the water from inside the MMDC, you can snorkel over giant clams lined up in underwater cages just offshore. Watch out for the spiny urchins that cling to the sides of the wall.

If you're stuck in town, snorkelling is OK in the shallow water between the long breakwater and the Malakal bridge, half a mile from the fork which leads from Koror to Malakal. There are lots of tiny tropical fish and some low thickets of coral. The other side towards a rock island is less interesting. Be careful getting in as the concrete ramp is slippery.

On the other hand no one really comes to Palau to snorkel in Koror. The real action is in and around the Rock Islands – and it's worth whatever it takes to get yourself out there!

Places to Stay

The *D W Motel* (tel 641; Box 738) is a family-run place popular with independent travellers. Owner Dave Williams is an amiable guy and a former language instructor for the Peace Corps. Beds have comfortable foam mattresses, some rooms have refrigerators, singles cost $25 and doubles are $30. There's free coffee and tea in the upstairs lounge all day long and free transport to and from the airport.

The *West Motel* (tel 218; Box 280) is also good value and quite comfortable. There are two locations, one is in Topside and the other on T-Dock near the water. The large rooms all have TVs and refrigerators and cost $30 a single or double. With cooking facilities they cost $35. Airport transportation can be provided if the room has been booked in advance.

The *Bai-Bal Inn* (tel 646), up the road past Desekel Mall, has a few nice two-room apartments with full kitchens for $25 a single or $30 a double. Long-term rates are less. It's a little off the main drag, but excellent value if rooms are available.

The four-storey *Palau Hotel* (tel 231; Box 339) is the highest building in central Koror. The 47-room hotel officially costs $50 a single and from $55 to $60 a double but the front desk clerk claims to discount these prices 25% for businesspeople and 30% for tourists! Each room has a TV, refrigerator and telephone, but there's a dark and deserted feel to the place.

If you're ready for a splurge, the 64-acre *Palau Pacific Resort* (tel 600; Box 308) may well be Micronesia's best resort hotel and its protected white sand beach is certainly Koror's finest. The 100 rooms have rattan furniture, block prints and private lanais. Rates are $100 to $120 for singles or doubles. There's a lounge with books and videos, a swimming pool, tennis courts and a duty-free shop (good place to pick up slide film). The NECO dive shop and tours work out of the resort and they also rent water sports equipment, including windsurfers for $10 per hour and canoes for $6. Local events such as native dance competitions and the Presidential

inaugural ball also take place at the Palau Pacific.

The *Hotel Nikko Palau* (tel 486; Box 310), which is owned by Japan Air Lines, is musty and neglected. The 56 rooms cost $65 for singles or doubles. That's supposedly the 'discount rate' for businesspeople, government workers and divers, but no one bothers to quote a higher price. The Nikko has a gorgeous setting on a hill overlooking some of the Rock Islands and was Palau's premier hotel until bumped out of first place by the resort. Now it has an air of abandonment typified by the algae-infested swimming pool.

For monthly accommodation rentals, try the Rock Island Apartments in the centre of town behind the BMC Club, or the Cave Inn Apartments near the commercial dock on Malakal Island. Both charge $350 per month.

All Koror hotels have private bathrooms and air-con and a 10% tax is added to room rates.

Places to Eat

Seafood, especially fish, crabs and shellfish, is an important part of the Palauan diet. Crocodile, giant clam and pigeon are some of the more unusual local delicacies, though these are unlikely to appear on restaurant menus. Most places in Koror have both western and oriental dishes. Noodles or hamburgers are cheap and fried chicken or fish don't cost much more.

The best food available is at the *Osel Plaza*, which is just a little more expensive than places in town. It has a nice atmosphere with an outside patio by the water and a good sunset view. Meals cost from $3 to $12, with many in the $4 to $6 range. Chicken with rice is $3.50. It's open daily for dinner only, but it occasionally closes down for private parties. To get there from Koror centre, take an immediate left at the end of the K-B Bridge just before reaching Babeldaob.

The *Olbukl Restaurant* on T-Dock has good, cheap food but you have to sit through the B-grade video movies that run non-stop. Fried fish or chicken dinners cost $3.25.

The *Carp Restaurant*, out on Malakal Island, has delicious seafood tempura for $5 and tofu vegetable stew for $3.50. Meals end with a fresh fruit plate, which is a welcome treat.

The *Furusato Restaurant*, which is an easy walk from the D W Motel, is a good place to try Japanese food. *Oyako domburi*, or steamed chicken and egg atop rice, costs $3.50.

The *Arirang Restaurant* is a Korean barbecue where you cook the food at your table.

The *Yokohama Restaurant* is neither as good nor as cheap as many other small cafés, but locals gather there when the electricity goes out to get the only shaved ice in town.

A cheap place to eat is the *Ben Yore Snack Bar* which is attached to the Family Mart opposite the sports ground. Their breakfasts are a good bargain for $2, the hamburgers are $1.50 and fried noodles cost $2.

You can try local food at the *Belau Central Produce Market* where fixed plate lunches, such as fried fish or chicken, rice, taro or tapioca, cost $2.50.

Yano & Sons, diagonally opposite the Palau Hotel, sells produce and freshly cooked Palauan-style food by the piece. You could easily put together a meal from the fried fish, sweet tapioca, coconut candy, bananas and papayas which are sold out of bulk containers. The selection and quality varies from day to day and rumour has it that prices are higher for foreigners.

The *Palau Pacific Resort* has average food at higher-than-average prices but you can eat it all in their open-air setting.

In Koror, be wary of drinking tap water especially if the water's been off for rationing. Water and sewage lines lay side by side and cross-seepage can occur. Ice and water are OK in most restaurants.

Entertainment

Small clubs come and go, so ask around to see what's hot these days. Many restaurants have a bar and serve drinks. The *Olbukl Restaurant* on T-Dock sometimes has a band in the evenings, at which time drink prices double, and just up the road the *Sakura Club* has a singer and other after dark entertainment.

A handful of small shops sell joints from under the counter for $1.

Traditional dance shows can be arranged for $75 to $100 per performance through tour agents or the tourist office.

Things to Buy

Storyboards are smaller versions of the long wooden planks carved with legends and local history that have traditionally decorated the beams and gables of men's meeting houses. A revival in this carving was started in 1935 by a Japanese anthropologist who suggested the smaller boards as a way to keep the art form and legends from dying out. Some of the best storyboards are made by the inmates of the local jail. You can go and watch them work in the afternoons and then bargain for a storyboard.

The women at the Old Age Center, next door to the D W Hotel, sit outside during the days and weave hats, purses and cigarette cases out of pandanus and coconut palm.

The Lebuu Gift Shop, on Lebuu St just down from the Air Mike office, has a selection of crafts, shells and T-shirts. Desekel

Mall has T-shirts and commemorative stamps, etc upstairs. The museum sells storyboards, T-shirts, artwork, carvings, and books and pamphlets on Palau and Micronesia. Both the Hotel Nikko and Palau Pacific Resort have overpriced gift shops. It's been said that storyboards that fail to sell for $60 at the museum get shipped up to the resort with a $120 price tag slapped on them.

Getting There

Palau is serviced by Air Mike, Air Nauru and SPIA. On Air Mike, the full fare from Guam to Palau, with a stopover in Yap, is $251 or $188 for a spouse. Direct flights between Guam and Palau are $125 on Sunday, Monday and Friday evenings. Other direct Guam-Palau flights are $150. The Thursday flight from Yap to Koror is $50; other days it's $103.

SPIA has an off-and-on flight between Guam and Palau. The last time it was flying it was $99 one way but they often cancel flights if there aren't enough passengers.

Air Mike's one-way flights between Manila and Palau cost $125. For more info see the Getting There chapter.

Air Nauru flies from Manila to Koror for $124.

Inter-island Transport

Air Competition between several small domestic airlines has left Palau Paradise Air (tel 348; Box 488) the winner. They fly six and eight-seater planes from Koror to Peleliu and Angaur. There are usually two

Storyboard carved with Palauan legends.

return flights a day, in the early morning and late afternoon, which allows for day trips. Sometimes extra flights are added if there's a demand. Palau Paradise provides free transportation to and from the airport from their office in Koror. Wednesdays are usually reserved for charter flights.

Boat Information on boats from Koror to Babeldaob, Peleliu, Angaur, Kayangel and the Rock Islands is provided in those sections.

Getting Around
Getting around central Koror on foot takes a while as it's a sprawling town. It's dangerous walking across the causeways to Malakal or Arakabesang islands because the narrow roads just drop off with no railings or sidewalks. Hitching is not common.

Taxis Taxis in Koror are private, not the shared group kind. There are no meters, but the going minimum rate of $1 covers most places around town.

Car Rentals Several car rental places in Koror have both Japanese sedans and pick-up trucks and some have booths at the airport. A few, including Toyota at T-Dock, offer optional insurance. If you're after a four-wheel-drive vehicle try West U-Drive at T-Dock. The D W Motel (tel 641) rents cars from $20.

King's U-Drive (tel 964) has cars from $18.50 per day, though the ones at the airport are apt to be $25. Older pick-up trucks start at $25.

Watch out for dips and bumps and sharp V-shaped rain gutters that can tear up car bottoms.

Boat Because Koror is the commercial centre, Palauans commonly commute between Koror and their home villages in private speedboats. You might be able to hitch a ride with someone by offering to help pay for petrol. Abby's Marine Shop near

the Fisheries is where most of the speedboats fill up, so look there first. T-Dock and M-Dock are other possibilities.

The Rock Islands

The Rock Islands are Palau's crowning glory.

More than 200 of these rounded knobs of limestone, totally covered with green jungle growth, dot the waters for a 20-mile (32 km) stretch south of Koror. The bases of the islands are narrower than the tops, having been undercut by water erosion and by grazing fish and chitons that scrape at the rock. They are often likened to emerald mushrooms popping up above calm blue seas.

From the air they are an absolute knock-out! Even if you don't want to go anywhere, flights from Koror to Angaur or Peleliu are worth the airfare for the scenic overview of the Rock Islands alone.

But that's only half of it. In the waters that surround the Rock Islands is some of the most abundant and varied marine life to be found anywhere.

Islands which have been undercut all the way round have no place for boat landings, but others have beach hideaways where soft white sands have washed up and stayed. Some islands have caves, rock arches and underground channels.

This is a superb place to lose the rest of the world for a while, hanging out on a speck of paradise and snorkelling the clear waters at whim.

Marine Lakes
The Rock Islands hold about 80 marine salt lakes, former sinkholes now filled with saltwater with a limited exchange to the sea. Variations in algae give them different colours and some have soft corals, fish, sponges or jellyfish.

The island of **Eil Malk**, for example, contains **Spooky Lake** which has stratified layers of plankton, hydrogen sulfide and gases. Eil Malk also has a hot water lake that reaches 100°F (37.4°C) just 15 feet (4.5 metres) down, as well as Palau's largest salt lake, **Metukercheuas Uet**, which is 1½ miles long and 200 feet deep (2.4 km and 60 metres).

Each lake is a different ecosystem. Travellers rarely get in to see them but marine biologists love 'em.

Diving & Snorkelling

Palau is one of the world's truly spectacular dive spots.

If coral reefs in crystal clear waters, blue holes, WW II wrecks and hidden caves and tunnels aren't enough, consider the more than 60 vertical drop-offs.

Palau is the meeting place of three major ocean currents that merge with their abundant food supplies to support an enormous variety of tropical fish and other marine life. There are four times the number of coral species in Palau than there is in the Caribbean, including immense tabletop corals, interlocking thickets of staghorn coral and soft corals of all types and colours. The sea temperature averages about 82°F (27°C).

Divers can see manta rays, sea turtles, moray eels, giant tridacna clams, grey reef sharks and sometimes even a sea snake or a rare dugong.

The **Ngemelis Wall**, also called the 'Big Drop-off', is considered the world's best wall dive. Starting in water just knee-deep, the wall drops vertically nearly 1000 feet (300 metres) with attractions all the way down. Divers can free float past a brilliant rainbow of sponges and soft corals whose intense blues, reds or pure whites form a backdrop for quivering nine-foot (three-metre) orange and yellow sea fans and giant black coral trees.

Blue Corners is known for its sheer abundance of underwater life, where you can expect to be totally bedazzled by the incredible variety of fish, including barracudas and sharks. Strong tidal currents nourish this chain of life. Only more experienced divers should dive here.

Both the **German Channel** and **Turtle Cove**, at the edge of the Rock Islands just north of Peleliu, offer dives that novices can feel comfortable with. Snorkelling is also good from the beach at Turtle Cove.

Jellyfish Lake, popularised by the National Geographic television special *Medusa*, is a different kind of experience. You'll need to hike a little through the jungle to reach this mangrove-bordered lake. If you mark your entry point into the lake you shouldn't have a problem finding your way back out. Be careful of slippery rocks around the shoreline where the water is murky and green. Further out, the water clears up and millions of harmless transparent jellyfish swim en masse following the sun. Snorkelling in this pulsating mass is an unearthly, somewhat eerie sensation.

Crocodiles are nocturnal creatures, but should you hear a low 'harrumph' you just might want to head quickly in the opposite direction, unless you plan to test the theory that the crocodiles in Jellyfish Lake are more afraid of people than vice versa.

Dive Shops *Fish 'N Fins* (tel 637; Box 142), owned by Francis Toribiong, is on M-Dock in Koror. A day's worth of diving the Rock Islands, including lunch and transport to and from the hotel, costs $65 if you have your own equipment, $75 if you just show up in a swimsuit. Snorkellers pay $35. Francis can certify divers in NAUI in four days for $400, including full-day dives and tours all around Palau while learning. If you just want to be certified, without the full treatment, it costs $250.

The *Palau Diving Center* (tel 978; Box 5), next door to the Carp Restaurant, also runs the Carp Island Resort. Their single tank day tour by boat, including equipment and lunch, costs $65. Double tank boat tours are $70 to $80. An introductory dive for beginners with a full day at Carp Island costs $120.

The *NECO Marine Dive Shop* (tel 600, ext 4122; Box 129) at the Palau Pacific Resort charges $65 for two dives on a full-day trip, including equipment. It's $45 for one dive.

All three dive shops offer night diving and rent tanks and equipment to those who want to go off on their own.

Places to Stay & Eat

The *Carp Island Resort* is booked through the Palau Diving Center, usually in conjunction with their dive trips. Six rooms in cottages with shared bath go for $45 a single and $55 a double (group rates are available). The boat to Carp Island costs $30 return, including a tour of the Rock Islands, and takes about an hour each way. If you bring your own food there are kitchen facilities available at no charge, or you can eat the seafood at Carp's informal restaurant.

The *Ngerchong Hotel* (tel 691), 45 minutes from Koror, has eight rooms at $20 per person and an open space area with sleeping mats and mattresses for groups. There's a small restaurant. The return boat ride to Ngerchong Island costs $80.

Camping The Rock Islands are possibly the best place for camping in all of Micronesia and the star gazing is tremendous. Some of the islands have nice sandy beaches and a few have shelters built by the Palauan government, though none have water and you'll need protection from biting sand gnats. There are no fees to camp.

Getting There

For $35 (the price of a full-day snorkelling trip) the Fish 'N Fins dive shop in Koror will drop you off at a deserted island at the end of a day's snorkelling and pick you up at an arranged date.

Francis is also open to doing an island pick-up deal which, once you've finished your sojourn on an island, allows you to join another group on its way to diving or snorkelling. The rates are the same as if you'd joined in Koror.

He weaves through the Rock Islands for most diving tours anyway and on the

return he can drop you back off at your rock. This is definitely one up on the free hotel pick-up service, as without the hotel bills the diving fees aren't as painful. If you go this route, arrange to have water dropped off as well.

Private speedboats go through and to the Rock Islands, so it's possible to hitch a ride with someone.

Several tour agencies offer full-day Rock Island boat tours that stop on an island for lunch and a bit of snorkelling, as well as shorter cruises that last just a couple of hours. The Palau Pacific Resort has a sunset cruise for $14 – but unless it's a great sunset, it's probably nicer to see the islands in the daylight.

Babeldaob

Babeldaob, or Babelthaup, is the second largest land mass in Micronesia and is ¾ the size of Guam. It has 10 states but a total population of only about 3500, with many of the younger people making an exodus to Koror in search of jobs.

Although it's a high volcanic island, the highest of its gently rolling hills, Mt Makelulu, has an elevation of only 787 feet (236 metres). Babeldaob's Lake Ngardok, which is about 3000 feet long and 12 feet deep (900 metres by 3.6 metres), is one of the few freshwater lakes in Micronesia. Parts of the island's dense jungle interior are virtually unexplored.

There are beautiful stretches of sandy beach on the east coast, particularly from Ngiwal to Ngaraard, while the west coast is largely mangrove-studded shoreline.

Ngarchelong State, at the northernmost point of Babeldaob, has two rows of giant basalt monoliths known as *Bairulchau*. There are a lot of stories about these stones. One legend says the gods put them there to support a bai that held thousands of people. There are 37 stones in all, some weighing up to five tons (4535 kg).

Many of Babeldaob's hillsides were

once elaborately terraced into steps and pyramids. Although their purpose remains a mystery, archaeological research suggests they were probably started around 100 AD and abandoned around 1600. Quite mysteriously, few villages seem to have been located close to the terraced hillsides. Bairulchau is the only known exception.

AIRAI STATE

Airai, at the southern end of Babeldaob, has Palau's international airport. The state's relatively good roads and its proximity to Koror, makes it a good area for exploration. The most visited attractions are two bais, one old and one new.

One mile after crossing over the K-B Bridge from Koror, the 1st class Grace Hotel pops up on the right. The opening of this hotel has long been delayed due to litigation between the overseas investors and the Palau government.

There are some crocodile pens about a ¼ of a mile ahead on the right, behind a store next to the Wash Land Laundromat. The storekeeper charges 25 cents for viewing and will toss fish to the crocs or spray them with water to liven up an otherwise sleepy show.

If you're heading to the airport you turn off to the left on the paved road ahead, if you're not then continue straight on.

There's the bombed-out shell of a Japanese administration building two miles from Wash Land, on the left just after the pavement ends. If you drive behind it you can see another old building, which is now an auto repair shop. The ruins of two generations coexist here, where dismantled cars sit inside the bombed building and a Japanese tank and gun rust in union with a heap of car parts outside.

Continue on down the main road, where it's quiet with tall grasses, red soil and an occasional ocean view. Just past a security gate the road splits and rejoins itself further on before coming to a new bai, which is made mostly of concrete though it's built in the traditional style. It's on the right, 4½ miles from the K-B Bridge.

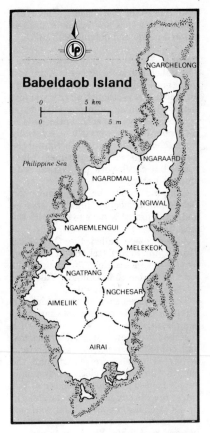

Just beyond, the road comes to a T-junction. The road to the right leads down to a speedboat dock and some mossy stone steps that lead back up to the concrete bai.

If you turn left at the T-junction, the road curves back around a bit before ending in front of a stone path. From there you can see a tiny bit of Palau's only remaining traditional bai, a few hundred yards down the path. The bai, about 100 years old, was constructed without nails using traditional native materials. There's a $5 charge just to walk up to it or $10 to take photos of the inside. There are traditional scenes and symbolic designs painted inside and outside both bais.

Places to Stay

The Babeldaob state offices in Koror can sometimes help you make arrangements for places to stay, though often if you just show up in a village someone will put you up. You can try local school principals as they sometimes take in visitors, especially if it's school holiday time. In Ngiwal the former magistrate sometimes takes guests but check with the Ngiwal state office in Koror.

Camping could be a problem on Babeldaob as people think it's strange and you'll probably have to deal with the local drunks.

A new place called the *Ongeluatel Traditional Resort* (tel 907 in Koror or write in advance to Box 773) is being built right on the beach in Ulimang Village on the east coast of Ngaraard.

Three cottages, each with two bedrooms, a living area and a cooking area have been completed, in traditional local style with thatched roofs and rough-hewn beams, and cost $20 per person. Showers and *benjos*, or toilets, are outside and the simple solar-powered electrical system is supplemented by kerosene lanterns. You can arrange in advance for local women to fix native dishes or you can bring your own food. There's a recreation facility with a bar and pool table. You have to arrange your own boat ride to Ulimang.

Ngaraard residents are used to seeing foreigners. Peace Corps volunteers train in this state and the local Christian girls school, which takes students from throughout Micronesia, has American teachers.

Getting There

Ollei, in Ngarchelong State, and Melekeok are accessible by fishing boats which leave from the Fisheries Co-op in Koror.

Most other boats to Babeldaob leave from Koror's T-Dock. If you're adventurous just go to the docks and ask when someone is going. It's generally $2 to $5 to go anywhere – though it often costs less for women.

One large boat, the *Kamome Maru*, makes weekly trips between Koror and Ngchesar, Melekeok and Ngiwal on the east coast of Babeldaob. The boat leaves T-Dock on Saturdays and returns on Sundays. The Palau Sea & Air Transportation Agency (tel 254) should have more information.

Getting Around

The few vehicle roads in Babeldaob generally follow the paths of the once-extensive road system constructed during the Japanese era. Some states have just a mile or two of roads which go through a main village and then stop. Because each state works on its own road projects, roads in one state don't always connect up with roads in the next.

Peleliu

Peleliu was the site of one of the bloodiest battles of WW II. The death toll from two months of fighting on this island, that measures only 24 square miles (61 square km), was 12,000 – almost equivalent to the total population of all Palau. Many of Peleliu's visitors these days are survivors of that campaign.

World War II

Some US military tacticians had worried that Japanese attacks from bases in Peleliu and Angaur might prevent a successful retaking of the Philippines. By mid-1944, however, American air bombings had reduced Peleliu to a negligible threat. It should then have been bypassed, as were other islands held by the Japanese, but Peleliu was captured at a terrible, unanticipated cost, with more than 8000 US casualties.

About 10,000 Japanese soldiers holed up in the natural and man-made caves honeycombed into Peleliu's jagged limestone ridges. Their goal was not to win, but to stall defeat. Far away from the beaches and the reach of naval bombardment, they tenaciously defended these caves to their deaths.

Rather than the expected quick victory, it took 2½ months for the Americans to rout out the last of the Japanese forces – often one by one with the use of flame throwers.

In the late 1950s, a Japanese straggler hiding in the jungle was discovered by an old woman as he entered her garden. Crouching low to see who had been stealing her tapioca, she froze and then screamed, thinking she was seeing a ghost. The man's uniform was torn into shreds, his hair matted and teeth streaked black. Police from Koror hunted the straggler down, bound him with rope and paraded him around for everyone to see. In that way, the last soldier left Peleliu.

Peleliu Today

In pre-war days there were settlements scattered around the island but upon returning from Babeldaob after the war, the people all resettled on the northern tip. The population is now about 550.

Several areas in Peleliu have been re-named in recognition of their military usage. Koska, at the southern end of Klouklubed, is not really a separate village but is the area where the Coast Guard, or the *kos ka*, personnel once stayed. Ngerkeyukl, the former village north of Orange Beach, is now called Sina, which is the Palauan word for China, and is named after the Nationalist Chinese that came to that area to buy jeeps and other WW II surplus.

During the fighting Peleliu's forests were bombed and burned to the ground. Today the island is alive with the whistles and songs of a great number of tropical birds that thrive on the secondary jungle growth of vines and leafy foliage that have grown up to cover the battle scars. If there weren't the occasional pillbox, rusting tank or memorial to stumble across, there'd be no immediate sense of this island's place in war history.

Peleliu is also known, in other circles, for its high-quality marijuana. Fertile soil is brought in from Babeldaob for pot planting in 50-gallon oil drums. Raids by US agents from Guam a few years back outraged the locals, who were indignant that anyone would consider such an attack on their economy.

Peleliu has much more to offer than just war relics. It's a fine place to kick back and take life easy for a while. The old name for Peleliu was *Odesangel* which means the 'beginning of everything'.

Orientation

The coral-surfaced 6000-foot (1800 metre) airstrip, dating from WW II, is about five miles (eight km) from the village.

The terminal is just a few benches covered with a tin roof. Sometimes there's a minibus that will give you a ride into town for a dollar or so. If not, get a lift from one of the people meeting the plane.

Many of the remnants of war are clustered north of the airport amidst a criss-cross of roads that can be confusing. It's helpful to have a guide, but if you don't care about seeing every war relic, the coral and concrete roads are in good condition and you can explore on your own. The island still has a scattering of live ammunition, so take care if you go off the beaten path.

Most of the best beaches are to the south.

KLOUKLUBED

The main village of Klouklubed is interesting more for its small-town atmosphere than for any particular sights, though there are a couple.

Palau's first president Haruo Remeliik, who was killed by an assassin in 1985, was from Peleliu. His grave is in the centre of the village, directly opposite the governor's office.

The multi-storey bombed-out Japanese communications centre is right in the middle of the village, tangled with vegetation and circled by homes. Kids

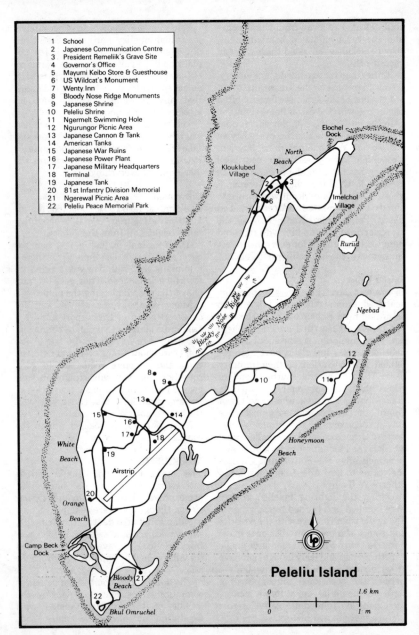

1   School
2   Japanese Communication Centre
3   President Remeliik's Grave Site
4   Governor's Office
5   Mayumi Keibo Store & Guesthouse
6   US Wildcat's Monument
7   Wenty Inn
8   Bloody Nose Ridge Monuments
9   Japanese Shrine
10 Peleliu Shrine
11 Ngermelt Swimming Hole
12 Ngurungor Picnic Area
13 Japanese Cannon & Tank
14 American Tanks
15 Japanese War Ruins
16 Japanese Power Plant
17 Japanese Military Headquarters
18 Terminal
19 Japanese Tank
20 81st Infantry Division Memorial
21 Ngerewal Picnic Area
22 Peleliu Peace Memorial Park

Elochel Dock

North Beach

Klouklubed Village

Imelchol Village

Ruriid

Ngebad

Bloody Nose Ridge

White Beach

Honeymoon Beach

Airstrip

Orange Beach

Camp Beck Dock

Bloody Beach

Bkul Omruchel

Peleliu Island

0   1.6 km
0   1 m

play inside the building and its roof is now a forest floor.

There's a small US military monument opposite Keibo's store and, towards the dock, there's a cave and a pillbox on the right.

Japanese War Ruins

The bombed-out shells of the Japanese power plant buildings are almost completely draped with vines hanging down from the upper ledges. Watch out for the wasp nests inside. The American-made generator off to the side has been used more recently. The whole place has an eerie feeling of abandonment but the seemingly orchestrated chorus of birds in the background there is amazing.

Nearby are the buildings that served as Japanese military headquarters, now little more than concrete crumbling around the steel reinforcement rods. You can walk up some steps to the 2nd floor. There are two rusting Quonset huts behind the main building.

Not far away, a small rusted Japanese tank sits at the convergence of three paths, all once paved. Other war wreckage, further on, includes a larger American tank with ferns and grass growing out the sides, two rusting American amphibs by the side of the road and a Japanese cannon guarding the entrance of a cave near a tiny Shinto shrine.

Bloody Nose Ridge

Below Bloody Nose Ridge, a sign points to a US Marine Corps monument, in a clearing to the right, from where there's a nice view.

To get to Bloody Nose Ridge, head uphill behind the sign taking the path to the left. It starts as a rough road and soon changes to steep narrow stairs with a chain alongside to use as a handrail. The climb to the top takes about five minutes. There is some old military machinery along the way.

At the top of the ridge there's a monument, a machine gun and a spectacular 360° view. There were once more than 500 caves dug into the limestone cliffs of Peleliu, many of them on this ridge.

Orange Beach

The first US invasion forces came ashore at Orange Beach on 15 September 1944. From concrete pillboxes the Japanese machine-gunned the first waves of Americans as they hit the beaches. Despite the barrage, 15,000 US soldiers made it ashore on the first day.

Today Orange Beach is a quiet picnic spot with a barbecue grill, sandy beach and water that's calm, clear, shallow and warm.

Just before the beach there are two grey coral monuments to the US Army's 81st Infantry Wildcat Division. Viewed from the platform to the side, the landscaping forms the letters 'USA'. Seabees regularly come down from Babeldaob to maintain Peleliu's memorials. There's a striking sense of stillness on this beach.

Camp Beck Dock

Behind Camp Beck Dock, where the water is a creamy aqua, there's a huge pile of mangled WW II plane engines, cockpits, pipes, tubing, fuselages, anchors and who knows what, all compacted into blocks of twisted aluminum and steel.

South Beaches

By constructing half a dozen chunky concrete tables the Japanese have turned Bkul Omruchel, at the south-west tip of the island, into Peleliu Peace Memorial Park. You can see Angaur Island to the south, there are some small blowholes nearby and aside from the crashing surf it's very peaceful.

Bloody Beach, despite its niche in history, is a calm circular cove with a nice sandy beach. Swimming is probably good at high tide. Ngerewal Beach Park is nearby and Honeymoon Beach is a fine beach with good seasonal surf.

At the end of the south-east tip of the

island is the Ngurungor picnic area, with some mangroves and tiny rock island-like formations just offshore.

Heading back from Ngurungor, off a grassy road to the right, is a small swimming hole of half-salt, half-fresh water that bobs up and down with the tides. A metal ladder hangs down the side of the pit, but local children just jump in.

Diving & Snorkelling

Peleliu Wall is one of the world's finest dives, an abrupt 900-foot (270 metre) drop that starts in about 10 feet (three metres) of water. It's a veritable treasure-trove of sharks, hawksbill sea turtles, black coral trees, mammoth gorgonian fans and an amazing variety of fish. The wall is to the south-west of Peleliu.

Many of Palau's best dive spots are in fact closer to Peleliu than Koror, but most people start from Koror because that's where the tanks and diving services are.

You can try snorkelling at Bloody Beach or by the dock.

Places to Stay & Eat

There are three guest houses in Klouklubed.

Wenty Tongmy runs the *Wenty Inn*, and has four rooms at $10 a single or $20 a double. Meals cost $2.50 for breakfast, $3.50 for lunch and $4 for dinner.

Mayumi Keibo rents three rooms next door to Keibo's store. The room rate is $32.50 per person with meals, or $13 per person without.

The Palau Paradise Air agent, Reiko Kubarii, sometimes rents rooms in her house a few doors down from the governor's office.

Peleliu has some small food stores but no restaurants.

Camping Peleliu is one of Micronesia's best camping areas. Some of the beach picnic sites have covered open-air shelters, tables, barbecue pits and outhouses but you'll need to bring water and a screened tent or insect repellent to keep the gnats at bay.

No permission is needed to camp, though if convenient it's a courtesy to check-in first at the governor's office. You can arrange in town for a car to drop you off and pick you up.

Honeymoon Beach is popular among backpackers. There's usually a good breeze accompanying the sound of rolling surf. It has a tin-roofed, open-air shelter and a barbecue area. At Ngrerewal and Ngurungor picnic areas and Orange Beach there are other camping possibilities available.

Getting There

Air Palau Paradise Air flies to Peleliu from Koror for $17 one way, and from Angaur for $11 one way.

Boat The *Peleliu Princess* makes scheduled boat trips between Elochel Dock in Klouklubed and the Fisheries Co-op on Koror. It leaves Koror on Monday and Friday mornings and returns from Peleliu on Thursdays and Sundays. The three-hour ride costs $1.50 each way. Apparently there is also a fishing boat with an irregular schedule.

Private commuting speedboats leave from the same docks. Joe's Mart (tel 908), on the causeway between downtown Koror and Malakal Island, is a hangout for Peleliu islanders and someone there might know of boats going down.

Getting Around

You can rent a pick-up truck, with or without a guide, for $25 to $30. A guide and mini-van costs about $35 or a larger van is $40. It may be possible to politely negotiate $5 or so off those rates or arrange for less than the full-scale tour. Cost is per vehicle, so the more people you pile inside, the cheaper it is. Make arrangements through the guest houses or in advance through the airline.

Mopeds or bicycles would be an ideal way to see the island; you might try asking around for one.

Angaur

For the independent traveller looking to get off the beaten track, Angaur has a certain timeless South Seas charm. It's a tranquil, hassle-free island with only one village. Angaur claims a population of just over 200, including Palau's President Lazarus Salii.

Angaur, seven miles (11 km) south-west of Peleliu, is outside the protective reef that surrounds most of Palau's islands. Open ocean pounds the north coast where in places the sea explodes through blowholes. The south end of the island is calm with sandy beaches.

The only monkeys in Micronesia are on Angaur. There are about 600 crab-eating macaques, the descendants of a couple of monkeys accidentally introduced by the Germans in the early 1900s. The macaques cause some agricultural damage and there is occasional talk of eradication programmes.

Orientation

If you arrive by air you're greeted by a dilapidated 'Angaur International' sign hanging from a tiny open-air shelter. The 7000-foot (2100-metre) paved airstrip dates from WW II. It's not too much of a hassle if you can't get a ride from someone meeting the plane as the guest houses and village are only about 10 minutes walk from the airport.

The coastal road circling the island is mostly level and in good condition. Angaur is just 2½ miles (four km) long and though it's possible to walk the outer road in a full day, the heat and humidity don't make it tempting. The hottest walking is around the village where the sun reflects off the crushed coral streets.

If you're on a day trip you'll probably want to rent a vehicle or be content with walking around just a portion of the island. Outside the village, tall trees and tropical growth close in, allowing for shady strolls.

Angaur Harbor

Angaur's well-protected harbour is so nearly enclosed that the calm waters look like a big swimming pool. There's good swimming inside the boat basin and you can snorkel outside.

Phosphate Mines & Ruins

The Germans started mining phosphate for agricultural fertiliser in 1909. Operations were later taken over by the Japanese and mining resumed for another decade after the war. After a 30-year lapse there have been recent negotiations to reopen the mines, but it's questionable whether there's enough phosphate remaining to make it worthwhile.

To get to the old mines, turn inland north of the harbour, take the left-hand road at each of three forks and then look closely on the right for a low horizontal iron ramp. It's not the mines that are visible below, but cool green ponds which formed when the excavations filled with water after the mining. The water is just a little salty, which is apparently how the resident crocodiles like it.

Back on the coastal road, look for the tall rusting iron girders of the conveyer belt that moved the phosphate down to the nearby harbour.

Japanese Lighthouse

Up ahead, there's an old Japanese lighthouse hiding in the jungle on a hill to the left of the road. It takes a sharp eye to find it, but when the road nears a hill with dense vegetation walk back toward the village about 50 yards and look for the rough start of a trail. The crumbling coral steps give way to concrete ones leading up to the lighthouse, which is a five-minute walk from the road. There's a good view from the lighthouse, though the uppermost tower has toppled off. Wasps have made thousands of little mud homes on the inside but they don't seem bothered by visitors.

Shrines & Monuments

Further north there's a miniature wooden

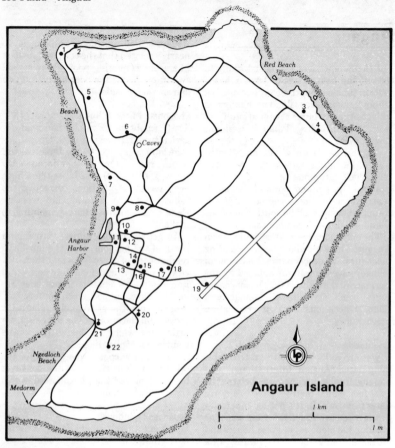

Angaur Island

Shinto shrine, no more than four feet high. It's set off to the right with jagged rock formations and twisting plant roots making an interesting backdrop. There's a nice beach across the way.

Around the north-west tip of the island is a statue of the Virgin Mary, erected to protect Angaur from stormy seas. A Buddhist memorial with markers honouring fallen Japanese soldiers is just ahead and if you walk down towards the ocean and look to the right you'll see a big blowhole.

Red Beach

On 18 September 1944, after five days of bombing, US Army troops stormed Angaur at Red Beach on the northern coast. The landings were unopposed. The US declared the island secured two days later, though hundreds of Japanese soldiers had merely retreated to caves in the north-west corner of the island.

Although the Americans were able to immediately move in and start building airfields, fighting continued until 23 October. By then 1500 Japanese and 240 US soldiers had been killed.

1	Virgin Mary Statue
2	Buddhist Memorial & Blowholes
3	Former Coast Guard Station
4	Aeroplane Graveyard
5	Shinto Shrine
6	Overview of Ponds
7	Lighthouse
8	Phosphate Plant Ruins
9	Phosphate Conveyer Belt Ruins
10	Store
11	Dispensary
12	Elementary School
13	Bai
14	Masao Endo's Guest House
15	Julio's Guest House
16	K Family Store
17	Governor's Office
18	School
19	Terminal
20	Catholic Church
21	Catholic Priest's House
22	Cemetery

Coast Guard Station

The well-manicured grounds of the former Coast Guard station have been returned to the former landowner who now lives in one of the buildings. If the phosphate mines reopen, workers may be housed there.

Aeroplane Graveyard

Look closely into the dense jungle left of the road about halfway between the Coast Guard station and the northern end of the airstrip to find the aeroplane graveyard. Pieces of wrecked WW II planes are blanketed with the soft needles of towering ironwood trees. A Corsair plane with both wings still intact is the most recognisable, but the incredible root structure of the trees and the dream-like setting are as interesting as the plane.

Swimming Cove

On the south-west side of the village there's a quiet swimming cove near the Catholic priest's house. A concrete slab and rock under a large shade tree are used to crack tasty 'Palauan nuts' found

scattered on the ground. The beach there and further south is called Ngedloch or sometimes Waikiki.

Spirit Respites

Beyond the priest's house is a cemetery with Palauan, Japanese and German graves and nearby, quite coincidentally, is an area where the souls of all Palauans go after death.

There's usually nothing to see, but within one or two days after a death it's said that a small waterhole appears so the spirit of the deceased can wash off all traces of earthly trappings and become totally free. The spirit then makes its way to Medorm at the south-west tip of the island, ascends a huge banyan tree and shoots off into the heavens. Fishermen in the area at night sometimes report seeing streaks of fiery light in the sky.

Diving

There's good diving around Angaur between January and July, but the rest of the year the water's too rough. You need to make arrangements in Koror, as there's no equipment on Angaur.

Places to Stay & Eat

There are two guest houses, both in modern concrete homes a short walk from the airport.

Julio's Guest House (Box 261, Koror, Palau 96940), next to the K Family Store (no sign), has three rooms with shared bathroom for $15/$25 a single/double, or mats on the living room floor for $12 per person. Meals are available and cost $5 for breakfast, $7 for lunch and $12 for dinner. The owner Julio Kazuo is also in charge of Angaur's tourism, what little there is. If you have any requests ask Julio and he'll go out of his way to help. He also has a speedboat to rent for fishing trips.

Masao Endo's house is around the corner. There's one bedroom for a single person or couple and mats are provided on the floor in a larger room for groups. Either way it's $10 per person. Meals are available, costing from $15 to $18 per day for breakfast, lunch and dinner and you eat whatever the family is eating, which is usually seafood. They prefer advance notice, which can be done through the airline, so if you're showing up on Angaur unannounced try Julio's first.

Angaur has a couple of small stores with basic provisions, but no restaurants. Locals proudly claim their fertile soil produces the best pot in Micronesia.

Camping Camping is easy and acceptable though there are no developed facilities. Take water and protection from insects. You could check with Julio for help in choosing a good camping spot, though for the most part no permission is necessary and you can pick your own beach.

Getting There

Air Palau Paradise Air flies between Koror and Angaur for $23 and between Peleliu and Angaur for $11.

Boat A state speedboat makes the 1½ hour trip between Angaur and Koror about once a week, usually on Fridays. Check at the Fisheries Co-op in Koror for details and expect to pay about $10 one way. Private speedboats sometimes commute, but not nearly as often as between Koror and Peleliu. The channel between Angaur and Peleliu can be very rough.

Getting Around

Ask at the guest houses about hiring a pick-up truck and guide. The rate quoted is $25 but it's often negotiable, especially if you're just going around for a few hours. Although you might be able to rent a truck without a driver to go off on your own, it probably won't be cheaper.

KAYANGEL

Kayangel, 15 miles (24 km) north of Babeldaob, is a picture-postcard coral atoll. It has four islands with sun-bleached beaches circling a well-protected

aqua lagoon. There's just one quiet village of 150 people, a predominance of tin houses, two small stores, no vehicles and no electricity. The main island is only ½ a mile wide and ¾ of a mile long, yet there are two chiefs – one for each side.

Kayangel is still fairly traditional. Visiting women should wear a T-shirt and shorts over a bathing suit for swimming and neither men nor women should wear shorts in public.

Woven handbags and baskets from Kayangel are in demand as they're made of a high quality pandanus leaf imported from Saipan. An average handbag costs $30 and lasts a couple of years.

Places to Stay

There are no hotels but you can ask at the Kayangel governor's house in Koror about the possibility of camping or staying with a family. Take rice, coffee or other provisions to give to people who help you. Bread is appreciated as there is none on Kayangel.

Getting There

State diesel boats called *bilas* leave Kayangel for Koror every other Thursday at payday time, returning to Kayangel from T-Dock the following Saturday.

Kayangel's one and only fishing boat travels to Koror about every five days. The schedule is irregular but the Fisheries Co-op will know if it's in. It's a smoother ride than on the state diesel boats.

Both take seven to eight hours and charge $3 one way. Private speedboats, if you can find one, take about three hours.

THE SOUTH-WEST ISLANDS

The tiny islands to the south-west stretch for 370 miles (596 km) beyond the main Palauan islands towards Indonesia. There are five groups, each of which cover less than one square mile of land. There is Sonsorol, with two islands, and the single islands of Pulo Anna, Merir, Tobi and Helen.

People from the south-west islands are related culturally to the central Carolinians and have more in common with Yapese and Trukese outer islanders than with people from the main islands of Palau. Their language is Sonsorolese. This is traditional island life at its purest, with thatched houses, carved canoes and fishing as a livelihood.

Sonsorol has about 80 people, Tobi about 70, Pulo Anna a dozen or two and the only inhabitants on Merir and Helen Reef are birds and sea turtles.

There's no official field trip ship to the south-west islands, though a Palauan fishing patrol boat heads that way occasionally.

Palauan storyboard carved with legends.

Guam

Guam is the metropolis of Micronesia. It's the region's largest island, covering 212 square miles (543 square km), and with about 110,000 people it also has the largest population. In appearance and in style it's not unlike a 'little Hawaii' mixed with the Americanised Hispanic flavour of East Los Angeles.

Guam has traffic jams, fast food restaurants, large shopping centres, a university, busloads of package tourists who stay in a row of resort hotels, and a substantial US military presence.

It also has tropical forests, sleepy villages, a mountainous interior, good sandy beaches and an abundance of butterflies and rainbows.

The way you view Guam depends on the direction from which you're coming. If you've just been island-hopping through the less developed FSM then Guam is big time, and perhaps spoiled and over-developed. It's a consumer playground and a place for a salad fix for those expatriates living on the outer islands.

On the other hand if you've just flown in from New York, Sydney or Tokyo, Guam is likely to appear slow, rural and laid-back.

Guam's prolific tourist bureau promotes the island both as 'Where America's Day Begins' and as the 'Gateway to Micronesia.'

Geography
Guam is about 30 miles (48 km) long and nine miles (14 km) wide. It narrows to about four miles (6.5 km) in the centre so it's shaped a little like a bow tie. It is the southernmost island in the Marianas chain.

The northern part of Guam is largely a raised limestone plateau, with some steep vertical cliffs dropping 300 to 600 feet (90 to 180 metres) to the sea. The south is a mix of high volcanic hills and valleys containing numerous rivers and waterfalls.

Reef formations surround much of the island. The beaches on the west side tend to be calmer than those on the east coast which get heavier seas. The southern tip of the island has a number of protected bays.

Climate
Guam's climate is uniformly warm and humid throughout the year. Daily temperatures average from a low of 72°F to a high of 85°F.

The most pleasant weather is during the dry season from January to the end of April when the dominant trade winds, which blow year-round from the east or north-east, are strongest. The humidity is also slightly lower then and the rainfall averages just 4½ inches (11 cm) monthly.

The rainy season is from mid-July to mid-November with an average of about 13 inches (33 cm) of rain a month. The annual rainfall averages 98 inches (249 cm).

Guam lies in the path of typhoons and strong tropical storms, which are most frequent in the last half of the year but can occur in any month. If you want to check on the conditions you can call tel 343-2991 for the latest pre-recorded weather information.

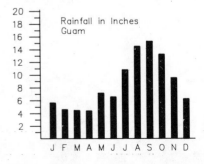

Rainfall in Inches
Guam

History
The ancient Chamorros inhabited the

Mariana Islands at least as early as 1500 BC. They were probably of Indonesian-Filipino descent, sharing language and cultural similarities with South-East Asians. The Chamorros were the only Micronesians to cultivate rice prior to western contact.

It was a matrilineal society of extended family households. Most farming, construction and canoe building was done by men while the cooking, reef fishing, pottery and basket making was done by women.

The social system had three main classes. The *matua* and *achoat*, or the nobles and the lesser nobility, owned the land while the *manachang*, or lower class, worked it. Only the nobles were allowed to be warriors, sailors, artists and fishermen. The manachang had to bow down in the company of nobles and were not allowed to eat certain foods including such basics as saltwater fish.

The island was divided into districts, each made up of one or more villages, mainly scattered along the coasts. The highest-ranking district noble, the *chamorri*, was in charge of local affairs but there was no central leader. The districts often fought each other, the villagers armed with slings and spears.

Foundation pillars called *latte stones* are the most visible remains of early Chamorro culture. The upright posts were usually quarried from limestone and the rounded top capstones were of either limestone or brain coral. Latte stones were used as supports for the homes of nobility and men's houses. The stones vary from a few feet high to as tall as 20 feet (six metres).

Chamorros were a tall, handsome and well-built people. Before the arrival of Europeans the men wore no clothing at all, except occasionally hats or sandals made of palm leaves. When women wore anything, it was only a waist cord with a type of thin grass skirt attached.

The Spanish Period The first western contact in the Pacific islands was in 1521 when Ferdinand Magellan dropped anchor at Guam's Utamac Bay during the expedition that made the first circumnavigation of the globe.

The Spaniards noted that the triangular sail design used on the Chamorros' outrigger canoes was superior in efficiency to the conventional European sails of the day. Magellan named the chain of islands *Islas de las Velas Latinas*, Islands of Latin Sails. He retained the native name *Guahan*, meaning 'we have', for the island of Guam.

The Chamorros provided the crew with food and water but in return they took whatever they could find on the ships, which prompted Magellan to quickly rename the islands *Islas de los Ladrones* – Islands of Thieves. The name Ladrones was still being used by sailors well into the 20th century.

The Guamanians claimed that what the Europeans saw as theft was in fact traditional reciprocity practiced in Chamorro society between hosts and guests. The Spaniards however, did not take the matter so lightly. Before they had left three days later, Magellan's group had killed seven people and burned 40 houses in the process of retrieving a stolen rowboat.

Miguel Lopez de Legazpi arrived in Guam 1565 and officially claimed the Marianas for Spain, before going on to establish the trade route between the Philippines and Mexico.

For the next 250 years Spanish galleons stopped at Guam to take on provisions during annual runs between Manila and Acapulco. In addition to galleon layovers, there were occasional visits by Spanish, English and Dutch explorers. Yet almost 150 years passed between Magellan's landing and any real attempt at European settlement.

In 1668 the Jesuit priest Diego Luis de Sanvitores arrived with a small Spanish garrison to establish a Catholic mission in the village of Agana. At first the mission was welcomed and Catholicism began to spread.

But the missionaries opposed traditions such as ancestor worship and the sexual initiation of young women in the communal men's houses. They insisted the natives wear clothing and blurred the traditional social system by accepting converts from all classes.

It took only a few years for the islanders to realise they were losing their traditions and this sparked rebellions and warfare that lasted for the next 25 years. Sanvitores was killed in 1672 after he baptised a chief's infant daughter against the chief's wishes. Spain sent reinforcements and the battles escalated.

By 1695 the fighting was over, but only because there were no more Chamorro men left to fight. Between the bloodshed and epidemics of smallpox and influenza, the Chamorro population dropped from perhaps 100,000 to fewer than 5000, virtually all of them women and children.

Spanish soldiers and Filipino men brought in to help re-populate the islands intermarried with Chamorro women, marking the end of the pure Chamorro bloodline.

As was the custom at that time, the man moved to the woman's house after marriage. This gave the women the chance to raise their children with some Chamorro influence. If not for this, the children would undoubtedly have grown up speaking Spanish and all traces of Chamorro culture would have been lost.

In addition to religion and disease, the Spanish introduced a written language, set up schools and taught construction and farming skills.

The American Period Although whaleships visited the Marianas as early as 1798, it wasn't until 1822 that any stopped at Guam. Some of the whalers were British, but most were American and during the peak whaling years of the 1840s there were hundreds of ships passing through.

In April 1898 the United States declared war on Spain. Two months later Captain Henry Glass sailed into Guam's Apra Harbor with guns firing. He was greeted warmly by the Spanish authorities who, having no idea that their two nations were at war, apologised for not having enough ammunition to return the salute. The next day the Spanish governor officially surrendered.

In August 1898 the Treaty of Paris ceded Guam (as well as Puerto Rico and the Philippines) to the US who maintained a largely unfortified naval control over the island until 1941.

The Japanese Occupation Japanese bombers attacked Guam from Saipan on 8 December 1941, the same day as the Pearl Harbor attack across the international date line. Guam was an easy and undefended target. On 10 December, within hours of 5000 Japanese invasion forces coming ashore, Guam's naval governor surrendered.

Two months earlier, in anticipation of such an event, many Americans on Guam had been sent home. Those that remained were taken prisoner and sent to labour camps in Japan.

The Japanese administration took over and began the task of teaching the Chamorros the Japanese language. They named the island *Omiyajima* which means 'Great Shrine Island'. Guam became part of an empire that the Japanese said would last for a thousand years. They held it for just 31 months.

In the beginning the Chamorros were mostly left alone. Food supplies were rationed, but islanders could live where they liked and workers were paid low wages for their labour.

Toward the end of Japanese control the military rule became quite harsh. Guamanians were placed in work camps to build fortifications and forced into farming to provide food for Japanese troops.

On 12 July 1944 the Japanese military command ordered all Guamanians be marched into concentration camps on the eastern side of the island. The people didn't know where they were going or why and considering the recent atrocities, some feared the worst. Particularly for some of the elderly and the sick it did indeed turn out to be a death march.

As it turned out the move saved many lives by concentrating the Guamanians away from the American invasion bombardment and subsequent fighting on the south-west side of the island.

In the final hopeless days there were incidents of massacres. The Japanese, hoping to kill as many Americans as possible before dying themselves, also took the lives of the Chamorros who they thought might compromise that aim.

In one of many incidents, 40 Chamorro men were taken abruptly at night from their camp to carry provisions as the Japanese retreated to the north. After arriving in Tarague, rather than allow the men to go back to their camp and give away their positions to the advancing US forces, the Japanese tied them to trees and beheaded them.

The Americans Return Pre-assault bombings by the US began on 17 July 1944. The US invasion came on 21 July, when 55,000 US troops hit Guam's beaches at Agat and Asan. The US secured Guam by 10 August after fierce fighting, with 17,500 Japanese and 7000 US casualties.

Agana was a city in ruins and many smaller villages were also destroyed. The population swelled tenfold, from about 20,000 local residents, as 200,000 US servicemen moved in to prepare for the invasion of Japan.

Large tracts of land, comprising roughly one-third of Guam, were confiscated by the US military at the time. When the war ended the military kept the land.

In 1986, a class action lawsuit for dispossessed landowners won a multi-million dollar settlement from the US government, but many found the terms unsatisfactory. To rub salt into old wounds, the military is now considering leasing out some of the land for farming – not to the families who were kicked off those farms, but to the highest bidders.

Twenty years after WW II, Guam's Andersen Air Force Base was a centre for B-52 bombing raids over Indochina during the Vietnam War. In 1975 more than 100,000 Vietnamese refugees were flown to Guam under the 'Operation New Life' programme before going on to the US. A decade later, a deposed Ferdinand Marcos took a similar route from the Philippines to the States, stopping long enough on Guam for his entourage to run up sizable unpaid bills at the base commissary.

Government

Guam is an Unincorporated Territory of the United States of America.

The Organic Act of Guam in 1950 installed a civilian government to replace the navy, including a 21-seat legislature and a judicial system. It also granted all Guamanians US citizenship. In 1962 security clearance restrictions on travel to Guam, which had been imposed by the US Navy, were lifted.

Guamanians chose their first elected governor, Carlos G. Camacho, in 1970. Although a part of the US, Guam does not have a voice on par with the 50 states. The islanders cannot vote in national elections and although in 1972 they were finally given the right to send a representative to the US Congress, he also has to sit on the sidelines without a vote.

With the US paying millions of dollars in leases for bases in the Philippines, many Guamanians question whether they're not being taken for a ride – token citizenship in exchange for free land use and control. It's a hot item in the local press.

Graft, corruption and payoffs are so widespread on Guam that in 1986 a federal investigation of local government resulted in more than 100 indictments, including many against department heads and the governor himself. It became a controversial issue among many Guamanians who argued that looking out for friends and relatives, as well as gift-giving to those in high positions, was a time-honoured Chamorro tradition. Considering only one of the first 50 defendants to be tried was acquitted, the argument doesn't seem to have much weight in affecting the outcome.

Economy

Before WW II Guam's economy was mostly subsistence agriculture. The establishment of large post-war military bases, however, opened up jobs in construction and support services.

The 1960s saw the beginning of economic growth and a rise in the standard of living. In 1962 Typhoon Karen hit Guam hard, destroying more than 60% of the buildings and much of the vegetation. Reconstruction aid and the building boom that followed gave another boost to the economy.

The Vietnam War and its related military expenditures provided more jobs and pumped in more money. Today the military is by far Guam's largest industry.

Among Guam's large naval and air force stations is a nuclear submarine base and a US Strategic Air Command headquarters. Guam is also a storage depot for an estimated 450 nuclear warheads, the largest stockpile of US nuclear weapons in the western Pacific.

The lifting of the security clearance in 1962 and the start of jet service in 1968 opened Guam to tourism and nearby Japan, then emerging as an economic power, provided the customers. In 1986 Guam had 394,000 tourists who brought in more than $200 million. About 80% of those visitors were from Japan.

GovGuam, as the local government is called, is an over-loaded bureaucracy employing 26% of the work force. If you add those on military bases an well as other federal jobs, the government payroll swells to include over 50% of all workers.

Guam is in the midst of a construction boom, with hotels, shopping centres, apartment buildings and you name it going up everywhere. In their attempt to cut labour costs, construction firms often hire overseas workers. Not only do they pay low wages but they attempt to get around labour laws, such as paying overtime, by threatening to have the workers deported if they complain. Some of Guam's most extravagant resort projects have been challenged by the Department of Labor over such practices.

People

When Guam was opened to settlement in 1962 it was largely Asians, not Americans, who started pouring in. The official 1980 census recorded a population of 105,979.

Although the 55,000 'Chamorro' Guamanians are still the largest ethnic group, indigenous rights groups are concerned that Chamorros will end up losing control of their island to outsiders.

About 30,000 residents are from the US mainland, 8000 of them permanent and 22,000 of them military workers and their families. The next largest groups are Filipinos (25,000), Koreans (4000) and Chinese (3000). Guam is also home to Japanese and a smattering of other Pacific peoples.

More than 90% of the population is Roman Catholic.

Language

Spanish never completely replaced the Chamorro language, although more than 75% of modern Chamorro words are derived from Spanish. Though it has more gutteral and repeated rhythmic sounds, Chamorro sounds a lot like Spanish too.

Chamorro was first written and printed by Spanish missionaries who, using their own language as a base, used 'y' for the Chamorro article 'the'. Western scholars then wrote it as 'i'.

Chamorro also has a unique sound

Designed in 1917 from a sketch by Helen Paul, the wife of a naval officer, the Guam flag features a sailing canoe, a coconut tree and the ocean below the cliffs of Two Lovers Point. The oval shape recalls the slingstones used as weapons by the ancient Chamorros and this central design was adopted as the official seal of Guam in 1930.

that's something like 'dz', which is spelt 'y' in the Spanish style and 'j' in the western style. There are still two systems for spelling Chamorro words, so you can expect to see both.

In theory Chamorro and English are both official languages as both are taught in schools and used in government documents. In practice however, English is taking over as the language of choice.

Many common Chamorro phrases are the same as in Spanish. 'Good morning' is *buenos dias* and 'goodbye' is *adios*.

The common Chamorro greeting is *hafa adai* (pronounced 'half a day'). Literally, it means 'what?' but it's sort of a 'hello, what's up?' and 'how are you?' all combined. *Hafa adai* is sometimes shortened to *hafa* or *fa*. 'Thank you' is *si yuus maasi*.

Holidays & Special Events
Guam celebrates the standard US holidays, as well as Guam Discovery Day on the first Monday in March; Liberation Day on 21 July; and the Feast of the Immaculate Conception on 8 December. Liberation Day is a day of feasts, fireworks and the largest parade of the year.

New Year's Eve is wild. Some Guamanians sit in their backyards shooting off guns and the Hilton Hotel has a fireworks display.

Guam has lot of activities going on all the time. The Guam Visitors Bureau publishes a free calendar of events, including fiesta dates, which is updated quarterly.

Fiestas Nowhere does the Spanish influence show up so profoundly as in Guam's Catholic traditions, particularly in its fiestas and celebrations.

Each village's annual fiesta honouring its patron saint is a community affair with feasting, games, music, traditional Mass and a parade around the village with the statue of their saint.

Fiestas are celebrated on the weekend closest to the saint's feast day so the dates vary slightly each year. If you're lucky

enough to be in Guam during fiesta time, it's a treat worth checking out. The idea is to attract as many people as possible to the festivities, so everyone is welcome.

Fiestas are held in the following places:

January
  Asan
April
  Barrigada and Merizo
May
  Inarajan, Malojloj and Santa Rita
June
  Tamuning, Ordot and Tumon
July
  Agat and Tamuning
August
  Piti, Toto, Barrigada and Agat
September
  Agana and Talofofo
October
  Mangilao, Yona, Umatac and Sinajana
November
  Agana Heights
December
  Dededo, Agana and Santa Rita.

Orientation
The airport is in Tamuning about a mile up from Route 1, which is also called Marine Drive and is the main island road. From the intersection of the airport road and Route 1, Agana centre is to the left. Tumon Bay, Guam's main resort area, is immediately below you, though you must first turn onto Route 1 (either way) before heading down to the bay.

The four-mile (6.5 km) stretch of Marine Drive from Tamuning to Agana has four-lane roads that get jammed with rush hour traffic. The ever-present road construction and detours compound the congestion.

A 50-mile (80.5 km) road circles the lower half of the island, which is the most scenic and historic part of Guam.

Most of the driving around Guam is on excellent paved roads, but tourist attractions are often poorly marked and street signs are scarce. It's more common to see signs pointing the way to 'Maria's Christening Party' or 'Roasting Pigs 4 Sale' than to a viewpoint or village.

Guam has numerous public beaches, some of them with showers, toilets and picnic tables.

AGANA

The capital city of Agana has been the centre of Guam since the Spanish period. With its parks and historic sites it's a pleasant place to spend an afternoon. If you have a car, it's easier to park in the public lot by the museum and visit many of the sites on foot rather than deal with the traffic.

Information

Most of Guam's main tourist and general business facilities, such as visitor info, government and post offices, as well as travel agencies, banks and laundromats are in Agana or in Tamuning and Tumon Bay, 2½ miles north-east of the main city area.

The Guam Visitors Bureau (tel 646-5278) on San Vitores Rd in Tumon Bay has free brochures and maps. Be sure to ask for the useful highway map put out by the Department of Public Works.

The modern public library is on the corner of Route 4 and West O'Brien Drive. It's open 9.30 am to 8 pm Monday to Thursday, to 6 pm on Fridays and from 10 am to 4 pm on Saturdays. The University of Guam also has a good general library in addition to its Micronesian Area Research Center.

All mail sent c/o General Delivery in Guam is delivered to the less-than-central Barrigada post office and can be picked up between 8.30 am and 5 pm Monday to Friday and from noon to 4 pm on Saturdays. The post office in central Agana is open weekdays from 8.30 am to 4.30 pm, and on Saturdays from 8 am to noon. Both post offices sell inexpensive boxes and padded envelopes useful for mailing things home.

Guam has two newspapers, the *Pacific Daily News* and the twice-weekly *Guam Tribune*, as well as several weekly and monthly publications.

Guam Now is a useful promo booklet with restaurant and entertainment listings, airline schedules, maps and mini-feature articles. It's free and readily available at the airport, hotels and car rental booths.

The *Guam USO Handbook* is quite similar in content, though geared more toward newly arrived GIs than tourists. You can pick one up at the USO in Piti.

It's not hard to find a bank on Guam and credit cards are widely accepted.

Four nations maintain consulate offices in Agana. Their addresses are:

Japan 6th floor, ITC Building, Route 1, Tamuning (tel 646-5220)
The Philippines
    4th floor, ITC Building, Tamuning (tel 646-4620)
Republic of Korea
    Suite 305, the GCIC Building, opposite the Agana Marina (tel 472-6488)
Nauru In the Ada Commercial Center, near the corner of Route 4 and Marine Drive, Agana (tel 472-8300). Air Nauru is also there.

Plaza de Espana

Plaza de Espana is a peaceful refuge of Spanish-style buildings, old stone walls and flowering trees.

The plaza was the seat of Spanish administration from 1669 and the centre of religious, government and cultural activities. Buildings once completely surrounded the central park area and included schools, a hospital, priests' quarters, governor's residence, military compound, arsenal and town hall. Most of the buildings were constructed of ifil wood and a concoction of lime mortar and coral called *manposteria*. They were roofed with clay tiles. Only a few of the buildings survived the American pre-invasion bombings in July 1944.

The Garden House, now the site of the Guam Museum, formerly served as a storage shed and servants' quarters.

The Chocolate House, the small white circular building with the pointed tile roof, was once where the Spanish govenors' wives served their guests refreshments.

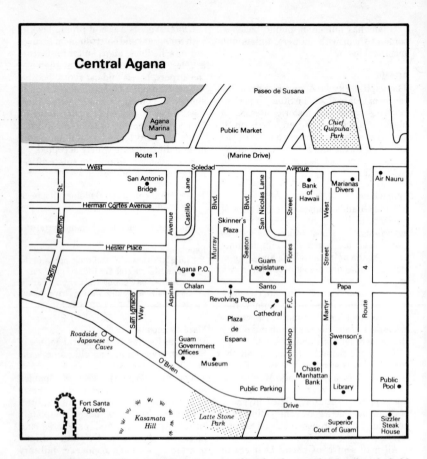

Central Agana

All that remains of Casa Gobierno, the Governor's Palace, is the raised, open-air terrace (west of the Chocolate House) called the Azotea. The small pavilion in the centre of the plaza is the Kiosko and the three stone arches, which date from 1736, were part of the Almacen, or arsenal.

The large tree with the gnarled roots in the south-east corner of the park is called the 'elephant's ear', perhaps because of its grey trunk and branches. Typhoon Karen partially toppled it in 1962 but it's still alive.

There's a statue of Pope John Paul II north of the plaza on the site where he held Mass in 1981. Don't get disoriented if you find that each time you go by the statue it's facing in a different direction. This pope revolves, making one complete turn every 24 hours.

Guam Museum

Guam's small museum features exhibits on Chamorro culture and history, including pottery and other archaeological finds. There are also displays of sea shells and other aspects of natural history.

One display is dedicated to the WW II

straggler Shoichi Yokoi, a sergeant in the Japanese army, who was discovered and captured in 1972. He had been hiding out in Guam's rugged interior for 28 years because no one had told him the war was over. One can only imagine how confused he must have been when he was brought to Agana which is cluttered with signs and billboards in Japanese and crowded with busloads of Japanese tourists!

The display records Yokoi's talent for survival. There's a skillfully woven jacket and a pair of pants made from wild hibiscus fibre, a rat trap made from wire (rat liver was his favourite food) and a frying pan cut from a discarded army water canteen. Many of the foods he ate and tools he made were similar to those used by the ancient Chamorros.

The museum, in Plaza de Espana, is open from 1 to 4 pm daily except Saturdays and admission costs $1.

Dulce Nombre de Maria Cathedral

The cathedral in the Plaza de Espana was first built in 1669, although the current building dates from 1955. Chief Quipuha and other Chamorro chiefs and church leaders are buried beneath the floor. Above the main altar is a statue of Santa Marian Camarin, which was found by a fisherman in the waters off Merizo.

The church is the main scene of activity during Agana's two annual fiestas, honouring the 'Sweet Name of Mary' in early September and the 'Feast of the Immaculate Conception' on 8 December.

Latte Stone Park

The latte stones in Latte Stone Park, at the base of Kasamata Hill, are thought to be house pillars dating from about 500 AD. They were moved to this site from an ancient Chamorro village in the south-central interior of Guam.

There are a number of Japanese caves, built by forced Chamorro labour, dug into the hillface in the park and further west along West O'Brien Drive. You can walk inside them. The ones in the park have been reinforced with cinder blocks and converted into fallout shelters.

Government House

Government House is the governor's residence, a Spanish-style building built in 1952 on Kasamata Hill. There's an excellent view of Agana from the lawn at the rear.

Fort Santa Agueda

All that remains of Fort Santa Agueda is part of its stone foundation, built of burnt limestone mixed with chunks of coral. The fort, which once had 10 cannons, was built in 1800 as a lookout, which is the best reason to visit it now – the view of Agana and the turquoise bay can't be beaten!

This is also the site of the first mission established in Guam in 1668. The fort is at the end of the first road on the right after heading uphill from Government House. It's a narrow street which dead-ends at the fort.

Skinner's Plaza

This park is named after Guam's first civilian governor, Carlton Skinner, and has memorials to Guam's war heroes. The feature of the plaza is a bust of General Douglas MacArthur, complete with his snazzy sunglasses but minus his pipe, which was stolen.

San Antonio Bridge

The San Antonio Bridge, also known as the 'Old Spanish Bridge' or To'lai Achu', sits in a downtown park, spanning a stagnant pool and surrounded by lots of flame trees. When the Agana River was diverted in 1800 this cut stone bridge was built to cross it. The river was filled in after WW II. A stone plaque on the bridge honours St Anthony of Padua.

In one of the pools is a statue of the mermaid Sirena. According to legend Sirena was a young girl of Agana who went swimming instead of gathering coconut shells as her mother had asked. When she didn't return on time the mother cursed her daughter saying, 'If the water gives Sirena so much pleasure I hope she turns into a fish!' Sirena's godmother intervened in time to say, 'Let the part that has been given to me by God remain human'. Sirena thus became a mermaid – half fish, half human.

Paseo de Susana

Paseo de Susana, the peninsula north of central Agana, was built during the reconstruction of the city after WW II, by bulldozing all the rubble and debris of the city to this area.

The Public Market with its food stalls and flea market is close to Marine Drive and behind it is the baseball stadium used by Guam's major league teams. All along the walkway there are stalls selling trinkets and T-shirts and on the waterfront at the northern tip is a tacky miniature replica of the Statue of Liberty.

The left lane of the road circling the baseball stadium has been designated for joggers and pedestrians only. The Agana Marina (also called the Agana Boat Basin) is to the west and beyond it surfers challenge the waves.

In the south-east section of the park, a statue of Chief Quipuha stands forever condemned to survey Agana's congested traffic on Marine Drive. Quipuha was Agana's highest ranking chief when the first mission was built on Guam. He was the first Chamorro adult to be baptised and donated the land for Guam's first Catholic church, the site of the present Dulce Nombre de Maria Cathedral.

TUMON BAY & POINTS NORTH

Tumon Bay is the tourist centre of Guam, jammed with hotels, nightclubs, restaurants, souvenir shops and all the usual trappings of resort life.

Ypao (Ipao) Beach Park

Ypao Beach is a public park in the midst of the resort hotels. It was once an ancient Chamorro village and in the late 1800s was the site of a penal and leper colony.

Gun Beach

Gun Beach is half a mile down a washed-out but passable coral road and straight through the open gates past the Okura Hotel. There's a rusted Japanese gun at the foot of the cliff on the north side of the beach just past the remains of a pillbox. Divers like to follow the cable out to the reef and it's popular for night dives.

Gun Beach is OK but past the gun and around the point to the north is a nicer crescent of white sand. At low tide it's possible to wade right around there or at high tide you can swim or snorkel. There was once an old Chamorro village in this area and latte stones can be found by following an overgrown trail heading inland.

Two Lovers Point

Two Lovers Point, or *Puntan Dos Amantes*, is at the top of a cliff just north of Tumon Bay.

Heading north on Route 1 towards Dededo, the turn-off to the point is marked by a telephone pole covered with small signs, including one to the VFW. Take a left there and another left at the stop sign. About a mile further up, take the left at the green building. Beware of the speed bumps as you drive down to the point.

As the story goes, two young Chamorro lovers entwined their hair and jumped to their deaths after being hunted down by the Spanish captain who had been promised the girl in marriage. A new, giant gilt statue graphically shows the two lovers entwining more than just their hair.

Another attraction at the point is a very deep basalt cave which drops down to the ocean. It's enclosed by protective fencing but you can look down into it.

Northern Beaches

Two of Guam's best beaches are Tarague Beach and Uruno Beach, on the northern coast of the island. However, although these beaches are public the only access to them is through the Andersen Air Force Base, so without a visitor's pass nonmilitary types can't get to them. On the other hand if you approach from the sea you're allowed to land.

One of the few stretches of northern coastline with public access is Tanguisson Beach, formerly known as NCS Beach. To get there, take the turn-off from Route 1 towards Two Lovers Point but instead of taking the final turn-off to the point follow the road past the sewage treatment plant. You then bear left when the road forks and you'll see a power plant to the left of the beach once you're there.

Heading north from Tanguisson Beach there's a dirt road that parallels the ocean which you can drive up for about ¼ of a mile to a picnicking spot. You can also continue hiking north from there on a trail that goes along the coast. There are sandy beaches along the way but the final one, called Shark's Hole, has a turquoise hole with good snorkelling. There are two channels into the hole so beware of the currents.

South Pacific Memorial Park
This park in Yigo is a memorial site for those who died during WW II. A chapel called the Queen of Peace is staffed by Japanese priests and nuns. The main monument is a 15-foot (4.5 metre) abstract sculpture of large white hands folded in prayer. It is surrounding by small, personalised memorial plaques, mostly in Japanese.

There are some steps leading down the hill from the monument to the caves which served as the last Japanese Army command post. On 11 August 1944 American soldiers detonated 400-pound blocks of TNT at the opening of the caves. When the caves were reopened a few days later more than 60 bodies were removed, including that of the Japanese commander, Lieutenant General Hideyoshi Obata, who had taken his own life.

The park is on Route 1 in Yigo and is open from 8 am to 5 pm daily. Heading south out of the park there are some former military Quonset huts on the left which are now private homes.

University of Guam
The university, which opened in 1952 and offers both undergraduate and graduate programmes, is on the east coast. Its Micronesian Area Research Center (MARC; tel 734-2921) has an excellent collection of books, papers, maps and documents on the Pacific region and the library staff are very helpful if you're interested in research. The university is also noted for its work in marine biology.

Guam's two-year community college is just to the north of the university.

SOUTHERN GUAM
If you had only one full day on Guam, you couldn't do better than to rent a car, circle the southern part of the island and take time to just stroll through the villages and catch the scenery along the way.

If you start in Agana and go down the west coast in the morning and up the east coast in the afternoon you'll keep the sun at your back for photography and views. Umatac and Inarajan are particularly worth exploring.

GovGuam at Adelup Point
South of Agana on the western coastal road is Adelup Point, site of the new Spanish-style government administration offices and adjoining beach park. The controversial complex was built by mainland Chinese construction labourers.

Route 6 Side Trip
At another time you might want to take the five-mile Route 6 loop from Adelup Point through the Nimitz Hill area to Piti. You'll get some excellent views of the west coast as well as the country in the interior.

War in the Pacific Park
This National Historical Park has its visitors' centre and display of war memorabilia in Asan, which is about a mile south of Adelup Point on Route 1.

The staff there present a 12-minute slide show which reviews WW II in the

Pacific, diplomatically presenting both the Japanese and American perspectives. They have a free brochure that gives a run-down of the war on Guam and maps out the sites for visitors. The centre is open from 7.30 am to 4 pm Monday to Friday, and 8.30 am to 3 pm on Saturdays. Admission is free.

Seven separate parcels of land, that were battlefield sites during WW II, have recently been acquired and added to the park's historical holdings. Only a couple are currently developed. One of them is just down the road from the visitors' centre and is an extension of the Asan Beach Unit, including Asan Point. It has pillboxes, gun emplacements and caves. Just offshore, a couple of pieces of rusting military paraphernalia can be seen at low tide.

Piti Bomb Holes

The Piti bomb holes, inside the reef, are ideal for beginner divers as they bottom out at around 30 feet (nine metres). They can be seen from the shore and look like dark blue circles surrounded by the aqua shades of shallower water. It's just local lore that the holes are bomb craters, they're actually natural sinkholes.

Snorkellers might enjoy the hard yellow corals around the edges of the holes, but the water is deep enough in the centres to make it difficult to see the bottom. The holes are about 100 yards (30 metres) out through shallow waters. Watch out for the strong currents around the holes furthest out. Closer to shore you'll see bright blue starfish, zebra damsels, pufferfish and other tropicals. The best time to go is high tide.

The parking area is on the right about ¼ of a mile after Asan Park, across the street from a metal warehouse.

Piti Guns

To get to the Piti guns, turn left off Route 1 just past the Mobil Station in Piti and at the stop sign turn right. Park under the big tree to the left of the first church building (it has a white cross on the front), and walk up the concrete steps behind that building. The path up to the Japanese coastal defence guns is fairly well defined although slightly overgrown with hibiscus bushes. It's only a few minutes up to the first gun which is amazingly well preserved.

Apra Harbor & Beaches

The US Naval Station encompasses Orote Peninsula and all of the land surrounding the huge, natural deepwater Apra Harbor. The harbour contains a number of sunken ships which makes it a popular diving spot.

There are good beaches and reefs out on the Glass Breakwater. This long and thin artificial extension of Cabras Island is named after Captain Glass who took Guam for the US in 1898. You can usually drive right out, although when ships come in it's sometimes closed for security reasons.

To get there turn right at the USO in Piti, go straight past the commercial port and take the upper road just past the Mobil Oil tanks. Family Beach is on the harbour side about halfway out the breakwater and at the grove of trees on the left you can climb down to a nice sandy stretch. Don't leave valuables in your car.

Dogleg Reef, just to the right of Family Beach, is clearly visible from shore. The top of the reef starts just two to three feet underwater and is a good place to see both soft and hard corals as well as anemone colonies with clownfish.

Back on Route 1, an artificial (hopefully!) Polaris missile guards the entrance to Polaris Point, part of the naval station.

To continue south around the island, you turn left at the traffic lights just past the US Army Reserve Center on the right. This is not well marked and if you miss the turn you'll wind up at a guarded US Navy gate. Route 1 becomes 2A there, then 2 and later 4. The yellow flowers along the roadside are called 'golden candles'.

Namo Falls Park

Turn left onto Bishop Olano Drive (Route 12) and follow the signs for one mile to get to Namo Falls. This pleasant park has two gentle waterfalls from the Namo River which are surrounded by gardens of flowering trees and bushes. Admission is $1.50 and it's open from 9 am to 5 pm on weekends and holidays and from 8 am to 1 pm on weekdays.

Gaan Point

The park at Gaan Point, back on Route 2 in Agat, marks the site of the southern WW II invasion, where US marine and army combat divisions came ashore to battle with the Japanese infantry.

From their coastal caves and pillboxes the Japanese easily cut down the US Marines in their landing crafts, until US tanks made it ashore and managed to knock the Japanese out from behind. There's an American WW II Amtrak underwater about 400 yards (364 metres) out and 50 feet (15 metres) down.

Nimitz Beach Park

You'll know you're near Nimitz Beach Park when you become aware of the pungent scent of a chicken farm. The park is just past that smell!

At low tide you can wade or snorkel about halfway out to Anae Island, just offshore, to get to Coral Gardens which is a popular dive and snorkelling spot. In amongst the tall coral pillars are triggerfish, parrotfish, sea urchins and other colourful sights. If you want lots of company in the water, take some bread out with you and feed the fish.

Be careful when the tide goes out around Nimitz as the water funnels off the reef into the channel that flows past Anae, and the pull of the current can be very strong. On the southern side of Anae Island there is part of a wrecked plane.

Taleyfac Bridge

In the late 1700s the Spanish built a bullcart coastal road to connect Agana with Umatac and other southern villages. The road, known as the *Camino del Real*, was connected by several stone bridges.

The best preserved bridge is in Agat at Taleyfac (Tailafak), less than half a mile from Nimitz Beach, on the ocean side of the road. Built in 1785, the bridge has twin stone arches that picturesquely span a small stream.

The Southern Coastline Trail

Where the road rises and begins to wind away from the shore you enter the Territorial Seashore Park.

Two miles from Taleyfac Bridge a sign reading 'Southern Coastline Trail' marks the start of a well-defined red clay walking track down to Sella Bay. The whole walk is wonderfully scenic but watch out for slippery mud and vicious sword grasses. An old Spanish bridge crosses the Sella River close to the coast. Give yourself about 1½ hours to make the hike there and back.

Some people prefer to make a day of it, continuing south from Sella Bay along the shore to Cetti Bay and then up the Cetti River Valley. The valley dead-ends at Cetti Falls, but before that point there's a turn-off to the left that goes up to the main road.

Cetti Bay Vista Point

A mile down the road from the Southern Coastline Trail sign is a spot with a superb view of the coconut palm-lined Cetti River Valley emptying into the crescent-shaped Cetti Bay. From there you can see the Merizo Barrier Reef, Cocos Island and the whole south-west coastline.

Mt Lamlam & Mt Jumullong Manglo

Behind the Cetti Bay Vista Point and crowned with crucifixes is Mt Jumullong Manglo, or *Humuyung Manglu'*, the final destination of cross-bearers during the annual Good Friday procession.

The parking lot on the inland side of the road is the starting point for a trail that goes up to Mt Jumullong Manglo. Midway between the parking lot and the lookout point, you head up the eroded hill and continue along the mostly well-defined trail. At the divide, go to the right to get to the crosses. There are excellent views of both the coast and the interior forests on the way and the hike should take about an hour.

A more difficult and more obscure trail continues left from the divide to the 1332-foot (399-metre) Mt Lamlam, Guam's highest point. Lamlam means 'lightning' and legends call it the source of the winds. Clouds move quickly over these mountains, constantly changing the light.

Memorial Vista

I Memorias Para I Lalahita Vista Point is a Vietnam War memorial, about one mile north of Umatac. Two latte stones mark the spot and there's a good view of the surrounding area.

Umatac

Umatac is an unspoiled, friendly village, steeped in history. It's definitely worth stopping there for a while to enjoy it.

Magellan's landing is celebrated annually in March by the people of Umatac with four days of activities, including a re-enactment of the event.

The Spanish used Umatac Bay for more than 200 years as a major port of call for their galleons, though little remains of the four forts that once protected the bay.

Fort San Jose was built on the east side of Umatac Bay around 1803. What remains can be reached by turning off on the dirt road to the right, at the fenced-in water pump, just before the Umatac village sign. You can climb the hill to the south, but there's really not much to mark the site.

The village centre is another half a mile. Opposite a white concrete monument to Magellan there are the ruins of the Saint Dionicio Church. The original church, built in the 1690s, was reconstructed in 1862 and destroyed by an earthquake in 1902. Bougainvillea, the official flower of Guam, surrounds the carved stone pillars. In Chamorro, bougainvillea is called *puti tai nobiu* which means 'it hurts not to have a sweetheart'.

The rusting skeleton of a Japanese midget submarine used to be visible offshore at the river mouth but it's now buried under the sand bar. There's a Japanese Zero in the bay about 150 yards (136 metres) from the beach and 50 feet (15 metres) underwater.

On your way out of town you'll see the new Bridge with its extravagant spiral staircase towers. It's supposed to symbolise Guam's Chamorro-Spanish heritage.

Fort Soledad

Fort Nuestra Senora de la Soledad, past the bridge on the right, offers a spectacular view of village and the bay as well as the coastline to the north. The fort was built in the early 1800s. Its four cannons were never fired.

If you've got a keen eye you can see the remains of Fort Santo Angel which built in 1742 on a rock jutting out on the north-west side of the bay.

Merizo

The Merizo Conbento, in the village of Merizo, was built by the Spanish in 1856, soon after the smallpox epidemic which killed almost two-thirds of the population. The building is still in use today, as a parish house, and like Agana's Plaza de Espana it was built of ifil wood and manposteria (burnt limestone mixed with coral rocks).

Next to the conbento is San Dimas Church. In the courtyard there's a monument to the 46 Chamorros who were executed by the Japanese in the Merizo hills in July 1944, one week before the US invasion.

Directly across the street is *Kampanayun Malessu'*, the Merizo Bell Tower, built in 1910 under the direction of Father Cristobal De Canals. It was restored in 1981.

Cocos Island

Cocos Island is three miles offshore in the Merizo Barrier Reef. The left side of Cocos has been developed into a 100-acre resort hotel specialising in water sports. The right

Top: Latte stones, Taga House – Tinian
Bottom: Divers in the Grotto – Saipan

Top: Natural swimming hole – Rota
Bottom: Overview of Agana – Guam

side is a public area and part of the territorial park system. Cocos has good beaches.

The return ferry trip to the resort costs $12 for tourists and $5 for locals. As long as you're not getting off a tour bus, you should be able to slide by as a local. There's also a $3 landing fee.

Boats go at least once an hour between 7.30 am and 10 pm or so, with the heaviest schedule between 9 am and noon. The trip out takes 15 minutes. You can get an idea of where the resort's coming from by its 'No Outside Food or Drinks Allowed on Cocos Island' sign.

To get to the public park you have to hike over from the dock on Cocos or find a private boat from Merizo.

Offshore Islands
About four miles from Merizo, the offshore islands of As-Gadao, Fofos and Agrigan come into view. You can wade out to the islands across the coral reef. The water is waist-deep in places.

Back on the main island at this point, the road is flat and follows the coast with nice beach views.

Inarajan Natural Pool
You shouldn't miss the Inarajan (Salugula) Natural Pool which is an extensive natural saltwater pool with diving platforms and arched bridges. Jagged grey lava rocks separate the calm pool from the crashing ocean surf beyond making it a great swimming hole!

There are fresh water showers facilities there and lots of families go there on weekends.

Inarajan Village
Inarajan Village, just down the road, is another sleepy village with a smattering of Spanish-era influence. Townspeople decorate their lawns with a remarkable assortment of plaster geese, elves and toadstools – à la '50s kitsch!

The body of Chamorro priest Jesus Baza Duenas is buried beneath the San Jose Church. Duenas, his nephew and two other Chamorros were tortured and beheaded by the Japanese for failing to reveal the whereabouts of US Navy radioman George Tweed who had survived the Japanese invasion and gone into hiding.

Near the end of town is a crumbling concrete Baptist church, built in 1925, which is apparently going to be renovated.

Next to it is a shiny new sculpture, depicting part of a story told about two powerful Chamorro chiefs, Malaguana of Tumon and Gadao of Inarajan.

It seems that one day Malaguana went by canoe to meet and kill Gadao. When Malaguana got to Inarajan a stranger invited him to dinner but unknown to him, that man was Gadao. When Gadao asked his guest to get a coconut for dinner, Malaguana shook a coconut tree and the coconuts fell like rain. Gadao then took a coconut and pulverised it with one hand.

After a few more contests of physical strength Malaguana became worried that if this common Inarajan man was so strong, what would his chief be like? So Malaguana asked the man to take him back to Tumon by canoe. Both chiefs got in the canoe but paddled in opposite directions. The canoe broke in half but Malaguana, in his urgency to leave the island, was paddling so fast that he didn't even notice until he was back in Tumon.

The statue shows Gadao paddling his half of the canoe.

Gadao's Cave
From the statue you can see some caves in the cliffs across the bay. One of them is Gadao's Cave and has ancient pictographs said to be the canoe story drawn onto the wall by Gadao himself.

To get there, drive north out of town on Route 4. Just across the bridge you'll see a little store on the left with a latte stone and phone booth. Take the road to the right, opposite the store, and park at the far end of the beach just before the road turns inland.

Walk along the beach and then take the trail across a meadow and up a cliff to the caves. The walk takes about 15 minutes. Some of this land may be private property, so if you see anyone along the way ask their permission to continue.

Talofofo Falls

Talofofo Falls is a two-tier cascade, with pools beneath each fall. There's a 30-foot (nine metre) drop on the top one, but it's gentle enough to stand beneath. The deeper and larger pool is at the base of the second fall. This is a popular swimming and picnicking spot.

To get there you travel about 2½ miles past Inarajan and take the turn-off to the left leading to Talofofo Park and the NASA Tracking Station (there should be a sign). About 1½ miles down, turn right onto a dirt road and the falls are about a mile further on.

Talofofo Falls are open from 9 am to 5 pm on weekdays and from 9 am to 5.30 pm on weekends. Admission is $2.50.

You can either park in the lot above the falls and walk from there or brave the steep winding one-lane road down to a lower parking area. If you walk, it will take less than 10 minutes to get down but probably double that to walk back.

Talofofo Beaches

Back on Route 4, Talofofo Bay Beach Park is just ahead. This is one of Guam's prime surfing spots, where the sand is chocolate brown. Guam's longest and widest river, the Talofofo, runs out into the bay at this point.

Ipan Beach Park, just down the road, is another popular swimming place with calmer water and nice shade trees.

Pago Bay Vista Point

A viewpoint, just past the town of Yona, looks over where the Pago River empties into Pago Bay. The inhabitants of a Spanish village at the mouth of the river were wiped out by the 1856 smallpox epidemic.

The area between Pago Bay on the east coast and Agana Bay on the west is the narrowest part of the island. According to

legend a giant fish who wanted to divide Guam in half used to visit the island and nibble away at this neck of the land. Guam was saved by the women of the island who cut off their long hair, wove a big net of their locks and scooped up the fish with the net.

Other Attractions

The road along Tumon Bay is the entertainment drag of Guam. During the day the focus is on water sports and other outdoor activities and at night the clubs, discos and bars come alive.

Guam has a greyhound dog track, motor-cross raceway park, legalised cockfights, two country clubs with golf courses, movie theatres, tennis courts, a public swimming pool, bowling alleys, windjammer cruises and Polynesian dance shows.

There are also several shooting galleries. The highest profile goes to the Wild West Gun Club where a 20-foot (six-metre) John Wayne replica rounds up Japanese tourists. Donning cowboy costumes and Indian headdresses they photograph their own shoot-outs.

There's a friendly funky zoo on Tumon Bay. To get there turn towards the ocean onto the road opposite St William's Church. It's a small zoo run by a guy called Jimmy Cushing who just seems to like animals. Japanese tourists largely bypass it, as it's geared more towards local kids, but it has a variety of small animals, a shark pit and sea turtles. It's open from 10 am to 5 pm daily and admission costs $1.50.

Hiking, Cycling, Running

The USO in Piti (tel 333-2022) sponsors 'boonie stomps' around Guam every Saturday and if you're at the USO by 12.30 pm and have $1 you can go along. From the USO you can probably share a ride with someone to the trail start. They usually return around 5 pm. The location and difficulty of each week's hike is announced in advance. These folks know their hikes well so this is a great way to explore Guam.

If you plan to hike on your own, it's definitely worth getting down to the USO and asking to see the hiking scrapbook kept behind their front counter. The book describes trails around the island, with directions, time required and ratings according to distance and terrain.

The Athlete's Foot (tel 472-1514), in the Agana Shopping Center, has information on the Guam Running Club and upcoming road races.

The bicycling club (tel 477-9711 or 472-8346) sponsors short easy rides on Saturday mornings, longer rides on Sundays and a number of races.

Water Sports

Surfing in Guam is best between December and June. Beginners might prefer to start off at Talofofo Bay, while the more experienced surf the channel at Agana Marina.

The Marianas Yacht Club (Box 2297, Agana 96910) at Apra Harbor sponsors several races throughout the year. These include the Guam-Japan Goodwill Regatta in February, the Rota and Return Race in late May and the Round the Island Race in late November. The club also has information about charter boats and sailing lessons.

Tumon Bay hotels and shops rent hobie cats, paddle boats, outrigger canoes, snorkelling gear, inflatable rafts and other water sports equipment.

Windsurfing is popular around Merizo and in Tumon Bay where boards can be rented. Cocos Island hosts a major international windsurfing competition in February.

Fishing Deep sea fishing boats leave from Agana Marina and Merizo Pier on the search for marlin, wahoo, yellowfin tuna, sailfish, barracuda and mahi-mahi. A 1153-pound (519 kg) Pacific blue marlin, caught off Ritidian Point by a Guamanian in 1969, broke the world record at the time.

For information on the Marianas Fishing Derby held in late July write to the Guam Fishing and Boating Association, Box 24023, Guam Main Facility 96921.

Diving & Snorkelling

Guam has a rich marine habitat with more than 800 species of fish and 300 species of coral (Hawaii lists only 100). You should check for jellyfish that occasionally float in especially during trade wind months.

There are a couple of dozen popular dive spots on the west coast, many in or south of Apra Harbor. One of the best known, for advanced divers, is the Blue Hole at the end of Orote Peninsula. It is 60 to 130 feet (18 to 39 metres) deep with good visibility.

One of the more unusual dives is to the *Tokai Maru*, a Japanese freighter bombed during WW II. It sank and landed on top of the *Cormoran*, a German cruiser scuttled during WW I, which is resting upside down on the ocean floor. At about 95 feet (28.5 metres) you can have one hand on each war.

Dive Shops Two large dive shops handle most of Guam's diving business. Dive tour rates include tanks and weights, and other gear can be rented. Snorkel and mask sets rent for $2.50 and filled tanks for $3.

Marianas Divers (tel 472-3232; Box 1116, Agana 96910) is on the corner of Marine Drive and Route 4, opposite the Chief Quipuha statue. They're open daily until 6 or 7 pm.

Their double-tank boat dives cost $65 (single tank $50), and include lunch and hotel transfers. Beach/reef dives cost $50 for two tanks, $40 for one. For $70, non-divers can try the beginner's scuba experience, usually to the Piti bomb holes. Snorkellers on the boat with divers are charged $25.

The instructors from Marianas Divers can certify divers in PADI in four full days for $200 to $225. If you have two weeks you can join a class and do it for $105.

The *Micronesian Divers Association* (tel 565-2656; Box 13005, NS Branch,

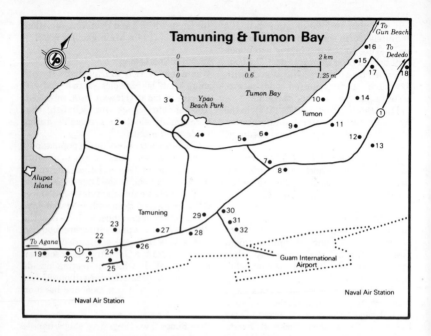

Tamuning & Tumon Bay

Agat 96915 is on Route 2 in Agat. Full-day diving (two dives and snorkelling) costs $65 including lunch and hotel transfers. Snorkellers are charged $30 and an introductory scuba dive costs $75.

The MDA's diver certification (usually NAUI) costs $90 to $110 and takes two to three weeks. They also rent underwater cameras (35 mm) for $15 per day.

Both dive shops have a space-available option for about half price. You need to have all your own gear and tanks (or rent theirs), show up at the boat ready to go and if there's room you get on at the last minute.

Nautical Charts The Coral Reef Marine Center, behind the ITC Building in Tamuning, has US Defense Department nautical charts and maps for all parts of Micronesia. Apparently this is the only place in Micronesia that sells them. Coral Reef also sells diving supplies but doesn't lead dive trips.

Places To Stay

Most of Guam's nearly 4000 hotel rooms are around Tumon Bay and most of them are usually completely booked out during Japanese vacation and honeymoon times in February, March, August, September and around the New Year.

Except where noted all rooms have air-conditioning, private bathrooms and an 10% room tax.

Places to Stay – bottom end

John Benavente rents three rooms with shared bathroom in his home which he calls the *Island Garden Guest House* (tel 632-5870; Box 2247, Agana 96910). It's a bit off the beaten track in a quiet suburb in Dededo, 3½ miles north of Tumon. Room rates are $20 a single and $35 a double and include tax and a breakfast of coffee, toast and juice. Arrangements can be made for other meals and tours.

John's an outgoing guy who knows Guam

1	Guam Memorial Hospital
2	Dog Track
3	Hilton Hotel
4	Pacific Islands Resort
5	Pacific Star Hotel
6	Dai-Ichi Hotel
7	Cool Spot Jr.
8	Japanese Anti-Aircraft Guns
9	Suehiro Hotel
10	Fujita Hotel
11	Joinus Hotel
12	St. John's Church/School
13	Pagoda Hotel
14	Guam Visitors Bureau
15	Reef Hotel
16	Okura Hotel
17	Guam Plaza Hotel
18	Guam Horizon Hotel
19	Ben Franklin Department Store
20	Pizza Hut
21	Taco Bell
22	Marty's Mexican Restaurant
23	Gibson's Shopping Center
24	ITC Building/Bank & Consulates
25	Coral Reef Diving Shop
26	Hafa Adai Marketplace
27	Denny's Restaurant
28	Hafa Adai Marketplace
29	McDonald's
30	Exxon/Thrifty Car Rental
31	Tamuning Post Office
32	Hotel Mai 'Ana

well and this might be a good way to experience Guamanian hospitality. Airport pickup costs $4 one way. To get there on your own you take Route 1 from Agana to Dededo and turn right at Winchell's Donut Shop. Where the road forks, nearly half a mile later, turn right and it's the second house on the left (yellow with gold trim, no sign), directly opposite a grassy parking area. Dededo is a large town with supermarkets, restaurants and modern facilities.

The *Kina Court Hotel/Motel* (tel 472-2557; Box 804, Agana 96910) in Barrigada, is a converted three-storey apartment building with friendly management and a coin laundromat. It has 24 units, each with full kitchen, living room, cable TV with HBO movies and free newspapers.

They cost $39 a single or double for one bedroom, or $42 for two bedrooms. This is a nice place if you're tired of cramped hotel rooms or want to do some cooking but the main drawback is aeroplane noise. Coming from central Agana on Route 8 you take the first right turn after the Naval Air Station's main gate onto unmarked Canada Rd. Kina Court is on the first corner on the left.

The new *Pagoda Hotel* (tel 646-1882) in Upper Tumon, opposite St John's School on Route 1, has 41 tiny but comfortable and clean rooms. They all have TVs and mini-refrigerators and cost $35 for a single or double, which includes tax, free soft drinks and morning coffee. The Pagoda is very popular, and if barring all the windows makes a place safe then the Pagoda is that too! The staff is loath to make reservations and when busy will break ones that have been made, even if a deposit's been given. Since Guam has lots of flights in the wee morning hours they try to rent rooms twice a day when they can. If the rates stay low and you can get in without a hassle it's a good value.

The *Hafa Adai Motel* (tel 646-6542), on Route 1 in Tamuning, has basic rooms with TVs for $30 a single or double, including tax. It's nothing fancy but the price is right and it's centrally located.

The *Micronesian Hotel* (tel 472-8156), on Route 8, is trying to shake its image as the place where two mass murderers ended their crime spree in a notorious shoot-out in 1983. The run-down collection of musty Quonset huts and little concrete boxes with peeling paint, was originally built as headquarters for the Trust Territory. Men can share a dorm room and bathroom with students and construction workers for $6 a day. Dreary private rooms, some with air-con and some 'tropical', start at $23 per day or $140 per week.

Places to Stay - middle

The *Downtown Hotel* (tel 477-7836), 470 West Soledad Avenue, Agana 96910, costs $38 a single and $43 a double. It's in the centre of Agana within walking distance of the historical sights.

The *Plumeria Garden Hotel* (tel 472-8831) on Route 8 has rooms for $39 a single and $42 a double.

The cheapest hotel on Tumon Bay's hotel row is the 38-room *Guam Suehiro Hotel* (tel 646-6835; Box 2767, Agana 96910). It costs $40 for singles and $45 for doubles.

Tumon's next cheapest is the 280-room *Fujita Tumon Beach Hotel* (tel 646-1811; Box FM, Agana 96910), which costs $50/$55 for singles/doubles. This is one of Tumon's better deals. The tile murals on the hotel buildings depict Guam's history and legends and are worth a look even if you don't stay there.

Across the road from the Fujita is the *Terraza Tumon Villa Hotel* (tel 646-6904) where the rooms are $55 for a single or double. The *Guam Horizon Hotel* (tel 646-6851), on Route 1 above Tumon Bay, has studios for $46 a single or double and two-bedroom suites from $60.

The *Hotel Mai'Ana* (tel 646-6961; Box 8957, Tamuning 96911) is on the right coming down from the airport, before reaching Route 1. Rooms start at $54.

The *Inarajan Shores* (tel 828-8343; Box 3308, Agana 96910) is at the southern end of the island on Route 4, about 5½ miles east of Merizo. Its four plain rooms, with sliding glass doors opening onto the beach, cost $50 a single or double. There's an open-air restaurant in a garden setting.

The *Cocos Island Resort* (tel 828-8691; Box 7174, Tamuning 96911) has cottages on Cocos Island with rates starting at $60 for singles or doubles. The resort has a tennis court and swimming pool and specialises in water sports, catering mainly to the younger Japanese set.

Places to Stay – top end
The deluxe 19-storey *Pacific Star Hotel*, a Republic of Nauru venture, is now Guam's biggest, fanciest, tallest and most expensive hotel. It has 436 rooms that cost from $800 down.

The *Hilton International Guam* (tel 646-1835; Box GPO, Agana 96910) is efficiently run with all the expected services. Rooms facing the ocean have balconies overlooking Tumon Bay and the rates start at $70 a single and $89 a double.

Tumon Bay has half a dozen other large high-priced hotels, most with swimming pools, restaurants, nightly entertainment, water sports equipment, gift shops and other standard amenities. They are Japanese-owned and operated and target their services to Japanese on three-day package tours. So before you decide to splurge on a meal in one of their restaurants consider whether you're really into dinner shows where the diners pop up in the middle of the meal and start reeling off their names and hometowns while the rest of their tour group applauds!

Camping Camping information is available at the Department of Parks and Recreation (tel 477-7825 or 477-9620), 490 Naval Hospital Rd in Agana Heights. The office is open weekdays. The staff will sell you $2-per-day camping permits they say are required, but beyond this seem completely at a loss as to why you might want to camp or which places are safer than others.

The truth is, camping is not that common on Guam. If you do camp it's advisable not to choose a roadside camp as there's apt to be a few rowdy drinkers cruising the roads at night. Guam's crime rate is high enough for potential campers to think twice. Camping in a group or in the wilderness shouldn't pose problems.

Cocos Island is one of the 15 approved camping locations in the park system and is one of the more frequently recommended spots.

Places To Eat
Chamorro food is a rich mix of Spanish, Filipino and Pacific dishes.

Kelaguen is minced chicken, fish, shrimp or Spam mixed with lemon, onions, pepper and shredded coconut.

Lumpia is similar to an egg roll, but dipped in garlic sauce or vinegar.

Pancit is a mix of shrimp, vegetables and garlic over noodles.

Ahn is grated coconut boiled in sugar water.

Poto is a ricecake of tuba, sugar and ricemeal. The red rice is soaked in *achote* seeds.

Other local delicacies include fruit bat soup, whole roast pig, tropical fruits, coconut crabs and anything barbecued. Thick tortillas often replace bread. To turn any dish into a Chamorro meal add *finadene*, a fiery red pepper sauce.

You'll find the best Chamorro food at village fiestas and private feasts. Otherwise, one of the few places where Chamorro food is served is the *Public Market* on Marine Drive beside the Agana Marina. It's open from Monday to Saturday and there are half a dozen food stalls lined up together. Fixed plate lunches of local favourites cost $2 to $3.50. Try a plate of spicy chicken kelaguen or barbecued spareribs. This is a popular place for Agana office workers to get a quick take-away meal.

The *Adventist Book and Food Center*, in the church across the street and up the hill from Government House, is a fully-stocked health food store. It's open from 9 am to 5 pm Monday to Thursday, and to 3 pm on Fridays. The lunch counter is open between 11 am and 2 pm on weekdays. Try the 'Hard to Handle' soybean burger for $2.65 and a fruit smoothie for $1.55.

The *Sizzler Steak House* has an all-you-can-eat salad bar, including nachos and fresh fruit, which cost $5.29 if you order cheese toast and a beverage in the afternoon (a bit more in the evenings). It's in the Agana Shopping Center and is highly recommended for salad lovers.

Uncle Sam's Restaurant, next to the Downtown Hotel, is a popular coffee shop. The hamburgers, which cost $3.25 at lunchtime, and the *mahi-mahi* plates, $4.50 at lunch or $7.50 at dinner, are local favourites.

Fast food enthusiasts can choose from *McDonald's, Kentucky Fried Chicken, Pizza Hut* and a host of others.

The snack bar at the *USO* in Piti is open to the public and features very cheap western fare including hamburgers for $1.20, grilled cheese for 50 cents and cheese omelettes for $1.10.

The *United Seamen's Service Club*, behind the USO on the right before the commercial port, is also a public place. One side of the club is a bar, the other an inexpensive coffee shop. Full dinner specials cost $3.95 and their Eggs Benedict on Sunday mornings cost $2.50.

China House in the Dai-Ichi Hotel has an all-you-can-eat Chinese lunch buffet for $4.75.

Marty's Mexican Restaurant in the Royal Lanes bowling alley building opposite the ITC Building has good Mexican food. If you just want a cheap burrito try *Taco Bell* across the street.

Guam's multi-ethnic population and thousands of tourists support more than a hundred restaurants in Agana alone. There are a lot of cuisines to check out including Japanese, Chinese, Korean, Chamorro, Mexican, Italian, French, Vietnamese, Filipino and Thai.

Things To Buy

With all its shopping centres and gift shops, Guam should have a better selection of handicrafts than it does. Instead however, there are the usual tacky slapped-together carvings, shell art and weavings made in the Philippines with 'souvenir of Guam' labels. There are some crafts from elsewhere in Micronesia, though quality ones are hard to find, and all carry a heavy mark-up. There are also the glitzy hotel shops with their typical duty-free lines.

In Guam you can buy any supplies you may need on other islands. The supermarkets and shopping complexes are fully modern.

Guam claims it is duty free but film is somewhat more expensive there than in the US or elsewhere. It's not a bad place to restock though, but even at the larger duty-free camera shops you should check the expiry dates. It's not advisable to purchase film from the stands set up in the market places or around tourist attractions.

US citizens returning to the States from Guam are allowed a higher than usual duty-free exemption on articles acquired abroad. They are permitted $800 worth of duty-free items ($400 is usual), 1000 cigarettes and four litres of alcohol. No more than $400 worth of these purchases are supposed to have been acquired outside Guam.

Getting There

Guam is one of the official gateways to Micronesia and is serviced by a variety of airlines with flights from the US, Japan, Indonesia, the Philippines, Australia, New Zealand, Nauru and Papua New Guinea.

For complete information on getting to Guam refer to the Getting There chapter at the start of this book.

Getting Around

Guam is difficult to get around without a car, especially if you want to tour the whole island, and hitchhiking is not a common practice.

Airport Transport A couple of the hotels in Tumon Bay, including the Hilton, provide airport transfers but most do not. You might see the ANA trolley bus cruising between the airport, central Agana and the hotels – it's strictly for passengers of All Nippon Airlines.

Car Rentals Budget, Hertz, Dollar and Toyota have rental booths at the airport. Thrifty has an office at the Exxon petrol station at the intersection of the airport road and Route 1. Avis (tel 646-1801) has an office next to the ITC Building. Some companies have drop-off points or branch offices downtown or in the hotels in the Tumon Bay area.

Most companies have a variety of discounted and business rates, but you have to ask for them as they won't always volunteer the information.

For 24 hours, with unlimited mileage, the prices start at $21.95 with Hertz, $22.95 with Avis, $23.95 with Budget and $24.95 with Dollar. Weekly rates are usually six times the daily rate. Optional collision insurance costs about $6 per day. Avoid the Japanese companies that add on an additional mileage charge.

For Americans, a US driver's licence is valid for 30 days. Other visitors need an international driver's licence. Unless otherwise posted the speed limit is 35 miles per hour.

Mopeds The Tumon Moped Center (tel 646-8116) on San Vitores Rd in Tumon Bay rents mopeds for $19 per day or $11 for two hours.

Tours At least two dozen companies (half in Japanese only) provide all sorts of tour options. Lam Lam Tours (tel 646-1028) has a 4½-hour sightseeing tour in English for $18.

Commonwealth of the Northern Marianas

The Northern Marianas have opted for closer political ties with the United States than have other Micronesian islands. It's now a US Commonwealth, similar in status to Puerto Rico, and is also the administrative headquarters for the fading UN Trust Territory.

Saipan, Rota and Tinian are the main islands. The centre of commonwealth activities is Saipan. It is also the largest island, has 87% of the population, dominates in economic development and political strength and gets most of the tourist trade. Rota and Tinian are unspoiled, quiet, friendly and have good beaches.

The Northern Marianas, scene of some of the Pacific War's most devastating battles, woos the Japanese these days by turning war ruins into sight-seeing spots, erecting peace monuments and encouraging the development of resort hotels.

New US passports in hand, the people of the Northern Marianas are hurtling head-long after the American dream. In the rush to look, eat and act American, much of their cultural heritage is being lost. Yet the traveller who chances upon a village fiesta or christening festivities can still get a glimpse of the more traditional Chamorro life.

Geography

The Mariana Islands rise more than seven miles (11 km) from the floor of the ocean, marking the dividing line between the Pacific Ocean and the Philippine Sea.

These islands are actually the world's highest mountains. They are about 10,000 feet (3000 metres) higher than Mt Everest when measured from their bases in the Mariana Trench, which is a canyon extending 1835 miles (2954 km) along the floor of the Pacific. The Mariana Trench also contains the world's greatest known ocean depth of 38,635 feet (11590 metres).

Guam is the southernmost island in the Marianas chain, but has a separate political identity. The Commonwealth of the Northern Marianas is made up of the other 14 islands in the archipelago which stretch 400 miles (644 km) northward from Guam in an almost straight line.

All the islands are high types of either volcanic or limestone formation and the total land mass is 184 square miles (471 square km). Saipan is 47 square miles (120 square km), Tinian is 39 (100) and Rota is 32 (82).

The defoliation of Saipan and Tinian during WW II was so complete that quick-growing *tangan-tangan* was aerially seeded to keep parts of the islands from washing into the sea. Today this pervasive shrub is the most prevalent plant on those islands. Although it has prevented major erosion, it is choking out native flora and has upset the natural pre-war ecosystem.

Northern (Outer) Islands Except for Aguijan which is just south of Tinian, the smaller islands run north of Saipan. From south to north they are Farallon de Medinilla, Anatahan, Sarigan, Guguan, Alamagan, Pagan, Agrihan, Asuncion, Maug and Farallon de Pajaros (Uracas). All are rugged volcanic rocks. Agrihan has an elevation of 3166 feet (950 metres) and is the highest point in Micronesia.

Pagan, which is 18½ square miles (47 square km), is the largest of these outer islands. Only Agrihan and Alamagan are inhabited, but even together have less than 150 residents. Maug is actually three islands, though is counted here as one.

Micronesia's only active volcanoes are among these islands. Following weeks of earthquakes, Pagan's volcano erupted in May 1981 shooting up flames, rocks and clouds of ash as high as 60,000 feet (18,000 metres). Almost half of all the arable land was covered with lava flows.

Farallon de Pajaros
(Mariana Is)

Maug Islands
(Mariana Is)

Asuncion Island
(Mariana Is)

Agrihan
(Mariana Is)

**Commonwealth
of the
Northern
Marianas**

Pagan
(Mariana Is)

Alamagan
(Mariana Is)

Guguan
(Mariana Is)

Sarigan
(Mariana Is)

Anatahan
(Mariana Is)

Farallon de Medinilla
(Mariana Is)

Saipan
(Mariana Is)

Tinian
(Mariana Is)

Aguijan
(Mariana Is)

Rota
(Mariana Is)

Guam
United States

MARIANA TRENCH

| 0 | 10 | 30 | 50 km |
| 0 | 20 | 40 m |

Evacuation planes sent to Pagan immediately after the eruption were not able to land or find any survivors. However, all 54 residents were alive and well and were rescued two days later by a passing Japanese ship. The island is now a restricted area.

The 1000-foot (300-metre) peak on Farallon de Pajaros' and Asuncion's 3000-foot (900-metre) mountain sometimes send up smoke and steam.

Climate
Saipan is listed in the *Guinness Book of World Records* as having the world's most equable temperature. It averages 81°F year-round.

The climate of the Northern Marianas is very similar to Guam's and, also like Guam, the islands lie directly in the typhoon track.

In December 1986, Typhoon Kim smashed the Northern Marianas with winds of up to 170 miles (274 km) per hour. On Saipan, the hardest hit, about 20% of the homes were severely damaged, trees were stripped bare of foliage, thousands of coconut trees were knocked down, roads were blocked and electricity and water were out for weeks.

History
Prior to European contact, the Northern Marianas were populated by the Chamorros whose culture and origins were the same as the people of Guam. (Information on early Chamorro culture is given in the Guam section.)

The Spanish Period First named the 'Islands of Thieves' by Magellan in 1521, the Mariana Islands were renamed 'Las Marianas' in 1668 by the Spanish priest Sanvitores, in honour of the Spanish queen Maria Ana of Austria.

Spanish galleons, on their annual routes between Acapulco and Manila, passed between Guam and Rota in early June. So that they would not have to pass by in darkness, the Spanish ordered that fires be lit nightly on Rota's (and Guam's) highest points. The Rotanese would sail out in hundreds of canoes to meet the ships, hoping to trade food for iron nails and tools.

Around 1700 the Spanish swept down through the Marianas and took all the Chamorros they found to Guam – to control them better. Several hundred Rotanese hid in the hills and avoided capture. Consequently some of the purest Chamorro blood in the Marianas today is in Rota.

The other Northern Marianas were left uninhabited. Explorers that landed on the abandoned islands (including the British captain Samuel Wallis in 1768, soon after 'discovering' Tahiti) sometimes took advantage of the wild cattle and chickens found there, but most went instead to Guam to stock up on provisions.

Around 1820 the Spanish allowed islanders from the western Carolines to move to the larger Mariana islands. The Carolinians managed Spanish cattle herds and maintained a presence on the islands at a time when Spain was skittish over German intentions in the area.

After the pope declared Spain's sovereignty over the Marianas in 1885, the subdued 'Spanified' Chamorros were encouraged to move back to the Northern Marianas from Guam. They were given land for farming, though the Carolinians who had moved in ahead had already claimed some of the best coastal land.

The German Period Germany bought the Northern Marianas from Spain in 1899, as part of its Micronesia package deal. Germany's primary interest was in copra production.

The Northern Marianas were never heavily staffed with foreign administrators during either the Spanish or German years, although a handful of teachers and priests did live on the islands. At any rate, there weren't many islanders to administer.

The Japanese Period When the Japanese took the Northern Marianas from Germany at the beginning of WW I there were fewer than 4000 Chamorros and Carolinians on the islands.

The Japanese had little interest in copra but had great expectations for sugar cane. They chopped down groves of coconut trees and cleared tropical forests and jungles to create level farmland. When latte stones from ancient villages got in the way, they were cast aside.

In the mid-1920s, after Saipan's sugar industry was determined a success, plantations were set up on Tinian and Rota. On all three islands sugar cane was loaded from the fields onto bullcarts and hauled to little narrow-gauge railroads where steam-powered trains carried the cane to mills for processing. Both sugar and alcohol made from the cane were major export items.

By the mid-1930s sugar operations in the Marianas were providing the Japanese with more than 60% of all revenues generated in Micronesia.

Many of the people who worked the cane fields came from Okinawa, where poor tenant farmers were recruited to work for low wages. The high influx of foreigners and the tendency of the colonisers to turn villages into miniature Japanese-style towns overwhelmed the native culture.

At the outbreak of WW II there were more than 45,000 Japanese and imported workers in the Northern Marianas – more than 10 times the number of Micronesians.

World War II One of the largest military operations in all of WW II was 'Operation Forager' which captured the Mariana Islands for the US. Beginning in Saipan and attacking Guam just days later, an American invasion force of 127,000 soldiers, 600 ships and 2000 planes took part.

On 15 June 1944 two US Marine divisions landed on Saipan's south-west coast. The Japanese had 31,000 soldiers waiting. Resistance was fierce but by evening the US had 20,000 men ashore.

That same night the Japanese First Mobile Fleet was detected in the Philippine Sea heading toward the Marianas. When squadrons of Zeros took off from those ships on 19 June, the US forces were ready. In the battle that became known as the 'Marianas Turkey Shoot' both sides took part in a wild all-out air fight west of the Marianas. In two days the Japanese lost 402 planes and three aircraft carriers. The Americans lost only 50 planes in the dogfights, but on the return 80 more crashed into the sea when they ran out of fuel.

With the defeat of their fleet, Japanese forces in the Marianas lost any chance of rescue or support. On Saipan the Americans advanced northward and into the mountainous interior. Garapan, the central city under the Japanese, fell on 3 July. When the battle for Saipan was declared over on 9 July, 3500 Americans, 30,000 Japanese defenders and 400 Saipanese were dead.

After the fall of Saipan, the Japanese had no hope of holding on to Tinian, but chose to fight to the death rather than surrender. American pre-invasion bombing attacks included the first-ever wartime use of napalm.

The Japanese had a military force of 9000 on Tinian. The Americans made their first beach landing on the north-west shore on 24 July 1944. They secured the island after nine days of heavy combat and the loss of 390 American and more than 5000 Japanese lives. US troops immediately began extending the Japanese airbase, using it to stage air raids on Japan, including the atomic bomb drops on Hiroshima and Nagasaki.

American invasion forces bypassed Rota. The US bombed the northern airstrips, but the Japanese held the island until the surrender and Rota came through the conflict relatively unscathed.

The Post-War Period The fierce fighting had reduced whole towns to rubble and in the years following the war there were no attempts to rebuild the sugar industry. The US administered the islands by giving hand-outs rather than by supporting economic development.

In 1948 the CIA closed off half of Saipan to islanders and outsiders alike, using the island for secret military activities. When the CIA moved out in 1962, the Northern Marianas were finally opened to visitors. The UN Trust Territory administration moved their headquarters to Saipan, taking over the CIA offices.

Government
In 1961 Saipan and Rota petitioned the US government, asking to become integrated with Guam. The requests were made nearly every year until 1969 when Guam voters rejected the idea. One reason cited for the rejection was that many Guamanians still harboured ill feelings toward the Saipanese who had acted as interpreters during Guam's occupation by Japan.

In June 1975 the people of the Northern Marianas voted to become a US Commonwealth, and in doing so became the first district to withdraw from the Trust Territory. The commonwealth agreement went into effect in January 1978 and in November 1986 the new commonwealth covenant became fully effective and islanders became US citizens.

The commonwealth's strategic position between Japan and the Philippines, the rather politically sensitive sites of some of America's largest overseas military bases, is seen by the US Defense Department as a back-up in the event they are booted out elsewhere. In an attempt to win the islanders' hearts, the US has long provided the Northern Marianas with more federal funding per capita than any of the 50 states.

Exercising a land-use option built into the commonwealth agreement, the US has leased two-thirds of Tinian for $33 million. The 50-year lease allows use of the land for weapons storage and military training.

Although the majority of Tinian

residents voted for the commonwealth package, complete with military lease options, not all Tinian landowners are happy with the current arrangement. A lawsuit trying to stop military exercises on Tinian, by claiming that the training violates federal environmental protection laws, has been brought before US courts.

The US Air Force has plans to build a radar station in the northern part of Saipan, overriding fears of some residents that it might make the island a nuclear target or emit hazardous levels of radiation.

The Northern Marianas elects its own governor, lieutenant governor and a legislature with nine senators and 14 representatives. Each main island has its own mayor. Although the people of the Northern Marianas are now US citizens they have no vote in US elections and the representative they send to Washington DC is merely an observer and lobbyist.

Economy
Under the new covenant agreement, the US has to provide $228 million in funds over the years 1986 to 1992 for capital development, government operations and other programmes. The government is the largest employer, providing about 2000 jobs.

The Northern Marianas imports a large number of low-paid Asian labourers, the majority from the Philippines and China.

Korean bars bring in Filipinas to entertain, often keeping their passports just to make sure they don't split. The women clean the bars during the day, entertain in the evenings and are only let out if they're escorted. Filipinas are also commonly brought in as low-paid house maids.

Saipan has about a dozen huge clothing factories, some employing as many as 600 people, mostly from mainland China. On paper, workers are paid the minimum wage of $2.15 per hour.

However, because they live in the factory dorms their rent, food and other expenses are taken out of their pay leaving them only a fraction of that. You sometimes see these

workers, in the back of company trucks wearing matching uniforms.

Tourism is the largest industry in the Northern Marianas. In 1985 for example, there were more than 142,000 visitors, 75% of whom were from Japan.

Most of Saipan's hotel rooms are pre-booked, with all expenses pre-paid in yen back in Japan. People travel in tour packs, stay an average of two to four nights and use vouchers to eat in hotel restaurants. With most hotels owned and run by Japanese, relatively few tourist dollars see their way into the Saipanese economy, except in the form of minimum wages paid to those who wait on tables or clean rooms.

People
Between 1970 and 1980 the population of the Northern Marianas nearly doubled, from 9640 to 16,780.

The 1985 estimate of 20,350 residents, placed 17,840 people on Saipan, 944 on Tinian, 1444 on Rota and 122 in the northern islands. Roughly 75% of the native population is Chamorro, the remainder are Carolinian. Most islanders are Roman Catholic.

Language
English is the official and dominant language, Chamorro and Carolinian are native tongues and Japanese is spoken in most hotels and some shops. *Hafa adai* is the standard greeting, as it is in Guam.

Holidays
The Northern Marianas celebrates US public holidays as well as Commonwealth Day on 9 January, Marianas Covenant Day on 24 March, Citizenship Day on 4 November and Constitution Day on 8 December.

Most villages have an annual fiesta in honour of their patron saint, which is the big village bash of the year. Rota and Tinian have one fiesta each, Saipan has eight.

Saipan

Saipan has only Guam as a rival in the crush of Japanese tourists that flock to its shores.

As a quieter and more laid-back version of Guam however, Saipan doesn't have the bigger island's annoying traffic or huge military bases though it does have the modern conveniences, good paved roads and almost as many major resort hotels.

Saipan has a resident population of about 19,000 people and about 10,000 alien labourers.

There are gentle beaches on the west and south coasts, a rugged and rocky east coast, a hilly interior and dramatic north coast cliffs. The island is about 14 miles (22.5 km) long and five miles (eight km) wide.

The airport is at the south end of the island and the major hotels are on Beach Rd which runs along the west coast.

Saipan's main sights are in Garapan and in the Marpi area at the northern end of the island. By car, most can be touched on in three to four hours but a more leisurely look around would take a full day.

Information

The one and only Marianas Visitors Bureau (tel 234-8325) is in Saipan but it has maps and brochures of Rota and Tinian as well. It's directly opposite the airport in the former Japanese communications station.

The Bank of Guam has offices in Garapan and Susupe, the Bank of Hawaii is in the Nauru Building in Susupe and the California First Bank is in Chalan Kanoa.

The main post office is in Chalan Kanoa. All mail to Saipan should be addressed to Saipan, CNMI 96950. (CHRB, used in some addresses following the box number, designates the Capitol Hill branch – it's the same zip code.)

Long-distance calls can be made from hotels, phone booths and the tele-communications office on Middle Rd, south of Garapan centre.

There are travel agents in the lobbies of the larger hotels. Richard at Tasi Tours in the Saipan Beach Hotel is friendly and competent and keeps on top of airline discounts.

Japan has a consulate office (tel 234-7201) in the Nauru Building.

The *Marianas Variety* and the *Marianas Review* are newspapers published weekly on Saipan. Guam's *Pacific Daily News*, flown in daily, has a weekly supplement on the Northern Marianas. San Antonio has a small public library, as does the college. Saipan has three radio stations and a 15-channel TV station which broadcasts 24 hours a day.

GARAPAN

Garapan was the seat of Japanese administration in the Marianas and had Shinto shrines, Japanese schools, a hospital and a jail. The town was bombed to smithereens by the Americans during WW II and is only now returning to its former position as Saipan's main centre, thanks again to the presence of the Japanese – this time as tourists.

Micro Beach

Micro Beach, Saipan's most attractive white sand beach, is travel poster material. The beach faces west, making it a great place to watch one of Saipan's spectacular sunsets unfold. You can just sit in one of the beach chairs and catch the show. The colours continue long after the sun has dropped into the ocean.

Micro Beach Park, just north of the Hyatt, has picnic tables, showers and restrooms. The water is shallow there but during high tide it's fine for swimming and its sandy bottom makes it quite pleasant for wading out to the deeper areas. Sea cucumbers dot the bottom.

Saipan's museum is just before the park entrance. Two tanks, three guns and a torpedo sit rusting in the parking lot, while the museum itself has been closed and neglected for years.

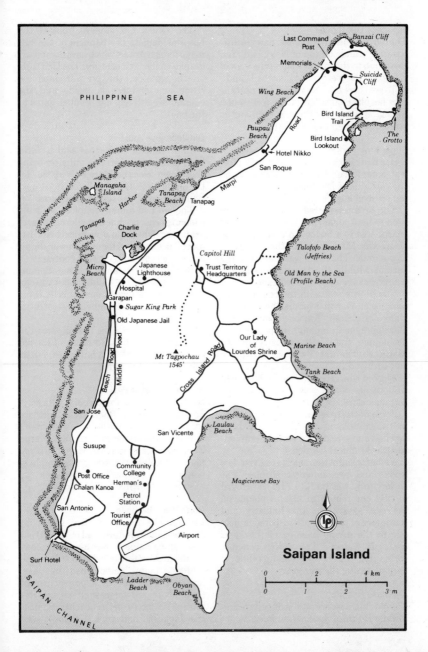

PHILIPPINE SEA

Last Command Post
Banzai Cliff
Memorials
Suicide Cliff
Wing Beach
Bird Island Trail
Road
Paupau Beach
Bird Island Lookout
The Grotto
Hotel Nikko
Marpi
San Roque
Managaha Island
Harbor
Tanapag Beach
Tanapag
Tanapag
Charlie Dock
Talofofo Beach (Jeffries)
Capitol Hill
Old Man by the Sea (Profile Beach)
Micro Beach
Japanese Lighthouse
Trust Territory Headquarters
Hospital
Garapan
Sugar King Park
Old Japanese Jail
Our Lady of Lourdes Shrine
Marine Beach
Mt Tagpochau 1545'
Tank Beach
Beach Road
Middle Road
Cross Island Road
San Jose
San Vicente
Laulau Beach
Susupe
Community College
Post Office
Herman's
Magicienne Bay
Chalan Kanoa
Petrol Station
San Antonio
Tourist Office
Airport
Surf Hotel
Ladder Beach
Obyan Beach

SAIPAN CHANNEL

Saipan Island

0   2   4 km

0   1   2   3 m

Japanese Lighthouse

The old Japanese lighthouse, now graffiti-covered, stands on top of Navy Hill. You can climb to the top for a sweeping view of Garapan, the reef and Managaha Island.

To get there take Navy Hill Rd, past the new hospital, turn left at the fork ¾ of a mile later, then take the next right and go straight through to the lighthouse.

Sugar King Park

Sugar King Park is a hodgepodge of historical, botanical and memorial sights. It's on the east side of Middle Rd and its bright red railroad engine makes it easy to spot.

The steam-powered engine was once used to haul sugar cane from fields in the Marpi area to a factory in Chalan Kanoa where the Mt Carmel Catholic Church now stands. The route was similar to the current Middle Rd, though none of the train tracks remain on the island.

The bronze statue in the centre of the park is of Haruji Matsue, head of the Nanyo Kohatsu Kaisha (South Seas Development Company), responsible for developing the sugar industry in the Marianas. The statue was erected in 1934 and survived the war bombings.

The old concrete building in the southwest corner of the park was a teacher's cottage before the war.

Some of the trees and flowering bushes in the middle of the park have been labelled and grandly called the Commonwealth Botanical Garden.

At the far end of the park is a red, riverless bridge and two Japanese shrines. The Katori Jinja was built in 1911, destroyed in 1944 and rebuilt in 1985. A plaque on the site says that 'the industry and commerce of this island prospered largely due to the divine blessing of the *kami* (god) of Katori'. The newer concrete shrine has interesting photographs of Saipan during the war years.

Japanese Hospital

The old Japanese hospital is directly across Middle Rd from Sugar King Park.

The school bus stop in front of the hospital depicts the banners of the two major foreign powers which have dominated Saipan in the 20th century. The US flag is on the outside, the pre-war Japanese rising sun emblem is inside and the commonwealth flag has been relegated to the back.

Old Japanese Jail

Aviator Amelia Earhart is said to have been held in the Garapan jail after being shot down over the Marshalls in 1937 by the Japanese. Don't fall for it, it just sounds good in the tourist brochures.

The jail had a main cellblock for male civilian prisoners while a smaller cell was set aside for geishas who stole from their customers' pockets and for women who didn't complete their employment contracts.

Bamboo and tangan-tangan are attempting a takeover of the buildings but you can still explore the damp concrete cells, some of which still have their barred steel doors attached.

To get there take the first dirt road to the right off Middle Rd south of the old Japanese hospital. The jail is just a little way down on the right.

NORTH OF GARAPAN

North of Garapan are the quiet villages of Tanapag and San Roque. The northern tip of the island, with most of Saipan's WW II tourist attractions, is called Marpi. There aren't any stores in Marpi, so if you plan to explore the area for a couple of hours you might want to pick up something to drink in San Roque.

North-West Beaches

Perhaps the most fanatical attack by Japanese soldiers during all of WW II took place along Saipan's north-west beaches. On the night of 6 July 1944, 4000 Japanese soldiers, many emboldened by *sake*, hurled themselves in a *banzai attack* (without regard for casualties) into the lines of US forces on the beaches. Some of the Japanese had guns, but most were armed just with clubs, bayonet sticks, bamboo spears and grenades.

The Japanese, honour-bound to die in the face of defeat, were intent on taking as many Americans with them as possible. Wave after wave of Japanese rushed down on the Americans, pushing them out into the water, across Tanapag Harbor and all the way back onto the reef – firing all the while at the unrelenting enemy. By the next morning it was all over and 5000 men were dead.

Paupau Beach, the first left heading north past Hotel Nikko, has good swimming and snorkelling.

If it's crowded at Paupau you could try Wing Beach, named after the US Navy aircraft wing that lay half buried in the sand for decades. The wing is gone now, pilfered during an aluminum recycling programme, but it's a good spot. Wing Beach lies midway between the Nikko and the Last Command Post.

Memorials

The memorial parks are lined up along the road starting about 7½ miles north of Garapan. The first is the Korean Peace Memorial, the second for Okinawans and the Last Command Post is straight ahead.

Banzai Cliff

Banzai Cliff, where waves crash onto the jagged rocks below, is one of the spots from where Japanese civilians jumped to their deaths as the Americans were taking over the island in 1944.

Whole families lined up in order of age. Each child was pushed over the edge by the next oldest brother or sister, until the mother pushed the oldest child and the father pushed his wife before running backwards over the cliff himself. Although US soldiers dropped leaflets and shouted through loudspeakers that those who surrendered would not be harmed, the mass suicides were deemed preferable to the shame of capture and to the torturings the Japanese had been convinced the Americans would inflict upon them.

Over the years the Japanese have put up a number of plaques and memorials to commemorate the spot.

The turn-off to Banzai Cliff is off Marpi Rd opposite the Okinawan memorial. The yellow blossoms along the road dry to become wood roses.

The Last Command Post

The Japanese Imperial Army, at the spot now known as the Last Command Post, had many well-hidden and fortified caves where they resisted American forces to the end.

It was there that Lieutenant General Yoshitsugo Saito admitted defeat and asked his remaining soldiers to each take seven American lives for the emperor, which triggered the suicide banzai attack at Tanapag Harbor. Saito then committed *hara-kiri* by thrusting his sword into his stomach while his aide shot him in the head.

Guns, torpedoes and tanks have been placed on the lawn below the concrete bunker which served as the command post. It was built into the rock face, cleverly concealed from the road. You can climb up inside and scramble around.

If you visit this place in the morning you'll find refreshment stalls set up for the tour buses about to arrive en masse. Bus after bus pulls up, the Japanese tourists pour out, grab Cokes, pose by the guns and get back on the buses. It all has the air of an amusement park.

From the Last Command Post the road climbs towards the north-east coast. The first fork, where you bear right, is unmarked but the second fork is marked: left for the Grotto and Bird Island, right to Suicide Cliff. The latter is almost two miles from there.

Suicide Cliff

The 800-foot (240-metre) sheer rock face of Suicide Cliff was another site for Japanese suicides. Below the lookout you can see the bits of paving that still remain of North Field, originally a Japanese fighter strip, while above you white terns swoop and soar in the wind drafts along the cliffside.

A small peace monument at the lookout reads:

The purpose of the Peace Memorial is to console the spirits of those who died, irrespective of nationality, in this historic area as well as to remind our posterities the tragic futility of war, with our sincere hope that everlasting peace and friendship may prevail amongst all mankind.

The Grotto

The Grotto, a popular spot for divers, is a sunken pool of cobalt blue seawater, filled by two underwater passageways. Sometimes the tunnels are calm and at other times powerful surges of water come whooshing in and out. The glowing blue light at the bottom of the rock wall is the tunnel to the open sea.

Once, locals who wanted to swim in the grotto had to climb down a rope but there are now steep concrete stairs down to the water. Tiny stalactites drip from above and massive spider webs hanging overhead make interesting photographs if caught in the right light. At the top of the stairs to the left is a viewpoint looking down into the grotto.

The left turn to the grotto is about ¼ of a mile past the Suicide Cliff turn-off, from where it's ¾ of a mile down to the grotto.

Bird Island

Bird Island, a rocky limestone islet sitting just beyond the beach, has a fair-sized colony of brown noddys (tropical terns).

From the windy lookout point you can see both sides of the island. The ocean surf smashes into one side while the inland coast is calm reef. The flowers to the left of the lookout are beach morning glory

You can hike down to Bird Island but not from the lookout. You head back the way you came and the start of the trail is about ¾ of a mile on the right, just before the turn-off to the grotto.

The start of the dirt footpath looks like an eroded driveway and leads down the

hill through a canopy of tangan-tangan. It requires climbing over some rocks but it's not too difficult. The water is clear and coral formations are nice between Bird Island and the cliffs. Currents are rough beyond the reef.

THE CROSS ISLAND ROAD

Cross Island Rd heads north of Garapan, turns inland to Capitol Hill, circles around Mt Tagpochau, goes south through San Vicente and then heads back for the west coast, passing the Northern Marianas Community College on the left and ending up on Beach Rd in San Jose.

About a mile after Capitol Hill, going toward San Vicente, there's a marker pointing left to a side road leading to Our Lady of Lourdes Shrine. The shrine was built inside a cave by villagers who had taken refuge there during the war.

Capitol Hill

Capitol Hill's complex of houses and office buildings was built for $25 million in 1948 by the CIA as a base for secretly training Nationalist Chinese guerrillas to fight against Mao Zedong. The soldiers were mainly trained in the Marpi area.

Capitol Hill has been the headquarters for the Trust Territory government since the CIA moved out in 1962. In recent years Trust Territory offices have decreased in size and staffing as responsibilities have largely passed on to local governments.

The area has its own post office and grocery store. Heading down to Garapan, there are good views of Tanapag Harbor.

Mt Tagpochau

You can drive right to the top of Mt Tagpochau which, at 1545 feet (463 metres), is Saipan's highest point. To get there drive up to Capitol Hill from Garapan and when you see the convention centre on your left, turn right on the crossroad. Then drive a short way up through the housing project and turn right up to the former Congress of Micronesia buildings, now marked as civil defence, disaster and energy agencies. Continue a few hundred yards beyond the buildings and take the dirt road heading down to the right. If it's been raining heavily you may need a four-wheel-drive vehicle from there otherwise a sedan takes about 15 minutes to the top.

You can also make the long hike up (take water) from the congress buildings, following in the footsteps of hundreds of Saipanese who carry a heavy cross to the top every Easter. There are excellent views of most of the island from the summit.

East Coast Beaches
Laulau Beach, on the north side of Magicienne Bay, is one of several good beaches on the less accessible east coast. Heavy seas beat against the rugged shoreline along much of the coast although there are some calmer areas.

For the more adventurous, Tank and Marine beaches can be reached by dirt roads and you can hike into Jeffries (Talofofo) and Profile beaches. Profile Beach has a limestone islet called Old Man by the Sea, which does look remarkably like the laughing head of an old man.

SOUTH OF GARAPAN
Susupe, Chalan Kanoa and San Antonio used to be distinct villages on Saipan's south-west coast until a decade of development turned Beach Rd into one continuous strip of nightclubs, porno shops, restaurants, shopping centres and offices.

Susupe is the government centre and prior to the recent high-rise hotel boom, its multi-storied Nauru Building was Saipan's tallest and most pronounced landmark.

Chalan Kanoa has the main post office, the island's only remaining movie theatre and the picturesque Mt Carmel Catholic Church. San Antonio is the quieter end of it all.

Southern Beaches
Ladder and Obyan beaches, south of the airport, are popular picnic and dive spots.

To get there head towards the airport, turn right after the Mobil petrol station, go behind and past the six large bunkers that were part of the Japanese communications station and continue around the tip of the runway by the towers. A road on the right runs down to Ladder Beach. Sometimes there's a sign, sometimes there's not.

Obyan Beach which is half a mile past Ladder Beach has a latte stone, carbon dated to around 1500 BC, and a huge concrete bunker.

Don't leave things unattended at these beaches. At least one diving tour has returned from the water to find the tyres on their van slashed.

MANAGAHA ISLAND
A white sand beach fringes the whole island of Managaha, which is off the west coast north of Micro Beach. This is Saipan's best snorkelling area as its clear waters harbour lots of colourful tropical fish and coral close to shore.

There are a few glass-bottom boats which shuttle between Saipan and Managaha, taking a zig-zag path to stop above Zeros and other war wrecks that can easily be seen on the ocean floor.

Managaha is important to Saipan's Carolinians who have put up a monument at the burial place of Chief Ahgrub, who was originally from Satawal in the western Carolines.

Managaha has no permanent residents but, for visiting day-trippers, there are picnic tables, toilet and shower facilities and food and trinket stalls.

Getting to Managaha There are numerous half and full-day tours to Managaha, arranged through Saipan's hotels and dive shops. You can expect to pay from $15 to $25, more if a lunch barbecue is included.

Managaha is a popular weekend picnic spot for locals and it's cheaper to go when they do. Boats (look for the *Santa Rosa*) cost $5 to $8 return on Saturdays and Sundays. They generally leave from

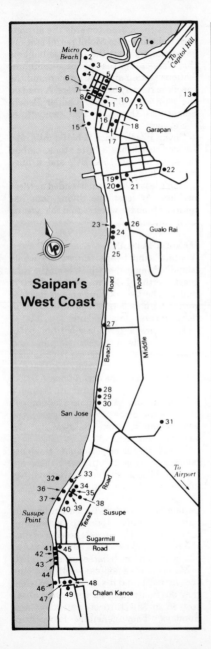

Saipan's
West Coast

1   Boats to Managaha
2   Micro Beach Park
3   Museum
4   Hyatt Regency Hotel
5   Police Station
6   Saipan Beach Hotel
7   Chamorro House Motel/Restaurant
8   Executive House Motel
9   Islander Inn
10   Captain's Lodge/MOE
11   Garapan Elementary School
12   Commonwealth Hospital
13   Japanese Lighthouse
14   Bank/Bakery/Market
15   Hafadai Beach Hotel
16   Poon's Restaurant
17   Laundromat
18   Water Sports
19   Old Japanese Hospital
20   Old Japanese Jail
21   Sugar King Park
22   Sugar King Hotel
23   Hong Kong Restaurant
24   Seasons Kitchen
25   Tropicana Motel
26   Telecommunications Office
27   Japanese Tank
28   National Car Rental
29   Bowling Alley
30   Toyota Car Rental
31   Golf Course
32   American Tanks (offshore)
33   Civic Centre Park
34   Marianas High School
35   Police Station
36   Saipan Diamond Hotel
37   Saipan Grand Hotel
38   Nauru Building
39   JoeTen Shopping Centre
40   Air Micronesia
41   Payless Supermarket
42   Town House Department Store
43   California First Bank
44   Kentucky Fried Chicken
45   Mt Carmel Catholic Church
46   Pacific Gardenia Hotel
47   Movie Theatre
48   Post Office
49   Farmer's Market

Charlie Dock, north of the Micro Beach area around 9 am and 1 pm, coming back at noon and 4 pm.

Diving & Snorkelling

You can snorkel out around a couple of US Army tanks which rest in the shallow waters south of Garapan where US invasion forces first came ashore.

Saipan's most unusual dive is the grotto with its tunnels to the open sea. Though it's a popular spot for locals to swim and for divers with a guide, it can be dangerous for the uninitiated.

Other popular dives are Tanapag Harbor, Laulau Beach and Obyan Beach. Obyan has caves and garden eels.

Dive Shops Saipan has several dive operations, most of them Japanese operated.

Water Sports (tel 234-6664; Box 31 CHRB) in Garapan is locally owned by Ben Concepcion. A full day of boat diving with two tanks costs $60 ($50 for beach dives), including gear, lunch and hotel pick-up. Divers can be certified (YMCA) in five full days for $250, with two dives a day.

Marianas Aqua Sports (tel 234-6965) offers beach dives for $30 per tank while their boat dives or dives for beginners cost $40 per tank.

Water Sports

Windsurfing is popular on Saipan as it's the only island in the Northern Marianas with a good-sized lagoon. Lessons and equipment rentals are available at most of the large hotels. The annual Micronesian Open Boardsailing Regatta is held in mid-February in front of the Hyatt.

Saipan hosts several sailing regattas, including one in mid-November and another at the end of December. Contact Bill Sakovich (Box 100 CHRB) for information.

Special Events

Village fiestas are held at Our Lady of Lourdes Shrine in early February, in San

Vicente in early April, in San Jose in early May, in Chalan Kanoa in mid-July, in San Roque in late August, in Tanapag in mid-October and in Garapan in late November.

The San Isidro Fiesta in mid-May honours the patron saint of Saipan's Carolinians.

The Flame Tree Festival is a two-week celebration at the end of June, when the brilliant orange-red blossoms of the royal poinciana trees are at their peak, which celebrates the American liberation of the islands. It ends on 4 July, US Independence Day, and features a parade, a queen contest, nightly entertainment, games and food booths.

There's an arts festival, an agricultural fair and a fishing derby in May. The Marianas Visitors Bureau publishes an annual schedule of fiesta dates and other events.

Places To Stay – bottom end

The *Sugar King Hotel* (tel 6164; Box 1939), up behind Sugar King Park, is a friendly place with small but comfortable rooms in duplex cottages. Rates for singles or doubles are $30 without TV, $35 with. Each room has a refrigerator, kitchen counter and sink. The owners provide free airport transfers as well as courtesy transportation to and from the beach. Guests can also rent bicycles for $5 per day.

The *Executive House Motel* (tel 234-3539) has four simple rooms for $25 a single or double but there's no hot water. The best feature is its location – right across the street from the expensive hotels at the end of Micro Beach.

The *Tropicana Motel* (tel 234-5550), south of the Hong Kong Restaurant, costs $30/$35 a single/double, including tax. Rooms have phones, refrigerators and TVs. It's clean but not fancy.

The *Captain's Lodge/MOE* (tel 234-6670) is above the MOE dive shop, one block from Micro Beach. Rooms are very neat and colourful but tiny and narrow as they're designed to resemble cabins on a ship, though it feels more like a submarine with two to four people squeezed into a room with bunk beds! Shared bathrooms are down the hall. Most customers come with package diving tours originating in Japan, but if there's room it costs $20 per person.

The rather drab *Islander Inn* (tel 234-6071; Box 95) is the 2nd storey of an office building on Beach Rd, a few blocks from Micro Beach. The 17 rooms cost $30 a single, $35 a double and they say they'll provide free airport transfers.

Places to Stay - middle
The new family-run *Chamorro House Motel* (tel 234-7361; Box 875), in the Micro Beach area, is only marginally more expensive than the cheap hotels but you get a lot more for your money. The rooms are large and pleasant and rates start at $35 a single and $40 a double. The Chamorro House Restaurant is in the same building.

The *Pacific Gardenia Hotel* (tel 234-3455; Box 144), also locally owned, is on a busy section of Beach Rd at the north end of Chalan Kanoa. The 14 rooms cost $48/$64 for singles/doubles and they provide free airport transfers.

Places to Stay - top end
The larger hotels, thriving on the package tour trade, have less need to be receptive to independent travellers and room rates are typically high.

Saipan's superior hotel is the seven-storey *Hyatt Regency Saipan* (tel 234-6811; Box 87 CHRB) right on Micro Beach. All 183 rooms have a balcony with sunset and ocean views. The rates start at $105 for singles or doubles for rooms on the 2nd floor but prices go up as the rooms do. However, if money is no object, this is definitely the place to be.

Next door, and sharing the same beach, is the *Saipan Beach Hotel* (tel 234-6412; Box 1029) which was formerly the Intercontinental. Rooms start at $68/$78 for singles/doubles.

Down the road, the *Hafadai Beach Hotel* (tel 234-6495; Box 338) has just added a 118-room wing, with a jazzy new glass elevator, to its 162-room main building. Rates start at $90 a single or double.

The atmosphere is more Tokyo than Micronesia at the *Saipan Grand Hotel* (tel 234-6601; Box 369) and at the *Saipan Diamond* (tel 234-5900; Box 66) which sit side by side in Susupe. The Diamond is built on the site of the former Royal Taga, Saipan's first hotel built in the late 1960s. The Grand's rates start at $70/$80 for singles/doubles and the Diamond's at $85 for either.

The *Surf Hotel* (tel 234-7976; Box 2370), just past the US Army Reserve Center at the southern end of Beach Rd, has 38 rooms and eight cottages on a quiet beach. Rates are $62 a single or double for the rooms and $80 for the cottages. Maui Airlines has hotel/air packages there.

A subsidiary of Japan Air Lines has started construction on the *Hotel Nikko*, a 320-room 13-storey self-contained extravaganza resort on the previously undeveloped north-west coast near San Roque.

All hotel rooms in Saipan have air-con, all but the Captain's Lodge have private bathrooms and most top-end hotels have the usual resort amenities like swimming pools, tennis courts, restaurants, nightly entertainment, lounge chairs and water sports equipment. Saipan has a 10% hotel tax.

Camping Camping on Saipan presents safety problems similar to Guam. Managaha used to be a great camping spot but the new development might make it more of a hassle. Officially you're allowed to camp there.

Places To Eat
Chamorro food is basically the same in the Northern Marianas as it is on Guam, except it's harder to find. The majority of package tourists eat at their hotels, seldom stepping outside to try the local restaurants. Still there's a proliferation of

small and often unfrequented eating places and as one closes another opens.

Chamorro House, a popular lunch spot in the Micro Beach area, has been serving quality Chamorro food for years. The $3.75 lunch special is a good deal.

The Hyatt's *Kili Terrace* has a big Sunday brunch, but it's a pricey $10. You could however, take the Sunday paper with you and spend half the day in the open-air terrace, eating your fill of fruit, breakfast and lunch entrees, pastries, salads and delicious desserts.

Herman's Modern Bakery, on the way to the airport, is popular and fairly cheap. Besides being a good place for coffee and donuts, the coffee shop serves breakfasts and full meal lunch specials for $3 and sandwiches for under $2.

Poon's in Garapan has Indonesian food. Gado-gado costs $3, beef or chicken satay is $4. Portions are small but the owners are actually Indonesian so the food is authentic. Their Chinese-style dishes can be disappointing.

The *Taipei Restaurant*, a revolving eating place on top of the Nauru building in Susupe, serves Chinese food. If you go between 4.30 and 6 pm you get half-price drinks (beer and mixed drinks are 75 cents), free popcorn and a 360° sunset view.

The *Hong Kong Restaurant*, one in a line of inexpensive Chinese restaurants along Beach Rd, has an excellent lunch special for $3.50 between 11 am and 1 pm on weekdays. It includes sweet corn soup, a choice of entree and ice cream for dessert. If you like it spicy, try the kung pao chicken. The restaurant is on the left one mile south of the Hafadai Hotel.

Seasons Kitchen, in the same area, is cheap for dinner. Roast duck or suckling pig with rice costs $4 and chicken or barbecued ribs with rice is $3.

The only fast-food franchise on the island is *Kentucky Fried Chicken* which is in the Town House shopping centre in Susupe. Where else does the Colonel serve his chicken with red rice cooked with achote seeds?!

Saipan Farmer's Market, or the 'co-op of the hardworking people', is opposite the post office in Chalan Kanoa. It has coconuts, bananas and other fruits as well as vegetables, Pohnpei pepper and sometimes alcoholic tuba. It's open 8 am to 6 pm on weekdays and Saturdays, and from 10 am to noon on Sundays.

Supermarkets sell almost everything you'd find in western stores, except that prices tend to be substantially higher and much of the produce is tired.

Entertainment

A few nightclubs and discos surround the hotels in Garapan.

Local residents like the *Marine Bar* in the Hafadai Hotel on Mondays, Wednesdays and Fridays when designated drinks cost 50 cents all evening long.

The low-keyed *Matau Bar*, in the Saipan Beach Hotel, has very good tropical drinks. From 5 to 7 pm you get free appetizers and all drinks are half price, mai-tais and pina coladas are only $2, and you can carry them out to the beach lounge chairs to catch the sunset.

There's a 12-lane bowling alley on Beach Rd in San Jose, public tennis courts opposite the Marianas High School, an 18-hole golf course at the Marianas Country Club in Marpi, nine holes at the Whispering Palms Country Club in Chalan Kanoa and a driving range at the Hyatt.

Cockfights are held at the Saipan Cockfight in Garapan.

Things To Buy

Virtually none of the carvings, woven wall hangings or other handicrafts in the shops are made in Saipan. Most are imported from the Philippines and generally the prices are high and the quality low. Postcards, T-shirts and plastic knick-knacks bearing the island's name are the only souvenirs 'unique' to Saipan.

A fair amount of shopping goes on in Saipan nonetheless, largely by the Japanese who are obligated to take souvenirs home. Duty-free shops with high-priced designer products are a big hit, Saipan has stylish tropical print cotton clothing and film is available.

Getting There

There are flights to Saipan from Guam, Tokyo, Osaka and Nagoya on Continental Air Mike and JAL.

Air Mike's regular Guam-Saipan fare is $55 one way but their discounted flights cost $27 on Monday, Thursday and Saturday mornings. The excursion fare between Guam and Saipan is $82 for stays of two to 14 days. If you're flying Air Mike to Guam from Koror or Honolulu you can sometimes add Saipan on for an additional $30.

Both Maui Airlines and SPIA have numerous daily commuter flights between Guam and Saipan, some of which stop over on Rota. There are lots of deals, including off-peak, round-trip and stopover packages.

For example, on Maui Airlines the full-fare tickets from Guam to Rota and then Rota to Saipan total $100. But if you were to take their midday 'Paseo Barato' flights you could pay $54 by getting a $39 Guam – Saipan flight, with a stopover on Rota for an additional $15. SPIA charges $51 for their Guam to Saipan flight.

Getting Around

Air Planes can be chartered for sightseeing. Tinian Air charges $155 per hour for a five-seater. Freedom Air is $125 per hour for three people.

Airport Transport Saipan's modern airport has half a dozen car booths, a small overpriced handicraft shop, a foreign exchange booth, a restaurant and a duty-free shop.

Tour buses meet all flights to pick up package tourists. If you're a good talker you might be able to get a free ride.

Taxi Taxis are private with rates calculated on distance, regardless of the number of passengers. Typical charges from Micro

Beach are $10 to the airport, $6 to the Nauru Building and $5 to Capitol Hill.

Hitching Saipan's main routes are quite good for hitching. In fact, it can be difficult to walk for any distance along Beach Rd without someone stopping to ask if you want a ride, even if you don't and your thumb's not out. Be wary of accepting one-way rides to secluded areas, both for the usual safety reasons and because it can be a very long time between vehicles when you want to get back.

Bus Check to see if the on-again-off-again public bus is running. It has a limited route, mostly up and down Beach Rd, stopping at bus signs, major hotels or wherever it's flagged down. The fare is 25 cents anywhere it goes and hopping on for the one-hour round trip is a pleasant way to get oriented to the area.

Car Rentals There are a number of car rental agencies at the airport and around the hotels. Hertz has air-con sedans for $24.95 plus $6 for optional collision insurance. Island Rent-a-Car and Avis are similarly priced. The Japanese companies generally add on a mileage charge as well.

Mopeds & Bicycles Small shops in front of the Hyatt and Saipan Beach Hotel rent mopeds for about $5 per hour and one-speed bicycles for $2 per hour.

Tours A number of tour companies with offices at the larger hotels offer land tours, sunset cruises, fishing excursions and trips to Rota and Tinian.

Gray Line of Saipan (tel 6434) has a three-hour island bus tour from 9 am on Wednesdays, Saturdays and Sundays. It goes to Sugar King Park, Banzai and Suicide cliffs, the Last Command Post and Bird Island. It's one of the few tours in English but it costs $18.

Tinian

Tinian, which is just three miles (4.8 km) south of Saipan, has a notorious place in history as the take-off site for the aircraft that dropped the atomic bombs on Hiroshima and Nagasaki.

The sleeper of Marianas tourism promotions, Tinian's handful of small hotels and restaurants are insufficient to support package tourists which makes them ideal for individual travellers. It is an attractive island with ancient latte stones, farmland with grazing cattle, secluded sandy beaches and scenic vistas.

Tinian is the second largest island in the Northern Marianas, about 12 miles (19 km) long and five miles (eight km) wide, and is also the least mountainous, with a top elevation of 690 feet (207 metres).

The island's rich farmland was used to advantage by the Japanese who levelled the forests and turned the island into a chequerboard of sugar cane fields. Its level terrain was also perfect for the airfields which came later. Only a few Chamorros lived on Tinian during the Japanese occupation and they were greatly outnumbered by the nearly 18,000 Japanese, Okinawans and Koreans, many of whom were farm labourers.

Homesick Americans who captured the island from the Japanese decided the shape of Tinian was not too different from New York's Manhattan. They named the roads Broadway, 42nd St and 8th Avenue and called one section of the island Harlem and another Central Park. Some of the road names are still used today, though having an 86th St seems a little out of place on an island that has little traffic and only a few paved roads!

After the war Tinian reverted back to a quiet rural lifestyle and ranching and farming took hold. The island became known for its beef and dairy products which were exported to neighbouring islands.

Tinian seems destined to become the next US military base in the western Pacific. The northern third of the island has been leased to the US for its sole control and use. The middle third is also leased to the military, but includes some areas in joint-use with the Tinian government (such as the airport and harbour) and other areas such as pastureland that can be temporarily leased back by Tinian residents.

Though there aren't yet any permanent military facilities, Tinian is used sporadically for US Marine Corps training, and access to the northernmost part of the island is restricted during those times.

Tinian may be on the endangered list, but in the meantime it retains an unhurried small-island charm long since lost on neighbouring Saipan.

SAN JOSE

The quiet village of San Jose, where most of Tinian's 1000 residents (and 250 alien workers) live, was once the site of an ancient village of 13,000 Chamorros.

Information

The Bank of Guam has an office in the Fleming Hotel which is open Tuesday to Thursday only. There's a laundromat next door.

There is no tourist office on Tinian but people at the mayor's office can be helpful. As you come into town from the airport, the office is on the left just past the police station and health centre. Tinian's only post office is down behind the mayor's office, next to the farmer's market. Address all Tinian mail to Tinian, CNMI 96952.

Taga House

San Jose's most important attraction is Taga House, an impressive collection of latte stones said to be the foundations of the home of the legendary Chamorro chief *Taga*. It has a dozen or so pitted limestone shafts with capstones. The only latte stone still standing upright has a sapling rooted atop its broken capstone. There are Japanese memorials on both sides.

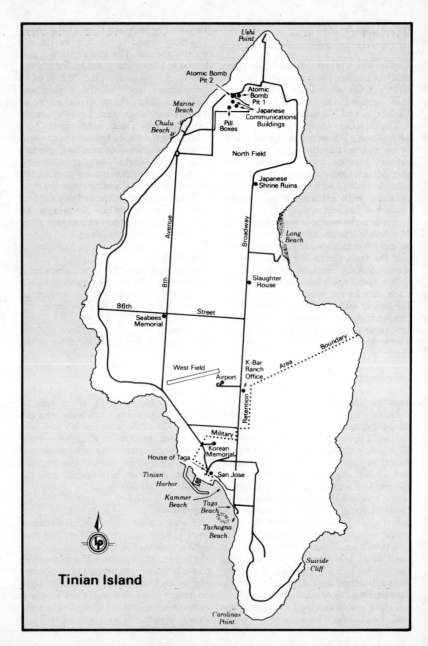

Tinian Island

Harbour & Beach

Tinian's deepwater harbour averages 15 tuna transhipment operations each month. Purse seines (large fishing nets towed between two boats to enclose a school of fish) move in and out, loading their catch onto mother ships which stay docked until full, then sail for home ports in the orient. Fish other than tuna that get caught in the nets are given away, so people on Tinian get to eat a lot of fish without having to catch it themselves.

Kammer Beach, a nice sandy stretch east of the harbour, is an easy walk from anywhere in town. A ship wreck, right up on the beach, marks the spot. Americans staged a fake diversionary landing there during WW II just hours before the actual invasion on the north-west shore.

SOUTH OF SAN JOSE
Taga & Tachogna Beaches

Taga Beach Park is one mile south of town on Broadway. From the cliff above the beach there's a striking view of San Jose and some of the most brilliant turquoise waters you can ever expect to see. Stairs lead down the cliff to a small sandy beach.

Tachogna Beach Park, immediately beyond, has a broad white sand beach and a good swimming area. The water may be a bit choppy at high tide, but at low tide you can wade right out to the shallow coral patch visible just offshore.

Suicide Cliff

To get to Suicide Cliff, follow the road inland from Taga Beach another four miles, bearing right first at the crossroads and then at the fork. Along the way there are excellent views of the south-west side of the island looking back toward San Jose. The grassy road to Suicide Cliff is usually passable in a sedan.

In the hills above the cliffs are the natural and man-made caves that were the last defence position and hide-out for the Japanese military. Though Tinian was secured by the US after nine days of combat, it took an additional three months to rout out the Japanese from these caves. Most of the 4000 Japanese defenders never accounted for are assumed to have committed suicide inside the caves.

It was mainly Japanese civilians who leapt from this spot on the cliff, now barricaded by a fence, in a smaller version of the suicidal jumps that took place on Saipan.

Cow patties in the area (step lightly!) attest to the grazing done there, Polynesian rats jump-hop across the road, there's a Japanese peace memorial and on a clear day you can see Rota.

NORTH OF SAN JOSE

Heading north on Broadway from San Jose there is lots of green pastureland which makes for a nice country drive. On the right side of the road the land was cleared of tangan-tangan and other brush for an agricultural project which never materialised. It's now prime grazing land.

Ranches

Though there are a number of small local ranches, Tinian's ranching is dominated by the Micronesian Development Company (the MDC), which grazes 4500 head of cattle on 7500 acres of leased land at the K-Bar Ranch. Their offices are directly opposite the airport turn-off.

Supermarkets in Guam and Saipan still sell K-Bar beef, but the dairy is gone and the MDC is trying to sell out for $4½ million.

Up ahead, the former Japanese communications building with its heavy metal window grates is now a slaughterhouse and, when need be, a typhoon shelter.

Japanese Shrines

About four miles from the airport turn-off a large Shinto shrine gate on the left, visible from the road, marks the entrance to the site of a former Japanese shrine.

Just ahead, the road circles a roundabout which has the wood and stone remains of another Japanese shrine in the centre. A restoration project is planned for this one.

Waves crash against the cliffs on the rocky east coast, sometimes bursting up through blowholes. Saipan can be glimpsed from there.

North Field

The main road circles North Field, a massive set of landing fields and crossroads. At the outbreak of the battle for the Marianas, the Japanese already had two 4700-foot (1410-metre) runways completed and three other airstrips under construction.

After Tinian was taken, the US Seabees immediately began building six airstrips, each 1½ miles (2.4 km) long. These strips were take-off sites for fire-bomb raids on Japan's home islands and later for the planes that carried the atomic bombs.

Once inside the field, there's a confusing maze of roads, airstrips and overgrown crossroads that all look the same. Watch out for monitor lizards basking in the sun.

Ushi Point

A road to the right, about eight miles past the airport turn-off, goes to Ushi Point which is the northern tip of Tinian. At the point, a cross and memorial stand in remembrance of Tinian fishermen who died at sea. The cross is replaced every Easter.

Atomic Bomb Pits

Back on the main road circling North Field there's an unmarked dirt road to the left leading to the loading pits for the atomic bombs that were dropped on Japan, bringing WW II to an end.

In the early evening of 5 August 1945 a uranium bomb code-named 'Little Boy' was loaded aboard the *Enola Gay*, an American B-29 aircraft. The four-ton bomb had been brought to Tinian from San Francisco aboard the heavy cruiser *Indianapolis*.

The *Enola Gay* and its 12-man crew took off from Tinian at 2.45 am on 6 August and headed for Hiroshima, 1700 miles (2737 km) away. The bomb was dropped at 9.15 am

Tinian time. It exploded above the city, forming a fireball which quickly mushroomed into a dark-grey cloud three miles (4.8 km) wide and 35,000 feet (10,500 metres) high. 75,000 people were killed and the age of atomic warfare had begun.

The second atomic bomb loaded on Tinian and dropped on Japan by the US was a 4½-ton plutonium bomb named 'Fat Man'. It was dropped on Nagasaki on 9 August 1945.

The road to the pits is about ¾ of a mile beyond the turn-off to Ushi Point and 4½ miles from the Japanese shrine roundabout. The pit sites are neat and sterile, marked with signs, plaques, plumeria and coconut trees. Some locals think the puny size of the coconuts indicates that radioactivity is present. Wood roses have taken over around the edges of the paving.

Japanese Buildings

There are some Japanese WW II installations nearby in the overgrown brush. Go south a few hundred yards from the loading pits until the road splits and turn to the left, the take the first right and first right again onto a runway. Continue on the runway until you notice a small overgrown road to the right which goes straight in to the complex.

A building at the right is the most obvious but hidden, straight ahead, is a large two-storey former communications building, once used in conjunction with an underwater cable system. Low concrete pillboxes with gun holes are concealed in the brush to the left as you face the main building.

Invasion Beaches

From the Japanese buildings turn right, back onto the runway, and at the end of the road turn left, then take the next right to Chulu Beach and, a little to the north, Marine Beach. These are the two places on the Tinian coast, dubbed White Beach I and II by American forces, where more than 15,000 US troops landed on in July 1944. These two beaches are so narrow it makes you wonder where they put them all.

A coastal road and the more direct 8th Avenue both lead back to San Jose.

Seabees Memorial
A memorial on the corner of 86th St and 8th Avenue has a map of wartime Tinian. The plaque reads:

To the men of the 107th United States Naval Construction Battalion and all the Seabees who in 1944-45 on Tinian, Mariana Islands, participated in the largest engineering feat of WW II. Seabees constructed four runways and created the world's largest air base enabling the US Armed Forces to end the war in the Pacific. We of the ex-107th Seabees consecrate this ground to our fallen comrades. May God help us to avoid WW III.

Korean Memorial
Seven miles south of Chulu Beach on 8th Avenue (just under half a mile north of Lizama's Store in San Jose), turn inland onto a grassy path lined with palm trees. Not far from the road is a memorial, built on the back of a carved stone turtle, honouring Koreans who died during WW II.

In the hills to the right are caves where the Japanese hid from invading US forces and through the grass, to the left of the turtle, is a brick oven which was a crematorium for Koreans who died before the war.

AGUIJAN ISLAND
Aguijan Island, which supports abundant birdlife, is less than five miles (eight km) south of Tinian. During the Spanish and Japanese administrations it was sporadically inhabited but now it's nicknamed 'Goat Island' after its current residents. Goat hunting takes place in season.

Aguijan is part of Tinian's political district and it's necessary to get a permit from the mayor of Tinian before visiting the island. The boat ride takes over 20 minutes, but there are no beaches and landings are usually made by jumping ship close to shore and wading in. Thorns can be a deterrent to exploring the interior.

Diving
Water Sports (tel Saipan 234-6664; Box 31 CHRB), one of the dive shops in Garapan on Saipan, has full-day diving trips to Tinian and Aguijan for $70.

Special Events
Tinian's fiesta is held on the first weekend in May in honour of San Jose, the island's patron saint. Everyone is welcome to the feasting and fun although finding accommodation at that time is a major problem.

A cliff fishing competition is held in November.

Places To Stay
Until recently the *Fleming Hotel* (tel 433-3232; Box 68) was the only choice on Tinian. The 15 basic rooms cost $28 a single and $32 a double downstairs, or $50 a single and $58 a double upstairs. There's a restaurant and bar, grocery store and bank in the same building. Fleming's (officially the Meitetsu & Fleming Hotel) caters to Japanese tourists.

A few doors down is the new *H-King Motel* (tel 433-3229) which is better value. There are five attractive and comfortable rooms, each with carpeting and refrigerator for $30 a single or double. There's a restaurant/bar behind the hotel.

A new hotel behind the Lori Lynn Restaurant has large rooms for about $30. At least one other hotel is in the planning stages.

All rooms on Tinian have private bathrooms and air-con and also add the 10% tax to room rates.

Camping Tinian is one of the better islands in Micronesia for camping, though the usual precautions apply. No permission is needed to camp on public beaches.

Kammer Beach, at the edge of town, has a sandy beach, running water, toilets, barbecue pits and picnic tables. There are even electrical outlets on poles though you'd need an extension cord to use them.

Taga and Tachogna beach parks, about a mile from town, are other possibilities.

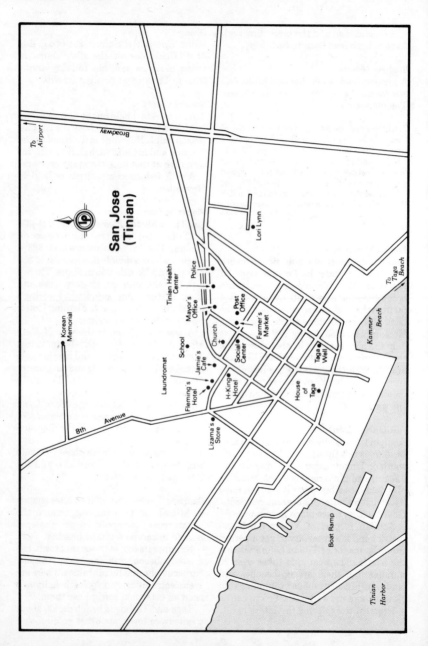

San Jose
(Tinian)

Both have picnic tables, and town water pipes have been extended as far as Taga Beach. You could find out from the mayor's office if the water is running yet.

If you want someplace more remote, try the white sands of Chulu Beach on the north-west coast but take water with you.

Places To Eat

The *Lori Lynn Restaurant* is a good place to eat. It's owned by a friendly local family who have a Japanese cook. Particularly recommended are the specials such as teriyaki, ginger pork or sashimi, with miso soup, rice and pickle. These meals cost $3.50 at lunch and $4.50 at dinner. A *bento* (prepared picnic lunch) costs $3 and breakfast is a mere $2.50. To get to the Lori Lynn, which is in the east part of San Jose, head towards Broadway from town and take the third right past the police station.

In the middle of the village there are three restaurants almost side by side, the *Fleming*, *H-King* and *Jamie's Cafe*. The H-King has cheeseburgers for $2.25, soba for $2 and breakfast is available for hotel customers upon request. Fleming's is open only during mealtimes and has a lunch special Monday through Friday.

Tap water is treated on Tinian and safe to drink.

Getting There

Air Flights from Saipan take about ten minutes. Three airlines are falling over each other competing for passengers, keeping fares low and providing several flights a day. The one-way fare is $18 on Tinian Air, $19 on Freedom Air and $25 on SPIA. A return flight is double.

SPIA also flies from Rota for $40 one way, from Guam for $51 one way and offers return excursion fares (two to 14 days) for $70 from Rota and $80 from Guam.

Surprisingly Tinian has a real terminal building with a snack bar. Customs and immigration are likely to be non-existent since most arrivals are from within the commonwealth.

Boat Ben Pangilinan's boat the *MB Monica*, ask for 'Benny's boat', runs between Charlie Dock on Saipan and the boat ramp in Tinian Harbor on Tuesdays and Fridays. It usually leaves Saipan before daybreak and returns from Tinian in the late afternoon, though Micronesian time prevails on this schedule as it's basically a cargo run. The trip takes about three hours and passengers are charged $10 one way. The channel between the islands is generally rough.

Getting Around

Airport Transport Fleming's provides airport transfers for $2 one way for customers with reservations and rental cars can be reserved in advance through the airlines. It is possible to hitch the 2½ miles from the airport to San Jose or you could ask the airline staff if they know of anyone going to town.

Hitching San Jose is OK for lifts, not that they're necessary as it's small and easy to walk around, but outside the village there isn't enough traffic to count on hitching. To get to Suicide Cliff or the sights to the north you really need a vehicle.

Car Rentals The H-King Motel rents older cars for $30 per day and new ones from $35. Tinian Rental Service (ask at the airlines) has older cars for $24 per day, new ones from $30.

The main island roads are paved and in good condition.

Mopeds The H-King rents mopeds at $2 an hour. This is a cheap and fun way to zip up to North Field and explore for a couple of hours.

Tours Fleming's offers guided tours of both the north and south ends of the island for $35 including lunch, or just half the island for $15, without lunch. Saipan tour companies can arrange one-day tours of Tinian from their end.

Rota

Rota, about halfway between Guam and Saipan, is just beginning to get an overflow of tourists from those larger islands. It is still however, a relaxed and friendly place.

The main village of Songsong has remained virtually unchanged for the past 20 years, with dusty unpaved roads and not a single gift shop or tourist nightclub.

Rota is roughly oblong, measuring three miles by 10 (4.8 km by 16) and has farms, good spring water, enough deer to have a hunting season and fiery orange sunsets that light the skies nearly every evening. Locals call the island Luta.

Rota is a one or two-day side trip for package tourists from Japan who stay at one of two small resort hotels isolated away from the main villages. They wear 'Rota – Adventure Island' T-shirts, swim in groups at guarded beaches and whiz around island roads in minibuses, jumping out just long enough to have their pictures taken at designated sites.

Few of Rota's 1500 residents seem to walk much. A trip to the local grocery store is an opportunity for the whole family to pile into the back of the pick-up truck for a ride. Almost without fail, drivers smile and wave at each other.

Rota's laid-back character is its leading attraction. Where else can you swim right in town and still have the beach to yourself?

SONGSONG

Songsong Village is spread along the neck of the island's south-west peninsula, at the end of which is Mt Taipingot. Overlooking the village, and rising to a height of 469 feet (140 metres), Taipingot is nicknamed Wedding Cake Mountain because of its layered look. Songsong is easily explored on foot – the potholed roads of the village are miserable in a vehicle anyway.

Just past the 'Welcome to Songsong' sign look out for the latte stones in some of the front yards.

Unain Man Amko Beach Park has a couple of large rusted boats right near the shore that attract small fish and make interesting snorkelling.

The San Francisco de Borja Church has a bell from the German period and a cross of German design. Behind the church is a cemetery.

Information

The Bank of Guam, in the Blue Peninsula hotel building, is open from 10 am to 3 pm Monday to Thursday, and to 6 pm on Fridays. There are laundromats nearby.

The post office and mayor's office are both up the hill a couple of blocks from the Blue Peninsula. All mail to Rota should be addressed to Rota, CNMI 96951. There's a public library in town.

Tonga Cave

Tonga Cave, a damp limestone cavern of stalagmites and dripping stalactites, some of them eight feet (2.4 metres) long, sits just above the village behind a grassy park. It's just a few minutes walk from the parking area.

The cave was used by the Japanese during the war as a hospital shelter and the Rotanese have used it as a refuge from typhoons. Beyond the cave is a good view of Songsong and Mt Taipingot.

Sugar Mill & Train

Down near the harbour are the remains of the Japanese sugar mill which was built of bricks made in Japan. Most of the original building was removed after the war.

Although Rota's soil was not as good for cane as the soil on Saipan or Tinian there was enough sugar to support two refineries, with distilleries for making whisky and port wine from molasses. In the mid-1930s Rota's sugar industry employed nearly 800 Chamorros and 5000 Japanese and Koreans.

A tiny locomotive, once used to haul

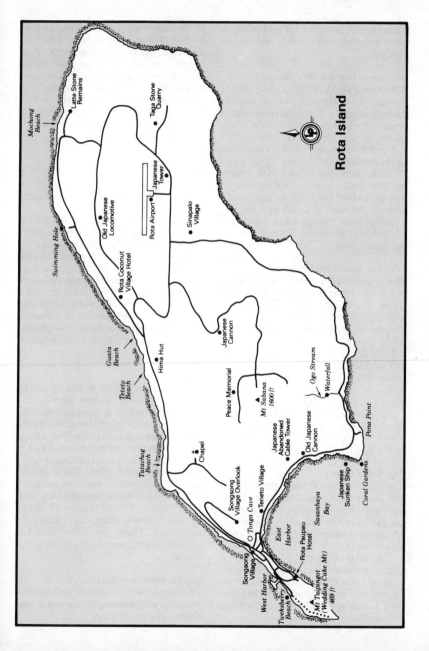

Rota Island

sugar cane from the fields to the mill, has been painted bright red and is on display.

Tweksberry Beach & Mt Taipingot

A dirt road south of the dock along the harbour leads through orderly rows of coconut trees to Tweksberry Beach, a protected white sand beach with picnic tables.

A trail made by the Youth Conservation Corps starts up Mt Taipingot from about 75 yards inland before the beach parking lot. The climb is steep but not too difficult and takes about two hours up and back. It ends on the edge of a cliff at a grove of ironwood trees and the views encompass Mt Sabana, Songsong, Pona Point and Sasanhaya Bay.

CENTRAL & NORTHERN ROTA

The remains of a two-storey Japanese building, probably once an observation tower, are on the left side of the road half a mile east of the airport. Another half mile along, a road to the right goes to the Taga Stone Quarry.

If you don't turn down to the quarry, the dirt road circles around the airport, past fenced-off farms, pastures and an old Japanese locomotive and continues on around to the main paved road.

There are sandy coves and beach parks all along Rota's west shore, alternating with scenic outcrops of craggy rocks and tidal pools.

Taga Stone Quarry

The Taga Stone Quarry has nine latte shafts and seven capstones still sitting in the trenches where they were being quarried before being inexplicably abandoned. Mosses, grasses and tiny ferns have grown up around them.

The early Chamorros were able to quarry the latte stones without the benefit of metal tools. It's believed they built fires in trenches around the stones and then used basalt stone adzes to cut into the softened limestone.

The quarry is half a mile from the main road and there are signs marking the way. Although there are other latte stone quarry sites around Rota most are on private property so this is the most accessible and the most impressive.

Legend says the ancient Chamorro king *Taga the Great* jumped from Guam to Rota and established a temporary kingdom on Rota.

Tatachog

In the 1930s there was a resettlement of Rotanese in the Tatachog area and the ruins of their buildings can be seen along the paved road.

There's a tiny chapel on the slopes above Tatachog which was built during the German era. To get there, take the road leading inland just south of Tatachog Beach Park and go right when the road forks. One mile from the beach park, turn left at a small path that leads through a bamboo gate to the tiny white chapel with its pink roof. The chapel is in a clearing that looks deserted, but don't be surprised to see candles burning or fresh orchids at the altar.

Beaches

Tatachog Beach Park is one of several beach parks along the west shore.

Teteto Beach is a popular place for package tourists, partly because Coconut Village shuttles guests there. Waves crash just outside the reef but inside it's calm and protected and snorkellers will find a good variety of fish. Hima Hut across the road sells sandwiches and cold drinks.

Guata Beach Park, just before the turn-off to Coconut Village, is being developed by the mayor's office for community recreation. There are some thatched shelters there, one with a nice loft inside.

Natural Swimming Hole

Don't miss the swimming hole at Agusan, 2¼ miles after turning off the main road toward Coconut Village.

This natural basin, a big scooped-out hollow in the rocks, is right on the shoreline. Unless the tide is high or the seas unusually rough this place is almost as calm as a swimming pool, with incoming waves just trickling in over the top and outgoing water pulled out through small cracks in the rocks below. It's a good place to snorkel as the fish are captive.

Mochong Beach
At the end of the turn-off road is Mochong Beach, the site of an ancient Chamorro village carbon dated to 640 BC, and the remains of latte stones. Exploration for the stones may prove frustrating as this land is all private property, there's usually a locked gate and what there is to see is hard to find. If the gate is open it's probably OK to go inside but ask permission if you see anyone.

Sabana Peace Memorial
Japanese peace memorials abound in Micronesia. Rota's was erected in 1973 near the top of the 1600-foot (480-metre) Mt Sabana. It's reachable by road and a sign near the airport marks the turn-off.

EAST OF SONGSONG
On the east side of Sasanhaya Bay the Japanese had a phosphate mill, loading site and ceramic factory. The remains of the old cable tramway towers, that carried the phosphate down the hill to ships in the harbour, can still be seen.

Japanese Cannon
An impossible to miss Japanese cannon points straight out to the harbour and Mt Taipingot from its concrete shelter on the road 2½ miles east of Songsong. The gun barrel can be moved from side to side but don't leave it sticking straight out or the next car going by could get whapped.

Beware of very steep drops along the edge of this road. They're often covered with vegetation and not always obvious and if you go off the side, the drop could well do you in.

A small road, there's a sign pointing the way, leads off to Pona Point, a wind-whipped rocky viewpoint. Further down, the main road passes above Ogo Stream which features some small waterfalls.

Diving
One of the highlights of diving Rota is the excellent visibility. Coral Gardens, in Sasanhaya Bay, is known for its huge platter corals and nearby is the wreck of the *Shoun Maru*, a Japanese freighter sunk during WW II. It lies offshore about 60 feet (18 metres) underwater.

Both of the larger hotels arrange diving tours and rent equipment. Coconut Village charges from $20 for reef dives and $35 for boat dives, depending on the number of people. The Pau-Pau Hotel has a mini-submarine that goes to 290 feet (87 metres) and costs around $150 an hour.

Places To Stay
The *Blue Peninsula* (tel 532-3541; Box 539), Rota's original hotel, has the only moderately priced hotel rooms on the island. These days it has an air of neglect and although the rooms aren't particularly good value the location is convenient, especially if you're trying to avoid renting a car. Anywhere in town, including the beach, is an easy walk. Rooms with fans and shared bathroom cost $20 a single and $26 a double but they're usually booked. With air-con and private bathroom it's $30/$36 for singles/double.

The new *Senora Apartment/Motel* (tel 532-3555 or 532-3442) in Teneto Village has four modern one-bedroom apartments with full kitchens for $40 a single or double. It's slightly less by the week. Senora has a booth at the airport or you can ask at Joe & Sons store in Songsong.

There's nothing intrinsically wrong with the modern *Rota Pau-Pau Hotel* (tel 532-3561; Box 503) but it's pricey and geared to packaged tourists. There's an expensive restaurant, an expensive gift shop (where you get the $15 'Adventure Island' T-shirts), a swimming pool, diving

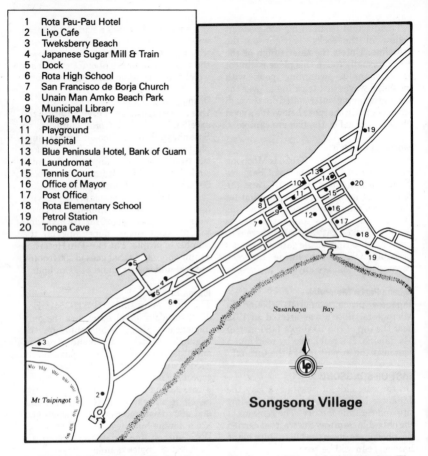

1   Rota Pau-Pau Hotel
2   Liyo Cafe
3   Tweksberry Beach
4   Japanese Sugar Mill & Train
5   Dock
6   Rota High School
7   San Francisco de Borja Church
8   Unain Man Amko Beach Park
9   Municipal Library
10 Village Mart
11 Playground
12 Hospital
13 Blue Peninsula Hotel, Bank of Guam
14 Laundromat
15 Tennis Court
16 Office of Mayor
17 Post Office
18 Rota Elementary School
19 Petrol Station
20 Tonga Cave

Sasanhaya   Bay

Mt Taipingot

Songsong Village

facilities and all amenities. The 50 air-con rooms start at $94 for singles or doubles. Maui Airlines sometimes has an air/hotel package deal there.

The *Rota Coconut Village* (tel 532-3448; Box 855) also caters to package tours from Japan, and has a swimming pool, diving facilities and restaurant, but it's cheaper and more relaxed than the Pau-Pau. The 10 duplex cottages are decorated in a sort of upgraded island style, with peaked roofs, wood trim and rattan furnishings. All 20 rooms have *ofuros* (individual hot tubs) in the bathrooms.

Singles cost $55 and doubles are $65. The beach opposite the hotel is not good for swimming but the hotel ferries small groups around to nearby beaches for $2 return. Airport transfers cost $5 return.

All rooms in Rota have private bathrooms and air-con, except where noted at the Blue Peninsula, and also add the 10% tax to room rates.

Camping Camping shouldn't be a problem at the beach parks, and the thatched huts at Guata Beach Park are also a possibility. Check at the mayor's office.

Places To Eat

The *Liyo Cafe* is open from 7.30 am to 8 pm with breakfasts for $2 to $5, sandwiches from $2 and most dinners from $5 to $6. The lunch special is the best deal as it's usually something from the dinner menu for $3.50.

The *Coconut Village* serves dinner Japanese style, with very small entree portions starting at $8, rice or soup for $1 extra and service so slow you might want to take a good book. The breakfast menu looks like a better deal.

At the *Pau-Pau* breakfast and lunch costs from $7 to $10 and dinner is anything from $12 to $30.

The *Blue Peninsula* has a restaurant and bar downstairs with irregular hours but reasonable prices. Two eggs, bacon and toast will set you back $3, grilled cheese sandwiches are $1.50 and dinners range from $5 to $7.

The *As Pari* is a restaurant and bar in Songsong. Breakfast costs around $5, a hamburger with fries is $3.50 at lunchtime and chicken or fish dinners are $6 to $7. It's open from 7 am to 1 pm and 6 pm to 2 am.

Despite claims of Rota's prolific fruit, you may be hard pressed to find any. Coconut Village and the Pau-Pau have 'fruit hunting tours', for $15 and $21 respectively, so maybe that's an indication of what's available.

Every fifth building in Songsong is a store of some sort so you'll have no trouble buying provisions, but check the expiry dates. Vegetables in the stores are commonly imported from California via Guam on, by the looks of them, a very slow boat.

Rota's water comes from a natural water cave and may be the best in Micronesia. They've even considered bottling it for export to other islands.

Entertainment

There are small bars around Songsong, including the *Blue Peninsula* and the *As Pari*. On weekends the *Hima Hut*, opposite Teteto Beach, has music and dancing.

Cockfights are held at 7 pm on Fridays and Saturdays in Sinapalo Village and on Sundays just north of Songsong.

Special Events

The largest and most popular fiesta in the Northern Marianas is held on Rota on the second weekend in October. It's a celebration in honour of San Francisco de Borja, the patron saint of Songsong Village. People flock from Saipan, Tinian and Guam for days of Chamorro food, drinks, religious processions, music and dancing. If you can secure accommodation, this is the island's finest hour.

Rota also hosts a fishing derby in September over the Labor Day weekend.

Getting There

On Maui Airlines you can fly to Rota for $29 on discounted midday flights from either Guam or Saipan. The full fare is $50 either way.

SPIA flies to Rota from Guam, Tinian and Saipan. The cost is the same from each: $40 one way or $70 for a return excursion fare valid for two to 14 days. There is also a $28 morning flight from Guam to Rota.

The airport is nine miles from Songsong. Upstairs in the *Mayflower Restaurant* there's a few interesting old photos from the Japanese administration period.

Getting Around

Hitching It's fairly easy to get lifts around the main parts of the island though traffic may be infrequent. Rota is just beginning to get paved roads. The stretch from the airport to Songsong is the best.

Car Rentals You can rent cars from Senora (at the airport) for $40 per day, or $45 for a 4-wheel-drive jeep, plus $6.75 for optional insurance. For an air-con sedan Coconut Village charges $35 for 12 hours, or $45 for 24 hours with petrol and insurance. Budget has an agent (tel 532-3438) but not an office.

Glossary

Bai – a traditional meeting house in Palau.
Bairulchau – giant basalt monoliths on Babeldaob, Palau.
Banzai attack – a mass attack of troops without concern for casualties, as practiced by the Japanese during WW II.
Beche-de-mer – a class of sea cucumber (also called trepang) with an elongated body, leathery skin and a cluster of tentacles at the oral end. They burrow in sand or creep on the sea bed and were gathered by early traders and sold in China and South-East Asia as a delicacy and aphrodisiac.
Benjo – an outhouse.
Betel nut – the fruit of the Areca palm tree which is commonly split open, sprinkled with lime, wrapped in a pepper leaf and chewed as a digestive stimulant and mild narcotic.
Breadfruit – a tree of the Pacific Islands, the trunk of which is used for lumber and canoe building. The fruit is cooked and eaten and has a texture like bread.

Chamorro – the indigenous people of the Mariana Islands.
Copra – dried coconut kernel, used for making coconut oil.

Dapal – a women's meeting house in Yap.
Dugong – a whalelike, herbivorous mammal inhabiting shallow tropical waters and often seen around Palau.

Faluw – a Yapese meeting house for men.

Jambos – Marshallese picnics or trips.

Kahlek – night fishing, using burning torches to attract flying fish into hand-held nets, practiced in Pingelap, Pohnpei.
Korkor – a Marshallese dug-out fishing canoe made from a breadfruit log.

Latte stones – the stone foundation pillars used to support ancient Chamorro buildings in the Marianas. The shafts and capstones were carved from limestone quarries.
Lava-lava – a wide piece of cloth of woven hibiscus and banana fibres, worn as a skirt by women throughout Yap and in Truk's outer islands.

Manposteria – a building material, used in the Marianas, made from burnt limestone mixed with coral.
Modekngei – the traditional religion of Palau.
Mwaramwars – head wreaths of flowers and fragrant leaves worn in Pohnpei.

Nahnmwarki – a district chief in Pohnpei.
Noddy – a tropical tern, or aquatic bird, with black & white or dark plumage.

Omung – perfumed love potion used in Truk.

Pebai – a Yapese community meeting house.

Rai – Yapese stone money.

Sakau – a mildly narcotic Pohnpeian drink made from the roots of a pepper shrub.
Saudeleur – member of a tyrannical royal dynasty that ruled Pohnpei prior to western contact with the islanders.
Seka – a narcotic, ceremonial drink (similar to sakau) of Kosrae.

Tangan-tangan – a shrub that was mass-planted in the Marianas to prevent erosion.
Thu – a loincloth worn by Yapese males.
Tridacna clam – the giant clam, *tridacna gigas*, is the largest known bivalve mollusc. It is collected and farmed in Palau for its edible flesh, and is poached throughout the Pacific for its valuable adductor muscle, considered a delicacy and aphrodisiac in the orient.
Trochus – a shellfish commercially harvested for its shell and flesh.
Tuba – an alcoholic drink made from coconut sap.

Udoud – traditional Palauan money, either beads of glass or fired and coloured clay.

Wunbey – a Yapese meeting platform.

Zories – rubber thongs, sandals, flip-flops.

Index

216 Index

MAPS

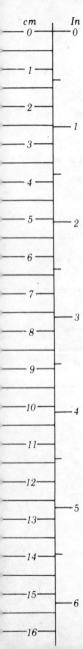

Temperature

To convert °C to °F multipy by 1.8 and add 32

To convert °F to °C subtract 32 and multiply by ·55

Length, Distance & Area

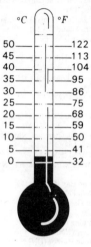

	multipy by
inches to centimetres	2.54
centimetres to inches	0.39
feet to metres	0.30
metres to feet	3.28
yards to metres	0.91
metres to yards	1.09
miles to kilometres	1.61
kilometres to miles	0.62
acres to hectares	0.40
hectares to acres	2.47

Weight

	multipy by
ounces to grams	28.35
grams to ounces	0.035
pounds to kilograms	0.45
kilograms to pounds	2.21
British tons to kilograms	1016
US tons to kilograms	907

A British ton is 2240 lbs, a US ton is 2000 lbs

Volume

	multipy by
Imperial gallons to litres	4.55
litres to imperial gallons	0.22
US gallons to litres	3.79
litres to US gallons	0.26

5 imperial gallons equals 6 US gallons
a litre is slightly more than a US quart, slightly less
than a British one

Lonely Planet

Lonely Planet published its first book in 1973. Tony and Maureen Wheeler had made a lengthy overland trip from England to Australia and, in response to numerous 'how do you do it?' questions, Tony wrote and they published *Across Asia on the Cheap*. It became an instant local best-seller and inspired thoughts of a second travel guide. A year and a half in South-East Asia resulted in their second book, *South-East Asia on a Shoestring*, which they put together in a backstreet Chinese hotel in Singapore in 1975. The 'yellow book', as it quickly became known, soon became *the* guide to the region and has now gone through five editions, always with its familiar yellow cover.

Soon other writers started to come to them with ideas for similar books – books that went off the beaten track and took an adventurous approach to travel, books that 'assumed you knew how to get your luggage off the carousel,' as one reviewer described them. Lonely Planet soon grew from a kitchen table operation to a spare room and then to its own office. It also started to develop an international reputation as the Lonely Planet logo began to appear in more and more countries. Always the emphasis has been on travel for travellers and Tony and Maureen still manage to fit in a number of trips each year and play a very active part in the writing and updating of Lonely Planet's guides.

Today over 20 people work at the Lonely Planet office in Melbourne, Australia and there are another half dozen at the company's US office in Oakland, California. Keeping guidebooks up to date is a constant battle and although the basic element in that struggle is still an ear to the ground and lots of walking, modern technology also plays its part. All Lonely Planet guidebooks are now stored and updated on computer. In some cases authors take lap-top computers into the field with them. Lonely Planet is also using computers to draw maps and eventually many of the maps will also be stored on disk.

At first Lonely Planet specialised extensively in the Asia region but these days it is also developing major ranges of guidebooks to the Pacific region, to South America and to Africa. The list of walking guides is also growing and Lonely Planet is producing a unique series of phrasebooks to 'unusual' languages. In 1982 the company's *India – a travel survival kit* won the Thomas Cook Guidebook of the Year award, the major international award for travel guidebooks and the company's business achievements have been recognised by twice winning Australian Export Achievement Awards, in 1982 and 1986.

The people at Lonely Planet strongly feel that travellers can make a positive contribution to the countries they visit both by better appreciation of cultures and by the money they spend. In addition the company tries to make a direct contribution to the countries and regions it covers. Since 1986 a percentage of the income from each book has gone to aid groups and associations. This has included donations to famine relief in Africa, to aid projects in India, to agricultural projects in Nicaragua and other Central American countries and to Greenpeace's efforts to halt French nuclear testing in the Pacific. In 1987 $30,000 was donated by Lonely Planet to these projects.

Lonely Planet guides to The Pacific

Australia – a travel survival kit
Australia is Lonely Planet's home territory so this guide
gives you the complete low-down on Down Under, from
the red centre to the coast, from cosmopolitan cities to
country towns.

New Zealand – a travel survival kit
Visitors to New Zealand find a land of fairytale beauty
and scenic contrasts – a natural wonderland. This book
has information about the places you won't want to miss,
including ski-resorts and famous walks.

Fiji – a travel survival kit
This is a comprehensive guide to the Fijian archipelago.
On a number of these beautiful islands accommodation
ranges from camping grounds to international hotels –
whichever you prefer this book will help you to enjoy the
South Seas.

Tahiti & French Polynesia – a travel survival kit
The image of palm-fringed beaches and friendly people
continues to lure travellers to Polynesia. This book gives
you all the facts on paradise, and will be useful whether
you plan a package holiday, or to travel the islands
independently.

Rarotonga & the Cook Is – a travel survival kit
Rarotonga has history, beauty and magic to rival Hawaii,
Tahiti or Bora Bora. Unlike those better known islands,
however, the world has virtually passed it by. The Cook
Islands range from mountainous islands to remote and
untouched coral atolls.

Papua New Guinea – a travel survival kit
Papua New Guinea is truly 'the last unknown' – the last
inhabited place on earth to be explored by Europeans.
This guide has the latest information for travellers who
want to find just how rewarding a trip to this remote and
amazing country can be.

Lonely Planet Update

We collect an enormous amount of information here at Lonely Planet. Apart from our research there's a steady stream of travellers' letters full of the latest news. For over 5 years much of this information went into a quarterly newsletter (and helped to update the guidebooks). The new paperback *Update* includes this up-to-date news and aims to supplement the information available in our guidebooks. There will be four editions a year (Feb, May, Aug and Nov) available either by subscription or through bookshops. Subscribe now and you'll save nearly 25% off the retail price.

Each edition has extracts from the most interesting letters we have received, covering such diverse topics as:
• how to take a boat trip on the Yalu River
• living in a typical Thai village
• getting a Nepalese trekking permit

Subscription Details

All subscriptions cover four editions and include postage. Prices quoted are valid until 1988.

USA & Canada – One year's subscription is US$12; a single copy is US$3.95. Please send your order to Lonely Planet's California office.

Other Countries – One year's subscription is Australian $15; a single copy is A$4.95. Please pay in Australian $, or the US$ or £ Sterling equivalent. Please send your order form to Lonely Planet's Australian office.

Order Form

Please send me

☐ One year's subscription – starting next edition.

☐ One copy of the next edition.

Name (please print) ....

Address (please print) ....

....

....

Tick One

☐ Payment enclosed (payable to Lonely Planet Publications)

Charge my ☐ Visa ☐ Bankcard ☐ MasterCard for the amount of $ ....

Card No .... Expiry Date ....

Cardholder's Name (print) ....

Signature .... Date..

US & Canadian residents
Write to Lonely Planet Publications, Embarcadero West, 112 Linden St, Oakland, CA 94607, USA

Other countries
Lonely Planet Publications, PO Box 88, South Yarra, Victoria 3141, Australia

Travel Survival Kits

Alaska
Australia
Baja California
Bali & Lombok
Bangladesh
Burma
Canada
Chile & Easter Island
China
East Africa
Ecuador & the Galapagos Islands
Egypt & the Sudan
Fiji
Hong Kong, Macau & Canton
India
Indonesia
Japan
Jordan & Syria
Kashmir, Ladakh & Zanskar
Kathmandu & the Kingdom of Nepal
Korea & Taiwan
Malaysia, Singapore & Brunei
Mexico
New Zealand
Pakistan
Papua New Guinea
Peru
Philippines
Raratonga & the Cook Islands
Sri Lanka
Tahiti & French Polynesia
Taiwan
Thailand
Tibet
Turkey
Yemen

Shoestring Guides
Africa on a shoestring
North-East Asia on a shoestring
South America on a shoestring
South-East Asia on a shoestring
West Asia on a shoestring

Trekking & Walking Guides
Bushwalking in Papua New Guinea
Tramping in New Zealand
Trekking in the Indian Himalaya
Trekking in the Nepal Himalaya

Phrasebooks
Burmese phrasebook
China phrasebook
Hindi/Urdu phrasebook
Indonesia phrasebook
Nepal phrasebook
Papua New Guinea phrasebook
Sri Lanka phrasebook
Swahili phrasebook
Thailand phrasebook
Tibet phrasebook

And Also
Travel with Children
Travellers Tales

Lonely Planet Distribution

Lonely Planet travel guides are available round the world. If you can't find them, ask your bookshop to order them from one of the distributors listed below. For countries not listed, or if you would like a free copy of our latest booklist, write to Lonely Planet in Australia.

Lonely Planet Distributors

Australia
Lonely Planet Publications, PO Box 88, South Yarra, Victoria 3141.
Canada
Raincoast Books, 112 East 3rd Avenue, Vancouver, British Columbia V5T 1C8.
Denmark, Finland & Norway
Scanvik Books aps, Store Kongensgade 59 A, DK-1264 Copenhagen K.
Hong Kong
The Book Society, GPO Box 7804.
India & Nepal
UBS Distributors, 5 Ansari Rd, New Delhi – 110002
Israel
Geographical Tours Ltd, 8 Tverya St, Tel Aviv 63144.
Japan
Intercontinental Marketing Corp, IPO Box 5056, Tokyo 100-31.
Netherlands
Nilsson & Lamm bv, Postbus 195, Pampuslaan 212, 1380 AD Weesp.
New Zealand
Roulston Greene Publishing Associates Ltd, Private Bag, Takapuna, Auckland 9.
Papua New Guinea see Australia
Singapore & Malaysia
MPH Distributors, 601 Sims Drive, #03-21, Singapore 1438.
Spain
Altair, Balmes 69, 08007 Barcelona.
Sweden
Esselte Kartcentrum AB, Vasagatan 16, S-111 20 Stockholm.
Thailand
Chalermnit, 108 Sukhumvit 53, Bangkok 10110.
UK
Roger Lascelles, 47 York Rd, Brentford, Middlesex, TW8 0QP
USA
Lonely Planet Publications, PO Box 2001A, Berkeley, CA 94702.
West Germany
Buchvertrieb Gerda Schettler, Postfach 64, D3415 Hattorf a H.